THE FIFTH EDITION

The Collectors Encyclopedia of

Fiesta

With Harlequin and Riviera

by
Sharon and Bob Huxford

THE FIFTH EDITION

The Collectors Encyclopedia of

Fiesta

With Harlequin and Riviera

by
Sharon and Bob Huxford

COLLECTOR BOOKS
A Division of Schroeder Publishing Co., Inc.
P.O. Box 3009 ● PADUCAH, KENTUCKY ● 42001

The current values in this book should be used only as a guide. They are not intended to set prices, which vary from one section of the country to another. Auction prices as well as dealer prices vary greatly and are affected by condition as well as demand. Neither the Author nor the Publisher assumes responsibility for any losses that might be incurred as a result of consulting this guide.

Additional copies of this book may be ordered from:

Collector Books
P.O. Box 3009
Paducah, KY 42001
or
The authors: Sharon and Bob Huxford
1202 Seventh Street
Covington, IN 47932

@$9.95 Add $1.00 for postage and handling.

Copyright: Sharon and Bob Huxford, 1984
ISBN: 0-89145-264-8

This book or any part thereof may not be reproduced without the written consent of the Author and Publisher.

TABLE OF CONTENTS

Foreword 4
About the Authors 5
Acknowledgments 6
The Laughlin Pottery Story 8
The Story of Fiesta 10
Identification of Trademark, Design and Color 19
A Word To The Wise! 22
That Radioactive Red! 25
Dating Codes and English Measurements 29
The Morgue Revisited 31
Fiesta 36
The Fiesta Casuals 88
Amberstone 90
Casualstone 92
Fiesta Ironstone 94
Fiesta Kitchen Kraft 96
Harlequin 104
Harlequin Animals 122
Riviera 124
Children's Sets 138
Decaled Century 142
Virginia Rose 144
Rhythm Rose 148
Priscilla Pattern Dinnerware; Dogwood 150
Serenade 152
Tango 154
Jubilee 156
Rhythm 158
Wells Art Glaze 160
Carnival 162
Epicure 163
Mexicana 164
Hacienda 170
Kitchen Kraft, Oven Serve 174
The American Potter 184
Laughlin Art China 192

FOREWORD

It's been ten years since we wrote our first book, *The Story of Fiesta*. This is our fifth edition — to us an exciting milestone! But in actuality, the story of Fiesta will soon be not ten, but fifty years old! To view Fiesta's success merely as a collectible would be from a narrowed perspective. For unlike nearly any other collectible on the market today, there has never been a time since it was introduced by The Homer Laughlin China Co. in 1936, that it was not appreciated. Those who had it kept it and continued to use it. Fiesta has always been a favorite of the American public, and as a product so closely aligned with the whims of fashion, it is certainly unique. It's simple, timeless design has remained perfectly attuned to the changing tastes of five decades.

Over two years have elapsed since our fourth revised edition was published. Although the market values reported in that issue remained fairly accurate during 1981 and part of '82 — a level effected no doubt by the country's poor economy — as the hope of a mid-year recovery became reality, dealers began to report a surge of enthusiastic buying. Prices rose to a point that we felt a new value guide was needed.

But the price increase was not all that was newsworthy. Though it seems unlikely that new finds could continue to surface after 10 years of avid collecting by an ever-increasing number of fans, amazingly enough, they do! Watch for these in the color plates — we'll be sure they're well marked so you won't miss them.

This year we have three new lines for you — all very exciting to us because they are in the solid colors, which after all is the style of dinnerware that primarily attracted us to Fiesta and prompted the publication of our books. These lines are Wells Art, a pre-Fiesta pattern; Epicure, a streamlined pastel glazed design of the fifties; and Carnival, a limited promotional assortment, but none-the-less special because of its Fiesta-like colors and styling.

We'll revise and correct the text as new information enables us to do so . . . and just because we wanted #5 to be special, we'll throw in some fantastic experimentals from the morgue at HLC.

ABOUT THE AUTHORS

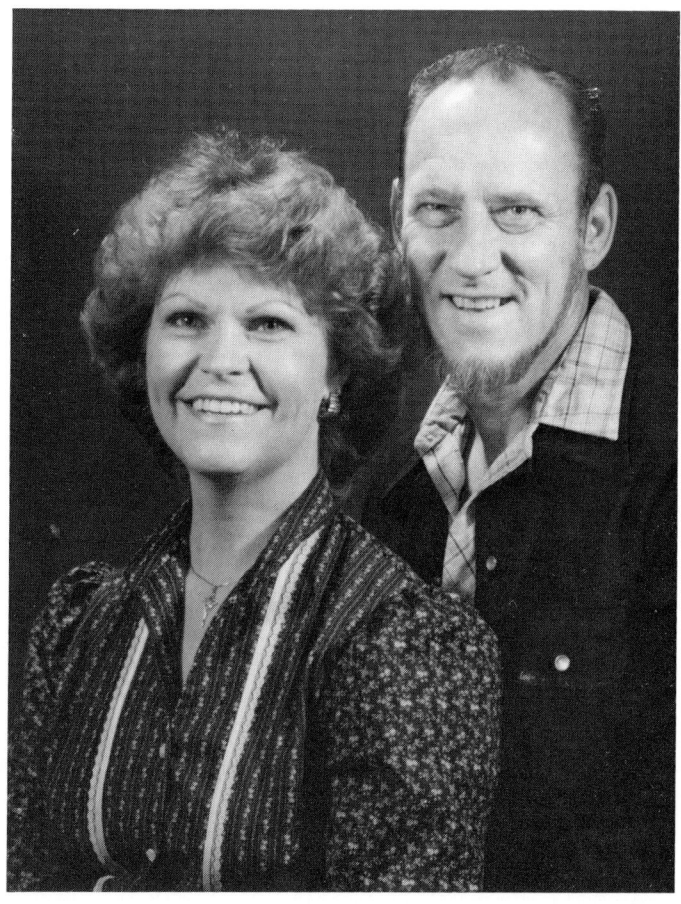

As a direct result of their first book *The Story of Fiesta*, written in 1974, the Huxfords became Pottery Editors for Collector Books and in that capacity wrote several other books on various Ohio potteries. *The Collectors Encyclopedia of Roseville Pottery* and *The Collectors Catalogue of Early Roseville* were published in 1976; new releases in 1978 included *The Collectors Encyclopedia of Mc Coy Pottery, The Collectors Encyclopedia of Brush-Mc Coy Pottery*, and *The Collectors Catalogue of Brush-Mc Coy Pottery. The Collectors Encyclopedia of Weller Pottery* was published in 1979, and in 1980 they wrote *The Collectors Encyclopedia of Roseville Pottery, Volume II.*

ACKNOWLEDGEMENTS

As you who began collecting Fiesta when it was first discontinued well know, it's not as simple as it once was! Harlequin and Riviera have both been popular lines almost as long as Fiesta. Rhythm, Jubilee, Serenade, Kitchen Kraft and the Mexican decaled lines were next to be noticed, and soon we were including Virginia Rose, Rhythm Rose, Priscilla and Tango in our growing little book! Some of these patterns — especially Rhythm, Jubilee and Serenade — have recently been 'awakened' from their 'sleeper' status, and have attracted a new band of followers who cite motives such as Fiesta's high prices, enjoying the challenge of reassembling sets of these less-produced lines, and simply appreciating each on their own esthetic merit. So from our early interest in three basic patterns, the field has expanded to now include many! Our personal grasp of so large a market would be totally inadequate, so we asked for help; and as they always have been, our fellow collectors were more than generous with their time, knowledge, experience and encouragement . . . and with their treasures!

Our questionnaires were sent all across the country — west to Seattle, Washington, and Carlsbad, California; east to New York and Washington, D.C. . . . New Mexico, Oregon, the Midwest states and many others were contacted. We asked for comments and criticism — signatures were optional and though kind not to criticize, some chose to remain anonymous. Those who did sign are listed below; we appreciate all who took part. Also listed are those who sent photos or brought things to the photography session, sent us new information, reported new finds, or in some other way contributed to the completion and the success of Fiesta #5.

Howard Marks
Barbara Seimsen
Kevin B. Thomas
Jean Jarrett
Debbie Merritt
Cassie Skalsky
Betty Carson
Jim Medeiros

Ken Brown
Diane Petipas
Robert A. Lamlein
Deane Bergsrud
Florence Ohlendorf
Ted Haun
Austin and Lucille Wilson
Paul Brache

Wayne Pyle	Ron Perrick
Rev. and Mrs. Leslie Wolfe	John Moses
Dick and Diane Knowles	Catherine Yronwode
Joyce Brooks	Chester Sturm
John Sanders	Ann Pace
Wendy Wilson	Barb Thye
Vicki Harmon	Peter Shalit
Jan Berryman	Charles Huddleston
Martha Gallih	

To Ed Carson of the Homer Laughlin China Company — again, 'Thank you, Ed', for allowing us to study company files thereby providing us with the only source of official information available. We especially appreciate the opportunity to photograph the experimental pieces in the morgue, traditionally 'Off Limits' to visitors.

To all of you, from us as well as from our readers, we send our sincere thanks and appreciation . . . and may God continue to bless!

THE LAUGHLIN POTTERY STORY

The Laughlin Pottery was formed in 1871 on the River Road in East Liverpool, Ohio — the result of a partnership between Homer Laughlin and his brother, Shakespear Laughlin. The pottery was equipped with two periodic kilns and was among the first in the country to produce whitewares. Sixty employees produced approximately 500 dozen pieces of dinnerware per day. The superior quality of their pottery won them the highest award at the Centennial Exposition in Philadelphia in 1876.

In 1879, Shakespear Laughlin left the pottery, and for the next ten years, Homer Laughlin carried on the business alone. William Edwin Wells joined him in 1889, and at the end of 1896 the firm incorporated. Shortly thereafter, Laughlin sold his interests to Wells and a Pittsburgh group headed by Marcus Aaron.

Under the new management, Mr. Aaron became President, with Mr. Wells acting in the capacity of Secretary-Treasurer and General Manager.

As their business grew and sales increased, the small River Road plant was abandoned and the company moved its location to Laughlin Station, three miles east of East Liverpool. Two large new plants were constructed and a third purchased from another company. By 1903, all were ready for production. A fourth plant was built in 1906 at the Newell, West Virginia, site and began operation in 1907. In 1913, with business still increasing, Plant 5 was added.

The first revolutionary innovation in the pottery industry was the continuous tunnel kiln. In contrast to the old batch-type, or period kilns which were inefficient from a standpoint of both fuel and time, the continuous tunnel kiln provided a giant step toward modern day mass production. Plant 6, built in 1923, was equipped with this new type kiln and proved so successful that two more such plants were added, Plant 7 in 1927, and Plant 8 in 1929. The old kilns in Plants 4 and 5 were replaced in 1926 and 1934 respectively.

In 1929 the old East Liverpool factories were closed, leaving the entire operation at the Newell, West Virginia, site.

At the height of their production, the company grew to a giant concern which employed 2,500 people, produced thirty thousand dozen pieces of dinnerware per day, and utilized 1,500,000 square feet of production area. In contrast to the early wares, painstakingly hand-fashioned in the traditional methods, the style of ware reflected the improved mass production techniques that had of necessity been utilized in later years. The old-fashioned dipping tubs gave way to the use of high-speed conveyor belts and spray glazing, and mechanical jiggering machines replaced for the most part the older methods of man powered molding machines.

In 1930, W. E. Wells retired from the business after more than 40 years of brilliant leadership, having guided the development and expansion of the company from its humble beginning on the Ohio river to a position of unquestioned leadership in its field. He was succeeded by his son, Joseph Mahan Wells. Mr. Aaron became Chairman of the Board, and his son, M. L. Aaron, succeeded him as President. Under their leadership, in addition to the successful wares already in production, many new developments made possible the oven-to-table wares, Oven Serve and Kitchen Kraft. Later, the creation of the beautiful colored glazes which have become almost synonymous with Homer Laughlin, resulted in the production of the colored dinnerware lines which have captured the attention of many collectors today — Fiesta, Harlequin, and Riviera.

On January 1, 1960, Joseph M. Wells became Chairman of the Board and his son, Joseph M. Wells, Jr., followed him in the capacity of Executive Vice-President.

Today, Homer Laughlin employs 1,600 workers, producing approximately 60 million pieces of dinnerware per year.

THE STORY OF FIESTA

In January of 1936, Homer Laughlin introduced a sensational new line of dinnerware at the Pottery and Glass Show in Pittsburgh. It was 'Fiesta' . . . and it instantly captured the imagination of the trade — a forecast of the success it was to achieve with housewives of America.

Fiesta was designed by Fredrick Rhead, an English Stoke-on-Trent potter whose work had for decades been regarded among the finest in the industry. His design was modeled by Arthur Kraft and Bill Bersford. The distinctive glazes were developed by Dr. A. V. Bleninger in association with H. W. Thiemecke.

This popularity was the result of much planning, market analysis, creative development, and a fundamentally sound and well-organized styling program. Rather than present to the everyday housewife a modernistic interpretation of a formal table service which might have been received with some reservation, HLC offered a more casual line with a well-planned series of accessories whose style was compatible with any decor and whose vivid colors could add bright spots of emphasis. Services of all types could be chosen and assembled at the whim of the housewife, and the simple style could be used compatibly with other wares already in her cabinets.

In an article by Fredrick Rhead, taken from the *Pottery and Glass Journal* for June, 1937, these steps toward Fiesta's development were noted: first, from oral descriptions and data concerning most generally used table articles, a chart of tentative sketches in various appealing colors was made. As the final ideas were formulated, they were modified and adjusted until development was completed. Secondly, the technical department made an intensive study of materials, composition, and firing temperatures. During this time models and shapes were being studied. The result was to be a streamline shape, but not so obvious as to detract from the texture and color of the ware. It was to have no relief ornamentation, and was to be pleasantly curving and convex, rather than concave and angular. Color was to be the chief decorative note, but to avoid being too severe, the concentric band of rings was to be added at the edges.

Since the early thirties, there had been a very definite trend in merchandising toward promoting 'color'. Automobiles, household appliances and furnishings, ladies' apparel . . . all took on vivid hues. The following is an excerpt from Rhead's article:

> *The final selection of five colors was a more difficult job because we had developed hundreds of tone values and hues and there were scores which were difficult to reject. Then, there were textures ranging from dull mattes to highly reflecting surfaces. We tackled the texture problem first. (Incidentally, we had made fair sized skeletons in each of the desirable glazes in order to be better able to arrive at the final selection.)*
>
> *We elimated the dull mattes and the more highly reflecting glazes first, because in mass production practice, undue variation would result in unpleasant effects. The dull surfaces are not easy to clean and the too highly reflecting surfaces show 'curtains' or variations in thickness of application. We decided upon a semi-reflecting surface of about the texture of a billiard ball. The surface was soft and pleasant to the touch and in average light there were no disturbing reflections to detract from the color and shape.*
>
> *We had one lead with regard to color. There seemed to be a trade preference for a brilliant orange red. With this color as a key note and with the knowledge that we were to have five colors, the problem resolved to one where the remainder would 'tune in' or form appropriate contrasts.*
>
> *The obvious reaction to red, we thought, would be toward a fairly deep blue. We had blues ranging from pale turquoises to deep violet blues. The tests were made by arranging a table for four people and, as the plate is an important item in the set, we placed four plates on various colored cloths and then arranged the different blues around the table. It seemed that the deeper blues reacted better than the lighter tones and also blues which were slightly violet or purple. We also found that we had to do considerable switching before we could decide upon the right red. Some were too harsh and deep, others too yellow.*

> With the red and blue apparently settled, we decided that a green must be one of the five colors. We speedily discovered that the correct balance between the blue and the red was a green possessing a minimum of blue. We had to hit halfway between the red and the blue. We had some lovely subtle greens when they were not placed in juxtaposition with the other two colors, but they would not play in combination.
>
> The next obvious color was yellow and this had to be toned halfway between the red and the green. Only the most brilliant yellow we could make would talk in company with the other three.
>
> The fifth color was the hardest nut to crack. Black was too heavy, although this may have been used if we could have had six or more colors. We had no browns, purples or grays which would tune in. We eliminated all except two colors: a rich turquoise and a lovely color we called rose ebony. But there seemed too much color when any fifth was introduced in any table arrangement. The quartette seemed to demand a quieting influence, so we tried an ivory vellum textured glaze which seemed to fit halfway between the yellow and the regular semi-vitreous wares, and which cliqued when placed against any one of the four colors selected. It took a little time to sell the ivory to our sales organization, but when they saw the table arrangements they accepted the idea.

In the same publication, a month earlier, Rhead had offered this evaluation of the popularity of the various colors with the public:

> When this ware first appeared on the market, we attempted to estimate the preference for one color in comparison with the others. As you know, we make five colors . . . Because the red was the most expensive color, we thought this might affect the demand. And also, because green had previously been a most popular color, some guessed that this would out sell the others. However, to date, the first four colors are running neck and neck with less than one percent difference between them. This is a remarkable result and amply bears out . . . that the 'layman' prefers to mix his colors.

New information taken from the August, 1936 issue of *China, Glass and Lamps* would seem to indicate that of the 54 items we have always considered part of the original Fiesta assortment, some may have actually been developed between the months of January and August. The following excerpt is from that publication:

> *New items in the famous Fiesta line of solid color dinnerware include egg cups, deep 8" plates, Tom and Jerry mugs, covered casseroles, covered mustards, covered marmalades, quart jugs, utility trays, flower vases in 8", 10" and 12" sizes, and bowl covers in 5", 6", 7" and 8" sizes.*

If this report is accurate, and we see no reason to doubt that it is, the original line, the above mentioned items excluded, must have then consisted of coffee pot, regular; teapot, large; teapot, medium; coffee pot, A.D.; carafe; ice pitcher; covered sugar; creamer; bud vase; chop plate, 15"; chop plate, 13"; compartment plate, 10½"; plate, 10"; plate, 9"; plate, 7"; plate, 6"; teacups and saucers; coffee cups and saucers, A.D.; footed salad bowl; nested bowls, 11½" to 5"; cream soup cup; covered onion soup; relish tray; comport, 12"; nappy, 9½"; nappy, 8½"; dessert, 6"; fruit, 5"; ash tray; sweets comport; candle holders, bulb type; candle holders, tripod; salt and pepper shakers; and tumblers. The article also dates the nested bowl lids, although it mentions only 4 of the 5 known sizes. (See color plates.)

Adding further to the selling possibilities of Fiesta, in June, 1936, the company offered their 'Harmony' dinnerware sets. These combined their Nautalis line decorated with a colorful decal pattern, accented and augmented with the Fiesta color selected for that particular set. N-258 featured yellow Fiesta, accenting Nautalis in white decorated with a harmonizing floral decal at the rim. N-259 used green Fiesta to compliment a slender spray of pine cones. Red Fiesta, in N-260, was shown together with Nautalis decorated in lines and leaves having an Art Deco flavor; and blue (N-261) went well with white Nautalis with an off-center flower-filled basket decal. These sets were composed of 76 pieces in this combination:

NAUTALIS SHAPE

8 9" plates
8 6" plates
8 teacups and saucers

8 5½" fruits
1 10" baker
1 9" nappy

FIESTA

8 10" plates
8 7" plates
8 6" plates
1 15" chop plate

1 12" comport
2 bulb candlesticks
1 pair, salt & pepper shakers
1 each, sugar & creamer

Retail price for such a set was around $20.00, with Fiesta red increasing the total cost by about $3.50. This offered a complete service for 8 and extra pieces that allowed for buffet and party service for as many more of the contrasting items.

For some time during the earlier years of production, beautifully accessorized 'Fiesta Ensembles' were assembled — you will see a picture of a display ad showing such a set in the color plates. It contains 109 pieces, only 40 of which are Fiesta:

8 9" plates
8 6" plates
8 teacups and saucers
8 5" fruits

Accessories include:

24 pc. glassware set with Mexican decals, 8 each: 10 oz., 8 oz., and 6 oz. tumblers
8 color coordinated swizzle sticks
8 glass ash trays
Service for 8, flatware with color coordinated plastic handles
1 serving bowl in red Riviera
1 15½" red Riviera platter
1 sugar and creamer in green Riviera

The silverware and glassware in these ensembles were manufactured by other companies and merely shipped to HLC to be reshipped with the Fiesta and other items included in the ensemble. Records fail to identify the company that may have manufactured these complimentary accessories. Included in the carton with the ensemble was a promotional poster advertising this set for $14.95.

The Story of Fiesta

Early in 1938, a sixth color — turquoise — was chosen to be added to the existing five.

By July 1, 1938, the covered onion soup and the small compartment plate had been dropped from production, and the stick handled creamer had been restyled with a ring handle before 1940. There is a 5" fruit listed on the 1937 list, however by 1939 the listing shows a 5½" and a 4¾" fruit. Possibly the 5" and the 5½" are the same size fruit, with the so-called 5" listed actual size in 1939, due to the addition of the 4¾" size. In comparing actual measurements to listed measurements, we found variations of as much as ¾". Assuming the smaller fruit to be the one added in 1939 would account for the scarcity of this item in red, since red was discontinued in 1943 and was not made available again until 1959.

Three other items made their first appearance on the 1938 price lists: the 12" platter, the sauce boat, and the disk water jug.

From 1939 through 1943 the company was involved in a promotional campaign designed to stimulate sales. This involved several special items, each originally offered for sale at $1.00. An ad from the February, 1940, *China, Glass and Lamps* magazine provides us with information concerning the campaign.

> *. . . dollar retailers in Fiesta ware include covered French casserole; 4 pc. refrigerator sets; sugar, creamer and tray set; salad bowl with fork and spoon; casserole with pie plate; chop plate with detachable metal holder; and jumbo coffee cups and saucers in blue, pink and yellow.*

But it also presents us with a puzzling question: what were the jumbo coffee cups and saucers? Sit 'n Sips perhaps? The colors mentioned, though dark blue and yellow were in production in 1940, sound pastel with the inclusion of pink. Anyone have an answer? We don't!

Another item featured in this selling campaign is described in this message from HLC to their distributors:

> *JUICE SET IN FIESTA . . . To help increase your sales! Homer Laughlin is offering an unusual value in the famous Fiesta ware...a colorful, 7 piece Juice Set, calculated to fill*

a real need in the summer refreshment field. The set consists of a 30 oz. disc jug in lovely Fiesta yellow, and six 5 oz. tumblers, one each in the Fiesta blue, turquoise, red, green, yellow and ivory. Sets come packed one to a carton, and at the one dollar minimum retail price, are sure to create an upward surge in your sales curve. Dealers who take advantage of this Juice Set in Fiesta will find it a potent weapon in increasing sales of other Fiesta items. At a nominal price, customers who have not yet become acquainted with Fiesta can own some of the ware which has made pottery history during the past few years. The result? They'll want to own more!

Although the other promotional items are relatively scarce, the yellow juice pitcher is very easily found. This flyer is the only mention of it being for sale during this period; neither it nor the juice tumblers were ever included on Fiesta price lists. A few pitchers have been found in red, and one was reported in light green — perhaps dipped in error or for some special order we have no record of. In 1952, the promotion was repeated — the juice pitcher in gray, the tumblers, according to company records, in dark green, chartreuse and yellow. Either this issue was not extensively promoted, or proved to be a poor seller judging from the scarcity of these items in the '50s colors. Rose tumblers are not at all rare, yet in this color they were not mentioned in either promotion. A factory spokesman explained this to us: while rose was not a standard Fiesta color until the '50s, it had been developed and was in use with the Harlequin line during the forties (see chapter on Harlequin). Since it was available in the dipping department, it was used to add extra color contrast to the juice set. (It also seems logical to assume that some were made in the fifties.)

The French casserole, individual sugar and creamer on the figure-8 tray, and the 9½" salad bowl were also unlisted except in this promotion. Each is standard in a specified color; on rare occurrences when they are found in non-standard glazes, their values are at least doubled! French casseroles were all to be yellow; however a dark blue one has been reported, and a lid has been found in green. Very recently, we received a letter telling us that an ivory one exists. Yellow was also standard for the 9½" salad, but a very few have surfaced in dark blue, red, ivory and light green. The individual sugars and creamers were to be yellow, the trays dark blue; one sugar has been found in turquoise, creamers in red are very scarce though not as rare as in turquoise, and trays are rare in both yellow and turquoise.

In 1943 our government assumed control of uranium oxide, an important element used in the manufacture of the Fiesta red glaze. As a result, it was dropped from production — 'Fiesta red went to war'. Perhaps the fact that Fiesta red was always listed separately and priced proportionately higher than the other colors was due in part to the higher cost of raw material, plus the fact that the red items required strict control during firing, and the losses that did occur had to be absorbed in the final costs.

The color assortment in 1944 included turquoise, green, blue, yellow and ivory. The '44 price list no longer shows the tripod candle holders, nested bowls, or the 10" and 12" flower vases.

Although the colors are listed the same on the 1946 price list, the following pieces were discontinued: bud vase, bulb type candle holders, carafe, 12" comport, sweets comport, 8" vase, 11½" fruit bowl, ice pitcher, marmalade, mustard, 9½" nappy, footed salad bowl, large teapot, tumbler and utility tray.

From 1946 through 1950 we have found no written information nor can the factory provide us with any. Perhaps at some time during these four years the color assortment was changed — we can't be sure. However, the October 1, 1951, price list does show these changes, and this may or may not have been the first year for them. Light green, dark blue and old ivory were retired from from active duty some time after the war was over. Their replacements were forest green, rose, chartreuse and gray, augmented by two old standards, turquoise and yellow.

If you have fallen into the habit of referring to these new colors as the 'war colors', as we have, they might be more accurately dubbed 'fifties' colors', since they and the listed assortment remained in production without change until 1959.

The big news in 1959 was, of course, the fact that Fiesta red had finished her patriotic duty and was welcomed back home with much ado! The Atomic Energy Commission licensed The Homer Laughlin China Company to again buy the depleted uranium oxide, and Fiesta red, the most popular of all colors, returned to the market in March of 1959.

The Story of Fiesta

In addition to red, turquoise and yellow, medium green was offered for the first time. Rose, gray, chartreuse and dark green were discontinued and the following items were no longer available: 15" chop plate; coffee cup and saucer, A.D.; coffee pot, regular; 10½" compartment plate; cream soup cup; egg cup; 4¾" fruit and 2 pt. jug. A new item made a first appearance — the individual salad bowl. During the sixties, no changes were made either in the line or the colors. Though retail prices had risen in 1965, by 1968 some items stayed the same while others had actually dropped just a little.

In the latter months of 1969, in an effort to meet the needs of the modern housewife and to present a product that was better designed to be in keeping with modern day decor, Fiesta was restyled and only one of the original colors, Fiesta red, always the favorite, continued in production.

As a footnote, we include a short chapter on Fiesta Ironstone, without which, perhaps, the story of Fiesta would be incomplete. Due to its very contemporary flair and modern colors, however, we feel reluctant to include it in our story, except as a sequel. However, in the days to come — perhaps even now in the minds of some — Fiesta Ironstone will come into its own as a collectible.

IDENTIFICATION OF TRADEMARK DESIGN AND COLOR

The original design, colors, and name are the registered property of the Homer Laughlin China Company. Patent No. 390-298 was filed on March 20, 1937, having been used by them since November 11, 1935. With only a few exceptions their distinctive trademark appears on every piece. These four seem to be the most common.

fiesta
HLC USA

H. L. C.
fiesta
MADE IN
U.S.A.

fiesta
MADE IN
U.S.A.

GENUINE
fiesta
H. L. Co.   USA
(Handstamped)

The indented trademark was the result of in-mold casting; the ink mark was put on with a hand stamp, after the color was applied and before the final glaze was fired.

Identification of Trademark, Design and Color

As many other manufacturers were following the trend to brightly colored dinnerware, the wide success and popularity of Fiesta resulted in its being closely copied and produced at one time by another company. Homer Laughlin quickly brought suit against their competitor and forced the imitation ware to be discontinued. To assure buyers they could buy with complete confidence, the word 'Genuine' was added to the hand stamp sometime before 1940. Genuine Fiesta was the exclusive product of Homer Laughlin.

There are some items in the Fiesta line which were never marked — juice tumblers, demitasse cups, salt and pepper shakers, and some of the Kitchen Kraft line. The teacups were never to have been marked as a standard procedure, but a rare few of these and the demitasses as well have been found with the ink stamp. Sweets comports, ash trays and onion soups may or may not be marked. Never pass up a 'goodie' such as these simply because they are unmarked! As you become more aware of design and color, these pieces will be easily identified as Fiesta.

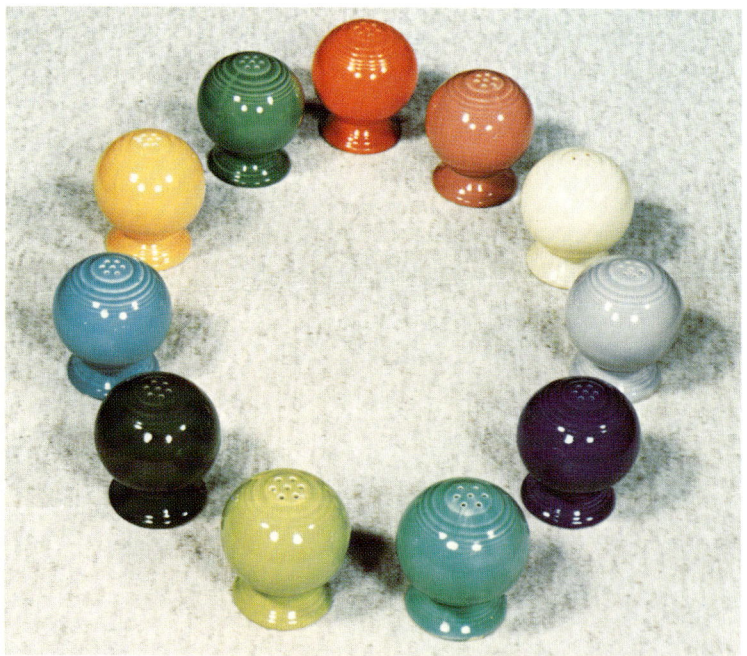

_____Identification of Trademark, Design and Color

Fiesta's design is very simple and therefore very versatile. The pattern consists of a band of concentric rings graduating in width, with those nearer the rim having the wider space between. The rings are repeated in the center motif on such pieces as plates, nappies, platters, desserts, etc. Handles are applied with slight ornamentation at the base. Vases and tripod candle holders, though designed without the rings, are skillfully modeled with simple lines, geometric forms and stepped devices that instantly relate to the Art Deco mood of Fiesta's clean uncluttered shapes. Flat pieces and bowls are round or oval; hollowware pieces are globular and many are styled with a short pedestal base decorated with the band of rings.

But of course, it's Fiesta's vivid colors that first capture your attention. The wide array of color provides endless possibilities for matching color schemes and decor. And if you find you love all eleven, you'll surely enjoy collecting a place setting in every color — Fiesta red, rose, old ivory, gray, dark blue, light green, chartreuse, forest green, turquoise, yellow and medium green. (See photo at left)

A WORD TO THE WISE . . .

Haven't we all had the experience of finding a likely looking piece of dinnerware . . . we ponder and study, turn it over and over, flip the rim to make it ring, compare color and glaze, weight and thickness . . . and still be at a complete loss???

Probably the most important lesson to be learned, especially in this area of collecting, is that no matter how good a piece looks, be extremely suspicious. Styles, designs, decorations, and even glazes were flagrantly copied from one pottery by another. Whole lines were stolen from pottery dumps!

By now, many of you have been collecting the various colored dinnerware lines of HLC for many years. You have become much more aware of the similar wares produced by Knowles; Taylor, Smith and Taylor; Bauer and many others; and you're better educated and equipped to determine which of the many 'look-alike' wares are indeed properly bred and truly deserving of a home in your exclusively Homer Laughlin collections.

But to the newer collectors, this can be very confusing to say the least! Once we become familiar with the wonderful glazes used for Fiesta and Harlequin, strange pieces in exactly those colors seem to 'come out of the woodwork' — coyly enticing — and in our enthusiasm it is sometimes difficult to place them in their proper perspective. Many manufacturers produced numerous lines of these gaily colored wares and it is impossible in most cases to determine the origin of any piece by the color or quality of the glaze alone. For instance, the Bauer Pottery of California produced their Ring pattern in some of the same colors as Fiesta. Taylor, Smith and Taylor made Vistosa, with its pastry crimped rims and hollowware handles each daintily accented with a tiny blossom, in Fiesta-like red, cobalt blue, yellow and light green! Caliente's streamline styling featured hollowware whose bases were designed with four petal-like feet, and its colors were also similar — tangerine, yellow, blue and green. There was Yorktown by Knowles, and a line by Stangl — at least three by the Paden City Pottery, not to mention others (even one from Japan). All were aimed at catching the 'magic ring' — at becoming the favorite of the American people who had fallen in love with color!

_____A Word To The Wise!

Nor was the 'band of rings' decoration exclusive with HLC. Bauer's Modern (1935) is very similar to Fiesta. Yorktown by Knowles . . . Hamilton Ross's look-alike . . . all were geared to the Deco movement — clean fluid geometry in precision arrangements of lines and angles.

So that you may easily recognize the Homer Laughlin wares, study the shapes in the color plates. This is the key. We still occasionally hear of those who refuse to buy unmarked ware. This practice is unnecessary. Although there have been many imitations, none of these lines have ever been copied so precisely that anyone who makes an effort to become familiar with their appearance cannot distinguish them from even their closest look-alike.

There are several items shown in the color section that are especially confusing to new collectors — others continue to surface. We once saw a turquoise casserole that looked exactly like the Fiesta casserole, except this one had no foot. It was marked 'Tricolator Products, U.S.A.' It seemed logical to assume that these were manufactured at HLC for Tricolator Products. But a company official cleared up the mystery with this statement: 'It is unthinkable that with the popularity of Fiesta, we would sell Fiesta items under another company's name.' Another imitation! There are bulb type candle holders very similar to Fiesta's, and salt and pepper shakers of many types. One curious set consisted of what appeared to be a genuine Fiesta salt shaker perched atop a little raised platform with handles, which was actually the pepper! (HLC had never heard of it!)

Then of course there are always 'Fiesta butter dish' stories from time to time. Here is HLC's report:

> *If you do find the butter in Fiesta, it will necessarily be a copy, because this certainly was one of the items that was never produced in this line, based upon all records available and the memories of those people involved in designing, manufacturing, and shipping Fiesta over the years.*

Although such reports have become infrequent, there may even yet be an undiscovered item or two . . . perhaps a one-of-a-kind whimsy created by an inventive craftsman. These things have always been. Even through the years of mass production, that desire innate in every man to make something with his own hands, using his own ideas, is

A Word To the Wise!

strong in the human breast. The temptation to create in an environment where all the necessary materials and equipment are available would be too much for the craftsman so inclined to put from his mind! In the color section you will see several lamps whose sections are fashioned from comport stems, casserole bowls, nappies and fruit dishes. A company spokesman recalls that some of their employees made lamps for themselves from carafe bottoms. Others used tall vases.

One last item that may be confusing some of you (it certainly did us) is the pie plate with an exact duplication of the Harlequin rings. We have seen one in green, and the color is a perfect match. This is a classic example. HLC says it is not Harlequin, nor did they produce it. So be cautious! We would welcome your inquiries if you have questions about identification. If there are new discoveries — and there may yet be — we will do our best to keep our fellow collectors informed and up to date!

THAT RADIOACTIVE RED!

Exactly when the first rumors began circulating, hinting that the red Fiesta could be 'hazardous' to your health, is uncertain. In most probability, it was around the time that Fiesta red was reintroduced after the war, and was no doubt due to the publicity given to uranium and radioactivity during the war years. Clearly another case where 'a *little* learning can be a dangerous thing'.

In any case, this worry must have remained to trouble the minds of some people for several years. Even today the subject comes up occasionally and remains a little controversial, even though most folks in this troubled age of acid rains, 25% unemployment, cholesterol-free diets, and constant reminders that 'cigarettes are hazardous to your health' don't really seem too upset by it any more.

The following letter appeared in the *Palm Beach Post Times*, in February, 1963. It was written 'tongue-in-cheek' by a man who had evidently reached the limit of his patience. HLC sent it to us from their files; it has to be a classic. Here it is . . .

> *Editor:*
> *After reading about the radioactive dishes in your paper I am greatly concerned that I may be in danger, as I had a plate with a design in burnt orange, or maybe it was lemon.*
> *This plate was left to me by my great grandmother, and I noticed that whenever she ate anything from it her ears would light up so we all had to wear dark glasses when dining at her house.*
> *I first became suspicious of this dish when putting out food for my dog on it I noticed the dog's nose became as red as Rudolph's and one day a seagull fed from it and all his feathers fell off; then one night when the weather was raw I placed it at the foot of my bed and my toenails turned black.*
> *Using it as a pot cover while cooking eel stew, the pot cracked; and reading the letters in your paper last week have concluded I am not the only person having a cracked pot in the house, so perhaps some of your other readers used a plate for a cover.*

> *I finally threw this plate overboard at a turn in the channel, now a bouy is no longer needed there, as bubbles and steam mark this shoal.*
>
> *Will you please ask your Doctor or someone if they think this plate was radioactive, and if so am I in any danger, and if so from what?*
>
> *(Name Withheld)*

Recently we were allowed the opportunity to search through old company literature in the event that some bit of pertinent information had escaped our notice. It was obvious from letters contained in these files that HLC had always been harassed with letters from people concerned with the uranium content of the Fiesta red glaze. Their replies were polite, accommodating and enlightening. Here in part is one of their letters:

> *Before 1943 the colorant, 14% by weight of the glaze covering the ware is uranium oxide (U-308) with the uranium content being made up of about 0.7% U-235 and the remainder U-238. With the probe of a nuclear measurements Corp GS-3 model Geiger Counter resting on ware found in our museum, we obtained a reading of 6 milliroentgens (mR) per hour of combined Beta and Gamma radiation. Between 1943 and 1959, under license by AEC, we have again been producing a red glazed dinnerware. However the colorant now used is depleted technical grade U-308 with the uranium content being made up of about 0.2% U-235 and the remainder U-238. Average recording is 4 mR per hour combined Beta and Gamma.*

Studies were conducted for us by Dr. Paul L. Ziemer and Dr. Geraldine Deputy (who is herself an avid Fiesta collector) in the Bionuclionics Department of Purdue University. The penetrating radiation from the uranium oxide used in the manufacturing of the glaze for the 'red' Fiesta ware was measured with a standard laboratory Geiger Counter. All measurements are tabularized in units of milliroentgens per hour (mR/hr).

ITEM	SURFACE CONTACT	4" ABOVE SURFACE	ALONG RIM
13" Chop Plate	0.8	0.35	0.1
9" Plate	0.5	1.5	0.07
Fruit Bowl	1.5	0.5	0.1
Relish Tray Wedge	0.8	0.2	0.02
Cup	1.3	0.2	0.03

In order to compare the above values to familiar quantities of radiation, we calculated the exposure of a person holding a 13" chop plate strapped to his chest for 24 hours. This gives 20 milliroentgens per day. Safe levels for humans working with radiation is 100 milliroentgens per week for a 5 day week or 20 milliroentgens per day as background radiation.

Some other measurements of interest for comparison purposes are:

ITEM	RADIATION
Radium Dial on a Watch	20 mR/hr
Chest X-Ray	44 mR per film
Dental X-Ray	910 mR per film
Fatal Dose	400,000 mR over whole body

So you see — unless you've noticed your grandmother's nose glowing — we're all quite safe!

One other small worry to put to rest (some have mentioned it): there is no danger from the fired-on glazes which are safe, as opposed to a shellac-type color which could mix with acid from certain foods and result in lead poisoning.

As recently as May, 1977, on an Eastern television station, an announcement was made concerning the pros and cons of the safety of colored glazed dinnerware. Fiesta was mentioned by name. We contacted the Department of Health, Education and Welfare, FDA, in Chicago, Illinois. This in part is their position, and is supported by HLC:

> *The presence of lead, cadmium and other toxic metal in glaze or decal is not in itself a hazard. It becomes a problem only when a glaze or decal that has not been properly formulated, applied or fired, contains dangerous metals which can be released by high acid foods such as fruit juices, some soft drinks, wines, cider, vinegar and vinegar containing foods, sauerkraut, and tomato products.*

HLC passed the rigorous federal tests with flying colors! In fact, the only examples of earthenware posing a threat to consumers were imported, and hobbyists were warned to use extreme caution in glazing hand thrown ceramics.

The FDA report continues:

> *Be on the safe side by not storing foods or beverages in such containers for prolonged periods of time, such as overnight. Daily use of the dinnerware for serving food does not pose a hazard. If the glaze or decal is properly formulated, properly applied, and properly fired, there is no hazard.*
>
> *. . . R.I.P.*

DATING CODES AND ENGLISH MEASUREMENTS

Many HLC lines often carry a backstamp containing a series of letters and numbers. The company has provided this information to help you in deciphering these codes:

In 1900 the trademark featured a single numeral identifying the month, a second single numeral identifying the year, and a numeral 1, 2, or 3 designating the point of manufacture as East Liverpool, Ohio.

In the period 1910-20, the first figure indicated the month of the year, the next two numbers indicated the year, and the third figure designated the plant. Number 4 was 'N', Number 5 was 'N5', and the East End plant was 'L'.

A change was made for the period of 1921-1930. The first letter was used to indicate the month of the year such as 'A' for January, 'B' for February, 'C' for March. The next single digit number was used to indicate the year, and the last figure for the plant.

For the period 1931-40 the month was expressed as a letter, but the year was indicated with two digits. Plant No. 4 was 'N', No. 5 was 'R', Nos. 6 and 7 were 'C', and No. 8 was listed as 'P'. During this period, E-44R5 would indicate May of 1944 and manufactured by Plant No. 5. The current trademark has been in use for approximately 70 years, and the numbers are the only indication of the specific years that items were produced.

Dating Codes and English Measurements

Collectors have long been puzzled over the origin and meaning of such terms as oval 'baker' and '36s bowl' — not to mention the insistent listings of 4" plates, when it has become very apparent that 4" plates do not exist! We asked our contact at HLC for an explanation. He told us that each size of bowl was assigned a number. Smaller numbers indicated larger bowls, and vice versa. The word 'baker', as used to describe a serving bowl, was an English potting term. It was also the English who established the unfortunate system of measurements based on some rather obscure logic where a 6" plate should be listed as 4". 7" 'nappies' (also an English term) actually measure 8¾"; 4" fruits are usually 5½"; 5", 7", and 8" plates are really 7", 9", and 10".

This practice continued through the fifties, until it became so utterly confusing to everyone involved that actual measurements were thankfully adopted . . . however, these may vary as much as ¾" from those listed on company brochures. For instance, 9" and 10" plates actually measure 9½" and 10½", and the 13" and 15" chop plates are 12¼" and 14¼".

The small incised letters and/or numbers sometimes found on the bottom of hollowware pieces were used to identify a pieceworker . . . perhaps a molder or a trimmer . . . and were intended for quality control purposes. More likely to appear on Harlequin, nevertheless these are sometimes seen on Fiesta as well.

THE MORGUE REVISITED

Several years ago on one of our visits to HLC we were allowed a rare treat — a visit to that dark, secretive room hidden behind a locked and barred door in the uppermost niche of the office building that has somehow down through the years earned the name of 'the morgue'. Dark and dingy it may be, but to a collector of HLC dinnerware it's filled with excitement! A Fantasy Island if indeed one ever existed.

We told you in previous issues of digging through boxes and shelves and finding fantastic experimentals, beautiful trial glazes and unfamiliar modifications of more standard forms. After spending an entire day photographing and cataloguing our 'finds', we left, tired and dirty, vowing to someday return with a professional photographer so we could share the fun with all of you.

The very first beautiful and unfamiliar piece of Fiesta we saw was the ivory individual teapot (see Plate 1). It is 6″ high and the lid is interchangeable with the demitasse pot. We learned that Fredrick Rhead, the designer, modeled several pieces that were never marketed due to the onset of the war — in fact, many already existing lines had to be cut back. Though this teapot was never mass produced, at least three — all in ivory — have been accounted for.

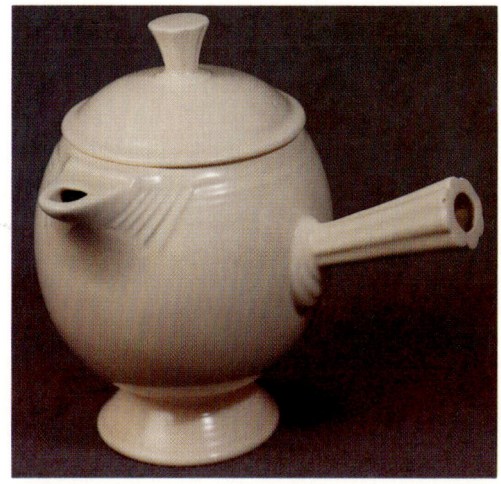

Plate 1

The Morgue Revisited

In Plate 2, at right, is a very unusual onion soup. This is, as far as we know, the only one of its kind, discovered just as we were wrapping up this edition. It differs from the standard onion soup in several ways: note that the handles are flat rather than rolled under; and the top of the base flares. Inside, this one has the band of rings device at the rim and in the bottom. The lid is less domical and ½" wider. The base is marked in the mold, 'Fiesta HLC'.

In Plate 3 is a very unique sugar and creamer set. It rests on the scarce figure-8 tray, which along with the standard individual sugar and creamer was part of a promotional campaign during the early 1940s. Though these (nor the onion soup in Plate 1) were not found in the morgue, we have included them here since they fall into the categeory of experimentals. This set has only recently been found; another creamer in ivory and a sugar bowl in a splotchy brown similar to some of the trial glazes we found at HLC are known to exist.

Somehow with all of our digging we missed the two items in Plate 4 on our first visit. The French casserole is a footed version of the more familiar yellow one; the bowl (isn't the foot a lovely addition) measures 9¾" tall by 6" across.

In Plate 5, left to right, is a divided relish molded in one piece; it measures 11" in diameter and has the look of Fiesta. The carafe, 10" tall, was sold with another HLC line, but this particular example was for some unknown reason dipped in the light green of the colored dinnerware lines we love. In the center is a magnificent Fiesta red 12" vase, over which wars would certainly be waged if it were up for grabs — which, we must stress, it is *not*, nor are any of these other fabulous pieces, so please don't even ask! They are all company property and will remain so. But there is a museum at the factory outlet in Newell, where some of them will be on display. The piece to the right of the vase looks very familiar, except for its size. It's 6½" tall, scaled to perfection to match the Fiesta syrup. Directly in front of it is the only marked piece we saw in the morgue. Most experimentals were merely marked with a number, or not at all. This one, however, was embossed 'Fiesta'. It's 5" across by 1" deep and has the band of rings on the flange.

The green relish section on the right was designed so that four would fit a large oval wooden tray. The coffee mug in yellow is 3" high, and except for the short tapered base is exactly like the standard mug.

The Morgue Revisited

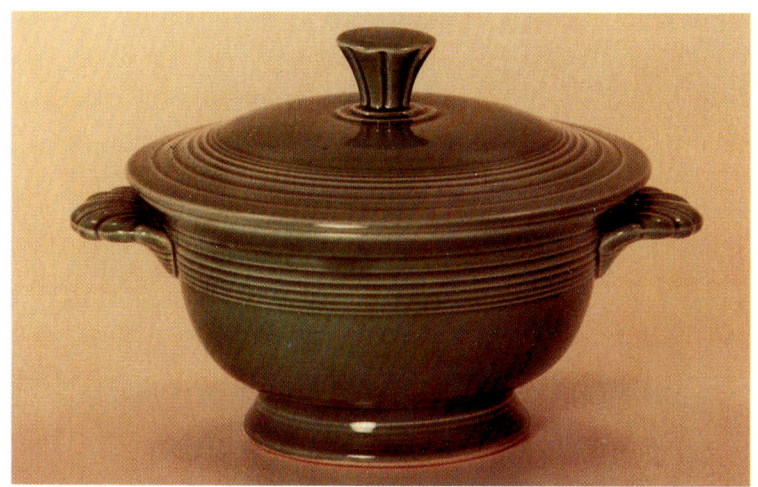

Plate 2

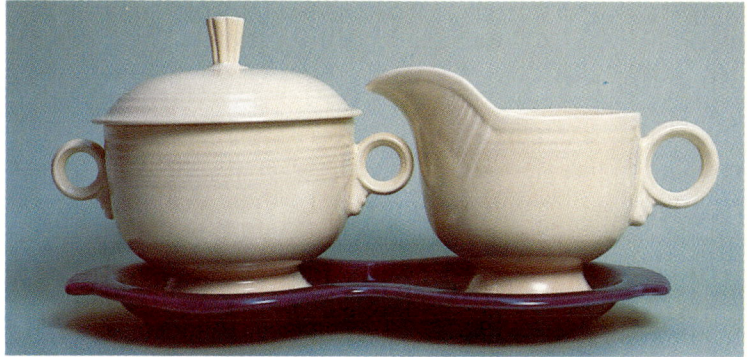

Plate 3

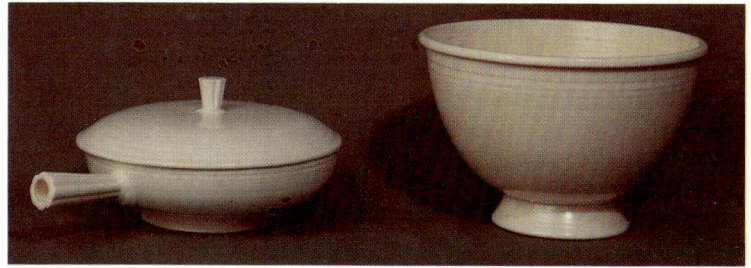

Plate 4

The Morgue Revisited

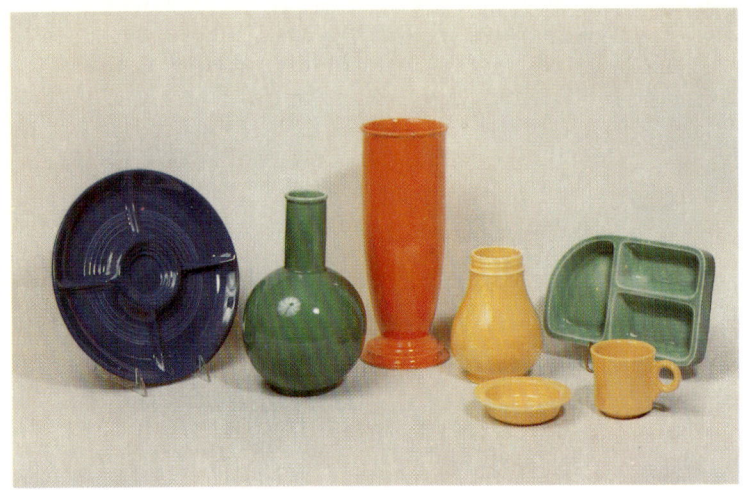

Plate 5

One piece we would have loved to show you but couldn't locate this time was a 6" ivory vase with a round upright disk body that looked like the joined front halves of two juice pitchers without their ice guards. There was a stack of Fiesta plates with unbelievable trial glazes — a pink beige, a spatter effect in dark brown on orange, a smoky delphinum blue, a dark red grape that might possibly be the rose ebony refered to in Rhead's article, a dark russet, a deep mustard yellow, and our favorite, black with four chromium bands.

Harlequin experimentals are shown in Plate 6. The nappy is 5" across and shaped like the small Fiesta fruits. Next, a sauce cup, perhaps, made from the demitasse cup mold. The deep dish in mauve blue is 2½" by 7½" — it has the Harlequin rings inside. On the far right, the yellow bowl measures 2½" by 5½" in diameter.

We looked for but couldn't find to photograph the two different styles of candle holders we had catalogued before. One pair was large and flat, 5½" wide and 2¼" tall in the center. The other pair were shaped like half of an inverted cone, 4¼" across the bottom and 3" tall. Both styles were lovely, but not quite as nice as our regular Harlequin candle holders.

One of the most exciting Harlequin pieces we saw was a demitasse cup and saucer in a beautiful high gloss black. Trial glaze plates included a light chocolate, deep gray, delphinum blue, vanilla, carmel and a luscious lavender.

The Morgue Revisited

The tall 6″ Riviera candle holders we fell in love with before were this time nowhere to be found. But the console bowl was! (See center Plate 7.) It's huge! 3½″ x 8½″ x 13″ long! The ivory Century piece is a one piece fast-stand sauce dish, 7″ across the attached tray. Although the butter dish is just the right size to hold a quarter pound stick of today's butter, it was the only one of the three sizes (this one is 7½″) never marketed.

We hope you have found this peek inside the morgue to be as much fun as it was for us to bring it to you. It is strictly off-limits to the public and we appreciate the opportunity of photographing these lovely experimentals for you to see.

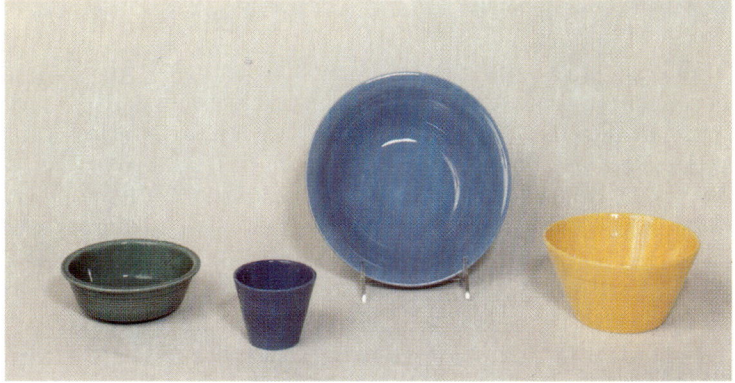

Plate 6

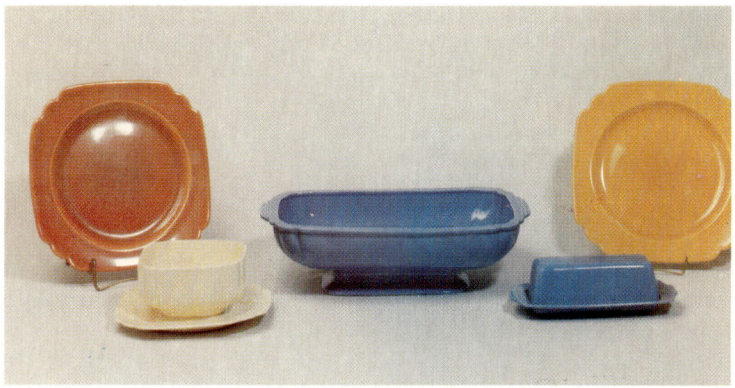

Plate 7

FIESTA

Values are suggested for items that are in mint condition... that is to say, no chips, 'chigger bites', or 'dings'! Bad glazing and scratches would also reduce the value. The three sager pin marks that are evident on the under side of many pieces are characteristic and result from the technique employed during the firing process. These should have no adverse effect. When varying market values warrant, prices are indicated for particular colors. The term 'original colors' will here refer to light green, yellow, ivory, dark blue and turquoise. Red will be mentioned specifically if it's included in the same price range, otherwise it will have a seperate listing.

Both chop plates were in the original assortment. The larger size was discontinued around 1959, while the smaller continued in production until the restyling. The large compartment plate was never shown on company price lists. They're a little hard to find; no turquoise has ever been reported, leaving us to believe that production began sometime after 1936 and ended before 1938 when turquoise was introduced. Not quite as scarce, the smaller size was listed in the 1936 assortment, but was dropped sometime before the advent of medium green. Plates have always been in good supply, however the 10" size is fast becoming less than abundant. The number of rings within the foot area on the back will vary — these identified the particular jigging machine that made it, and were used in quality control.

Plate 8. Chop plate, 15", fifties colors: $22.00-26.00; original colors: $12.00-15.00; red: $16.00-20.00. Chop plate, 13", fifties colors and medium green: $18.00-22.00; original colors: $9.00-12.50; red: $12.00-16.00.

Plate 9. Compartment plate, 11½": $18.00-22.00. Compartment plate, 10½", fifties colors: $16.00-20.00; original colors: $9.00-12.00; red: $15.00-17.50.

Plate 10. Plate, 10", medium green: $18.00-22.00; original colors: $7.00-9.50; red and fifties colors: $10.00-14.00. Plate, 9", original colors: $4.00-6.00; red, medium green and fifties colors: $7.50-10.00. Plate, 7", original colors: $3.50-4.50; red, medium green and fifties colors: $4.00-6.00. Plate, 6", original colors: $2.00-3.00; red, medium green and fifties colors: $3.00-4.50.

Fiesta

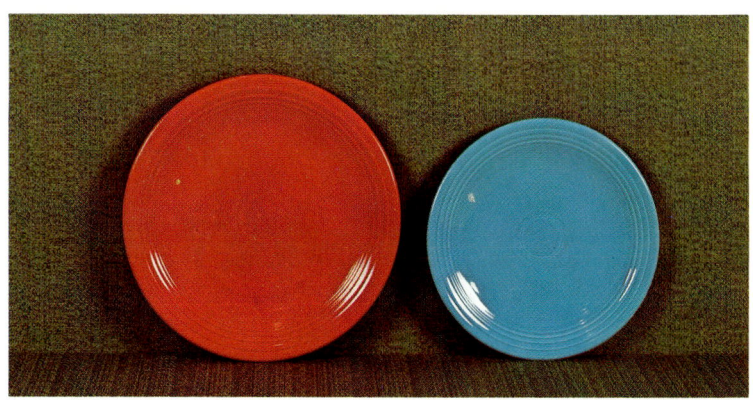

Plate 8

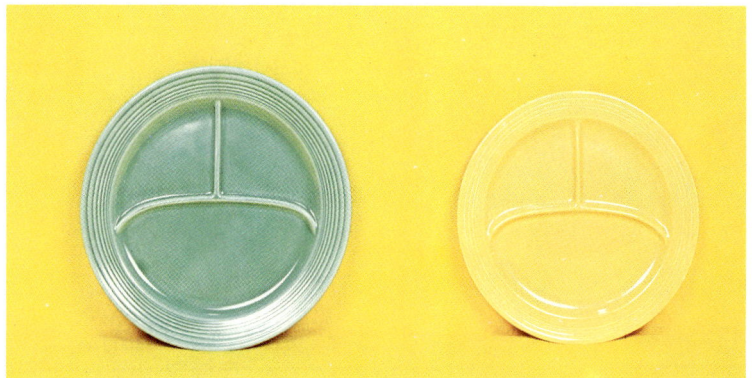

Plate 9

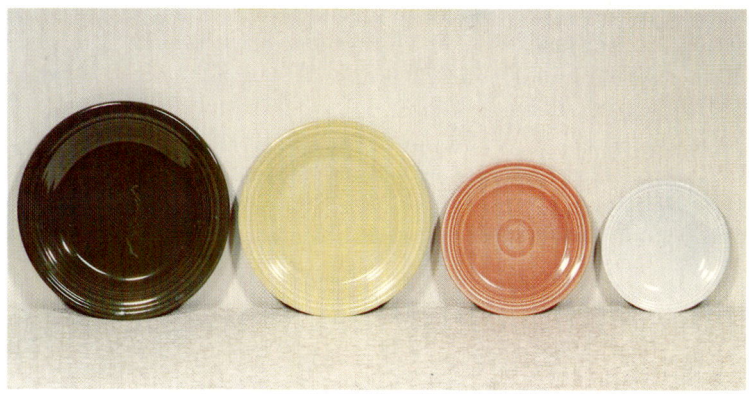

Plate 10

The deep plate was an August, 1936, item that continued in production until the restyling — it's found in all eleven colors. Cream soup cups and 6" deserts (1936 to 1959) are rare in medium green. A later addition, the individual salad bowls were not produced until 1959, and were of course made only in the colors of that period — red, turquoise, yellow and medium green. Occasionally you may find one with no rings in the bottom, probably produced toward the transition into Fiesta Ironstone when such modifications were finalized. Individual salad bowls are easier to find in red and medium green; nevertheless expect to pay a premium for medium green, regarded by collectors as Fiesta's 'rare color'. Of the 4¾" and 5½" fruits, one was the original 5" bowl, the other was added in 1939. We believe the smaller to be the 1939 bowl, due to the scarcity of that item in red. If so, then it would have been produced in red for four years only, before Fiesta red went to war in 1943. Although not appearing on the 1959 price list with the new color assortment, a few have been found in medium green. A rare find recently reported — four small fruits in Serenade blue!

Plate 11. Center top: deep plate, 8", original colors: $9.00–12.00; red, medium green or fifties colors: $15.00–18.00. Left: cream soup cup, fifties colors: $18.00–22.00; medium green: $50.00–60.00; original colors: $12.00–15.00; red: $16.00–20.00. Right: dessert bowl, 6", fifties colors: $12.00–16.00; medium green: $40.00–48.00; original colors: $9.00–12.50; red: $16.00–20.00. Center: individual salad bowl, 7½": $30.00–35.00; medium green: $35.00–40.00. Bottom left: fruit, 4¾", fifties colors: $7.00–10.00; medium green: $25.00–30.00; original colors: $5.00–8.00; red: $9.00–12.00. Bottom right: fruit, 5½", medium green: $15.00–18.00; original colors: $6.00–9.00; red and fifties colors: $10.00–13.00.

Fiesta

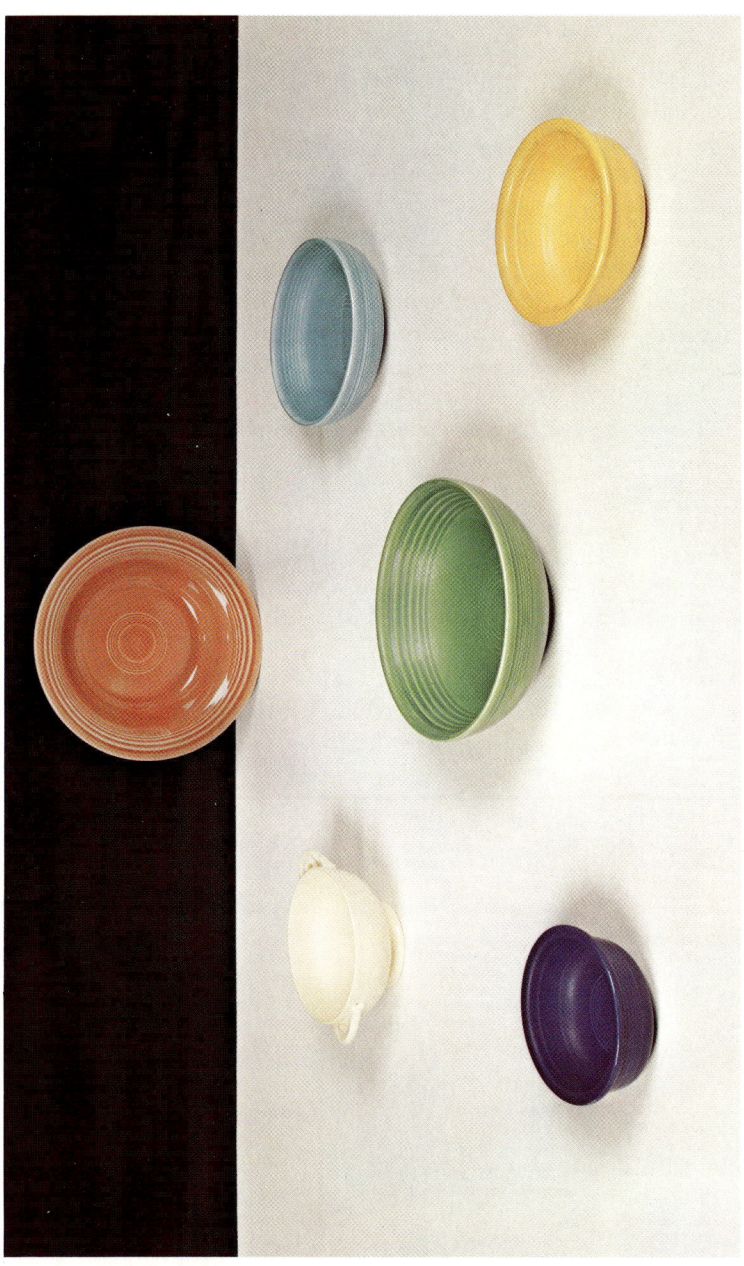

Plate 11

The coffee pot can be found in all of Fiesta's colors except medium green, since it was not made after 1959. We have no information concerning the unusual example in Plate 12 below in ivory with blue bands — but a fruit comport, footed salad bowl, and bulb and tripod candle holders with red stripes on ivory have also been reported. Of course, teacups are always in demand! Those with the inside rings are the oldest — these also have a hand turned foot. A rare few of this type have been found in medium green. Egg cups were made from 1936 until just prior to 1959. They're available in 10 colors (no medium green), and collectors report that chartreuse and gray are the hardest to find. For several years the Lazarus Company issued Fiesta items such as the yellow egg cup (shown opposite) to commemorate their anniversaries. Fruits, plates, tumblers, and recently a green Tom and Jerry dated 1937 have been found; the latest date reported so far has been 1941. Tom and Jerry's (coffee mugs to many collectors) have always been very popular. They were made in all eleven colors, though ivory ones are scarce. Maroon, of course, was never a Fiesta color, so the example in Plate 17 is extremely unusual. It is one from a punch set containing 12 mugs and a large salad bowl, all in maroon. Although it is impossible with so few available to establish an accurate market value, the owner reports a standing offer of $500.00 for her mug.

Plate 13. Coffee pot, original colors: $40.00–45.00; red and fifties colors: $50.00–58.00. Teacup, original colors: $10.00–13.50; red and fifties colors: $14.00–16.50; medium green: $18.00–22.00. Saucers: $2.00–3.00.

Plate 14. Egg cup, fifties colors: $35.00–40.00; original colors: $16.00–20.00; red: $25.00–30.00.

Plate 15. Egg cup, Lazarus commemorative: $25.00–30.00.

Plate 16. Tom and Jerry mug, original colors: $16.50–22.50; red, medium green and fifties colors: $35.00–45.00.

Plate 12

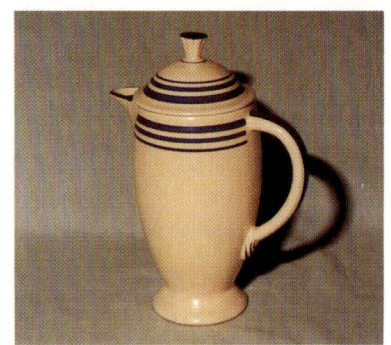

Fiesta

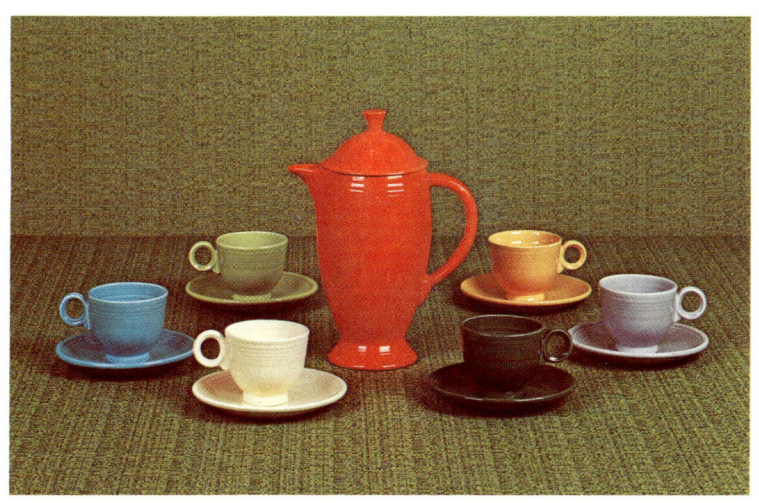

Plate 13

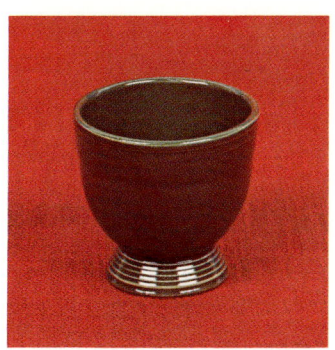

Plate 14

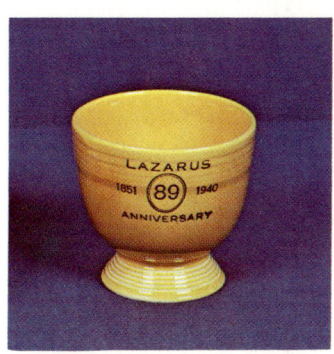

Plate 15

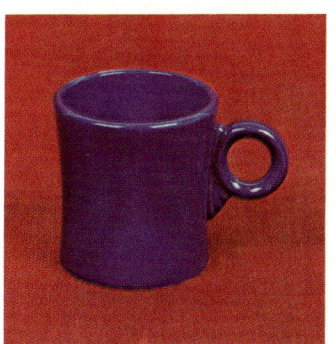

Plate 16

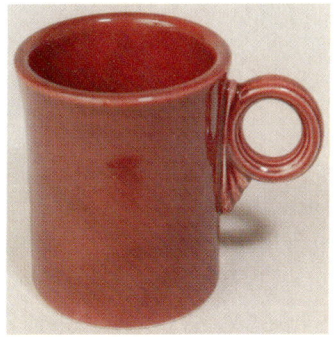

Plate 17

Not original, but added to the line in 1939, the disk water pitcher continued to be made until the end of production. It is most scarce in medium green and chartreuse, followed by the other fifties colors. The tumblers were discontinued in 1946, having been made since the beginning — so they are found in the original six colors only, with turquoise perhaps a little scarce.

The stick handled creamer was also original; sometime between 1938 and 1940 it was restyled with the ring handle . . . found in the first six colors only, it's scarce in turquoise. The utility tray (1936 to 1946) may be a little hard to find, especially in red. See the chapter on *Identification of Trademark, Design and Color* for a photo of the salt and pepper shakers, one in each of the eleven colors. Aside from the larger Kitchen Kraft shakers, this is the only style made in Fiesta. You may find a good imitation with holes on the side, but they are not genuine Fiesta.

Plate 18. Tumbler, 10 oz., red: $24.00–28.00; original colors: $17.00–21.50. Disk water pitcher, original colors: $24.00–28.00; red: $34.00–38.00; medium green and fifties colors: $45.00–50.00.

Plate 19. Covered sugar, fifties colors: $12.00–14.50; original colors: $7.00–9.50; red and medium green: $16.00–20.00. Creamer (regular), original colors: $4.00–6.50; red, medium green and fifties colors: $9.00–12.00. Stick handled creamer, original colors: $9.00–12.00; red: $12.00–15.00. Utility tray, original colors: $10.00–13.00; red: $16.00–20.00. Salt and pepper shakers, original colors: $8.00–10.00, pr; red, medium green and fifties colors: $12.00–16.00, pr.

Fiesta

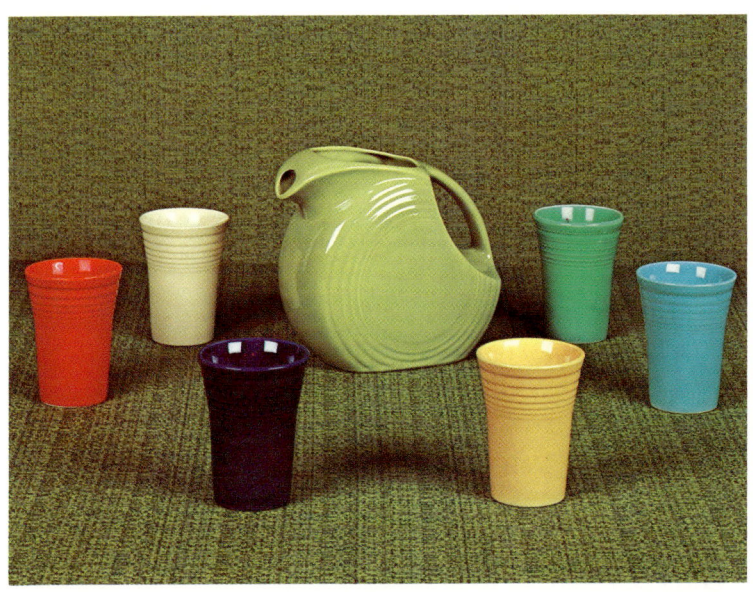

Plate 18

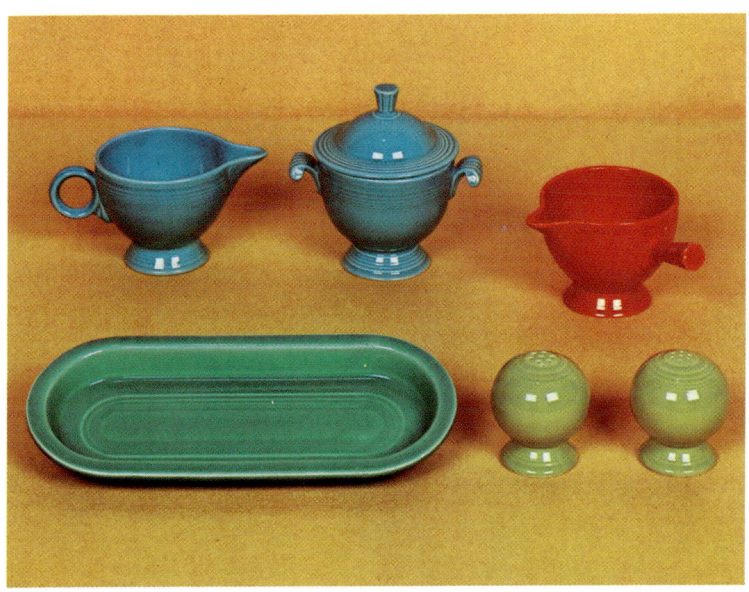

Plate 19

The platter was first listed in 1939 and continued in production until restyling when it was enlarged to 13″. Both nappies were in the original assortment, but the larger size was dropped in 1946. The smaller (8½″) carried through until the line was restyled in '69. Although the 9½″ salad bowl was never listed on the price pamphlets, a trade paper from 1940 reported on a Homer Laughlin sales campaign that offered this bowl along with the Kitchen Kraft spoon and fork for only $1.00. The ad copy indicated that these bowls were yellow — they're scarce even in that color, but a rare few have been reported in ivory, red and dark blue.

The 10″ cake plate is completely flat, and very, very rare. We've never found it mentioned in any of the company's literature, but since it has been reported in five of the six original colors (no ivory as yet) it has to be an early piece.

The 11¾″ fruit bowls are hard to find, especially in red. They were made for only seven years — from 1939 to 1945 — in the six original colors

Plate 20. Platter, 12″, original colors: $9.00–13.00; red, medium green and fifties colors: $16.00–20.00. Nappy, 9½″, original colors: $14.00–18.00; red: $18.00–23.00. Nappy, 8½″, original colors: $10.00–13.00; red, medium green and fifties colors: $14.00–18.50. Salad bowl, 9½″ , yellow: $30.00–35.00.

Plate 21. Cake plate, 10″: $65.00–85.00.

Plate 22. Fruit bowl, 11¾″: $70.00–80.00.

Plate 23. Salad bowl, 9½″, dark blue, ivory or red: $80.00–90.00.

Fiesta

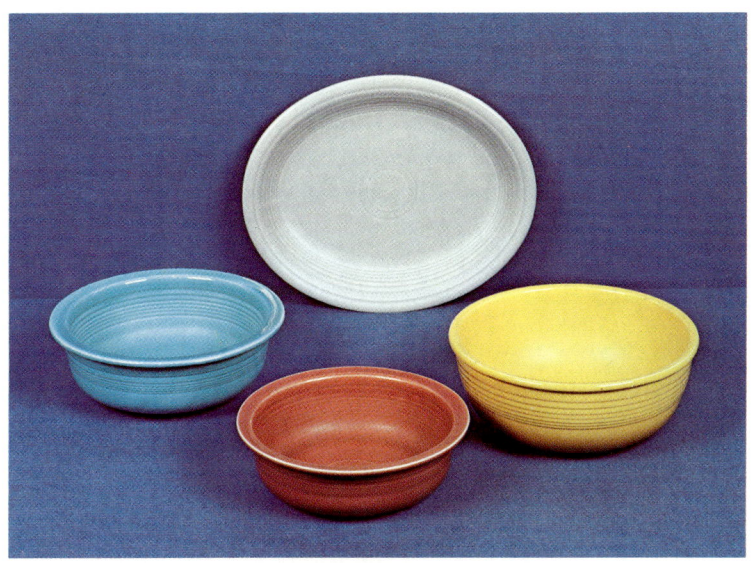

Plate 20

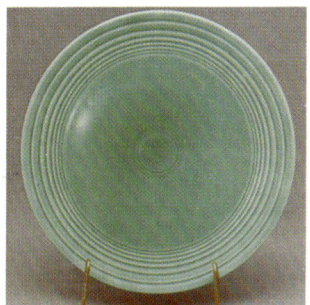

Plate 21

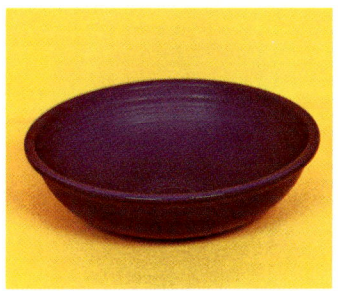

Plate 22

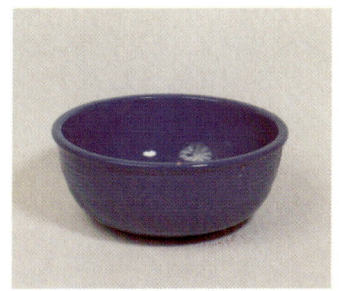

Plate 23

Fiesta

Some of the most exciting news to come along for awhile, a New York dealer has found the #5 nested bowl lid. (Since this is the only one we know of, it's not possible to report an accurate market value.) These lids were only offered during the early forties promotional campaign. The nested bowls (1936 to 1943) are each numbered in sequence on the bottom, #1 being the smallest. They are rather scarce and very heavy — stacked together they weigh nearly 20 pounds!

The sauce boat was produced from 1939 to 1973 in eleven colors, with red and the colors of the fifties the most difficult to find.

Considering that production of the covered casserole was continuous from 1936, they're not especially easy to find. Medium green and the fifties colors are at the top of the price range with red just below.

Rather hard to come by, the footed salad bowl was made from 1936 to 1946 in the first six colors — ivory and yellow are the hardest to find. The unusual decaled example is decorated inside and out with lovely florals and green piping. It's doubtful that it was decorated at HLC, but not entirely impossible. They did make the chop plate with the turkey decal there, though other decaled items have been found with the backstamp of such decorating firms as Pearl China and Royal China.

Plate 24. Nested bowls, #1, 5": $20.00–25.00; #2, 6": $18.00–23.00; #3, 7": $22.00–27.00; #4, 8": $24.00–29.00; #5, 9": $35.00–40.00; #6, 10": $40.00–45.00; #7, 11½", any color: $75.00–85.00. Add 25% to values for #1 through #6 for red. Lids, #s 1, 2, and 3: $60.00–75.00; #4: $70.00–80.00.

Plate 25. Sauce boat, original colors: $12.00–16.00; red, medium green and fifties colors: $16.00–20.00.

Plate 26. Covered casserole, original colors: $38.00–42.00; red, medium green and fifties colors: $58.00–80.00.

Plate 27. Footed salad bowl, original colors: $90.00–100.00; red: $120.00–135.00.

Plate 28. Footed salad bowl with decals: $90.00–100.00.

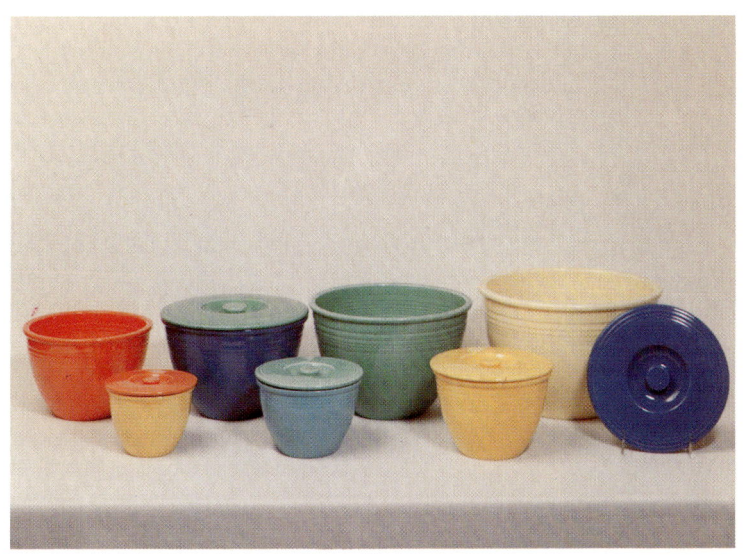

Plate 24

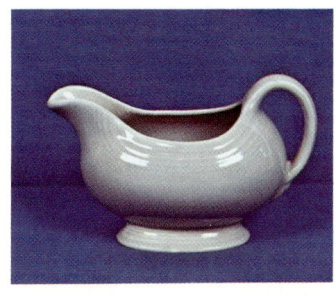

Plate 25

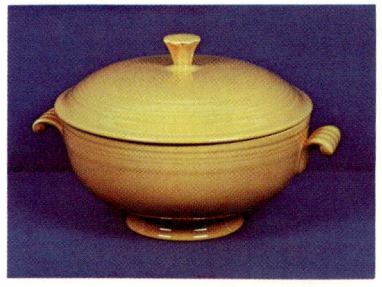

Plate 26

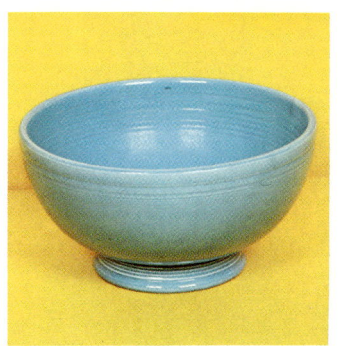

Plate 27

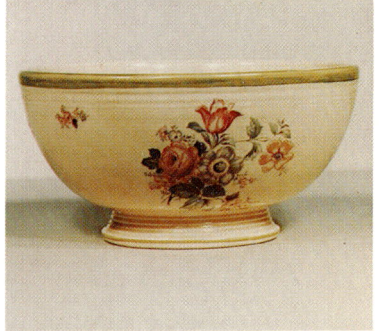

Plate 28

Five individual sections fit into the base of this relish tray, made in the six original colors only (1936 to before 1946). The base has often been mistaken for a pie plate; and even though those center sections would work nicely as coasters, they were never produced or sold for that use. The 12" comport was made from 1936 until 1946, in the six original colors.

Although the demitasse pot was dropped from the line before 1944, the cups and saucers continued to be made until about 1951. You'll find the pot in the original six colors, with red, turquoise and ivory rather scarce. Cups were made in ten colors (no medium green) with the fifties hardest to find and selling at a premium. Below, in Plate 29, a most unusual pot — copper lustre over red — one of a kind, as far as we know, and the decorator remains a mystery. If you're lucky enough to find a similar one, expect to pay at least double the going rate. Another has been reported in a rich burgandy wine. Demitasse cups and saucers decorated by Royal China have been found with a 22k gold overall pattern of cherries and leaves, featuring an 18th century garden scene with a suitor playing upon a flute to a properly demure lady with her fan, both elegantly attired in period costumes.

Plate 30. Relish tray, mixed colors: $54.00–58.00. Comport, 12", original colors: $38.00–42.00; red: $55.00–60.00.

Plate 31. After dinner coffee pot, original colors: $80.00–85.00; red: $90.00–100.00. After dinner cups, fifties colors: $54.00–58.00; original colors: $16.00–20.00; red: $22.00–26.00. After dinner saucers, fifties colors: $14.00–18.00; original colors: $4.00–5.00; red: $6.00–8.00.

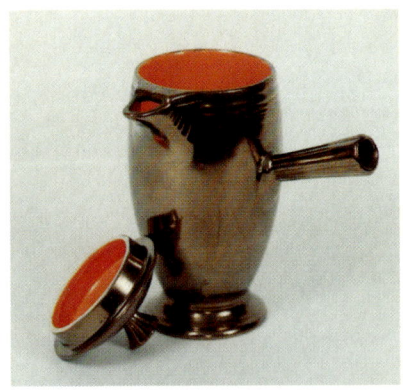

Plate 29

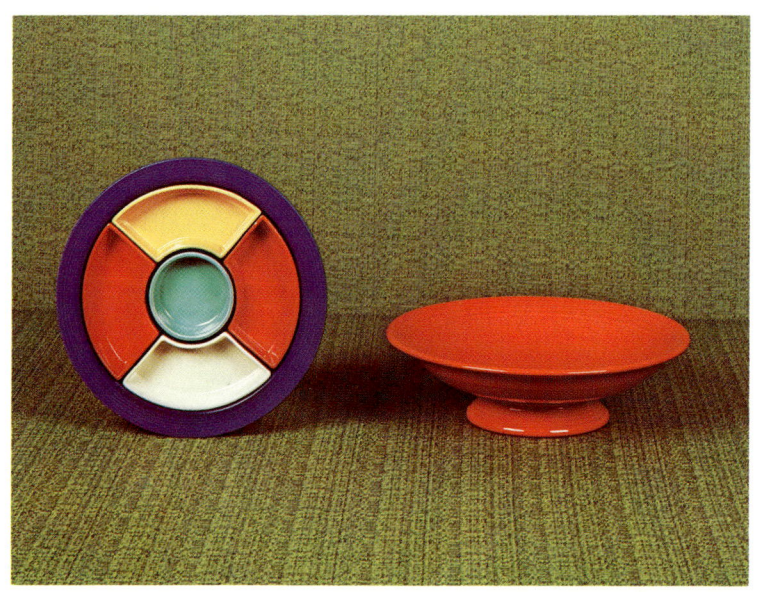

Plate 30

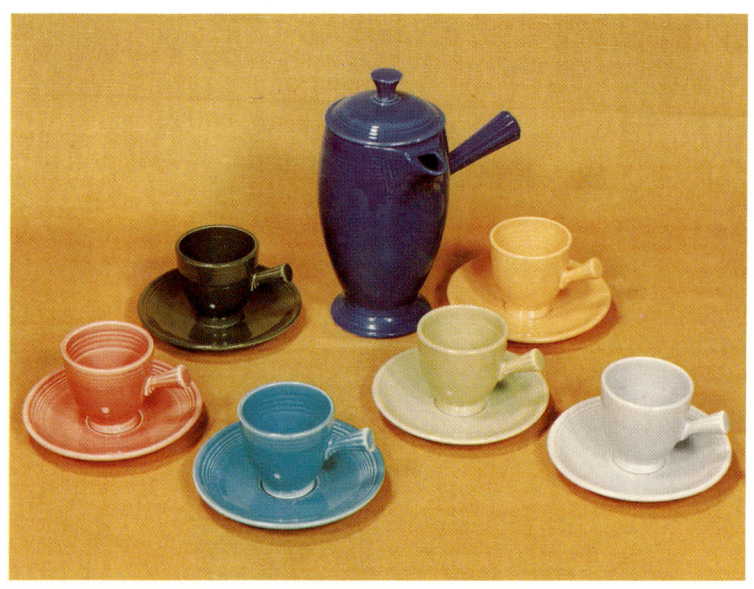

Plate 31

The carafe was an original item, but was no longer listed by 1946. The stopper has a cork seal, and its unique shape makes it a favorite among collectors. You'll find it in the first six colors, with red and ivory most scarce. Made from 1936 until 1946 in the original colors only, the ice pitcher is a little hard to find in ivory, but it's red that tops the price scale; and though its looks seem to suggest otherwise, it does not take a lid.

The 2 pint jug was in the original assortment; it was made until 1959 in all but medium green. It's most scarce in red and the colors of the fifties. Imagine a life style that required a covered onion soup bowl! If the number that remains to the present day is any indication, the housewifes of the late thirties found them to be a little ostentatious, too! They're very scarce — especially in turquoise, since that color was introduced in 1938 and the onion soups were no longer listed by 1939. In a recent poll, only a few collectors reported ever having seen one that was marked.

Plate 32. Carafe, 3 pt., original colors: $58.00–62.00; red: $70.00–85.00. Ice pitcher, 2 qt., original colors: $28.00–32.00; red: $45.00–50.00.

Plate 33. Jug, 2 pt., original colors: $20.00–23.00; red and fifties colors: $28.00–32.00. Covered onion soup, ivory, yellow, light green, and dark blue: $120.00–130.00; red: $140.00–150.00; turquoise: $250.00–300.00.

Fiesta

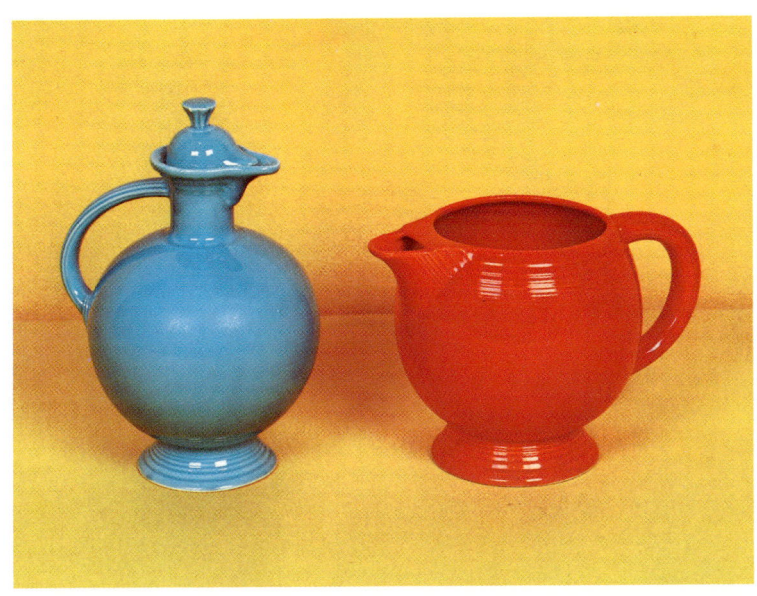

Plate 32

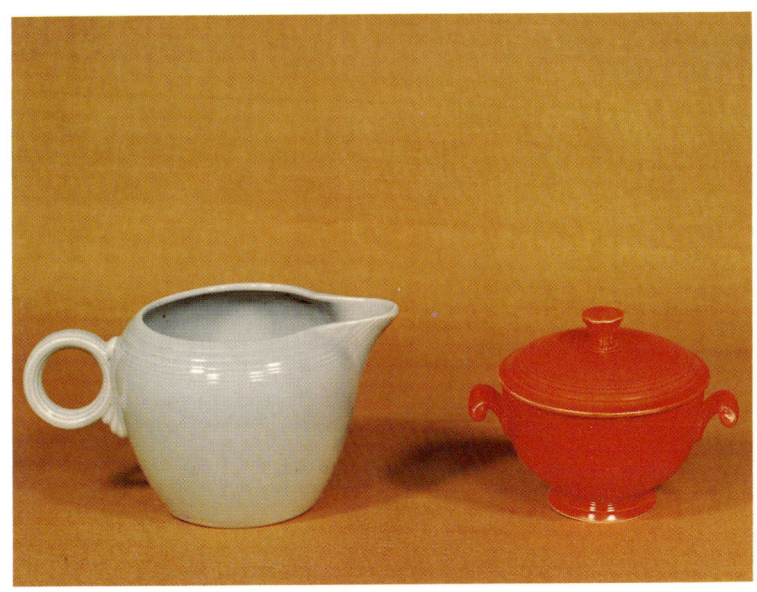

Plate 33

Fiesta

We found that the sweets comport, mustard and marmalade had been discontinued before 1946. (Spoons are not original.) Mustards and marmalades are always in demand. Red mustards are harder to find than red marmalades, and are usually very high! The ash trays were produced from '36 to '73. Syrups rate high with collectors, and the two very similar bottoms below prompt a rather unlikely but true tale! This is the only piece of Fiesta that Rhead did not design — and considering the carefull attention he paid to detail throughout the line, it seems strange that he at least did not alter it to include the band of rings. The mold was bought from the DripCut Company, who made the tops for HLC. The blue one is glass — marked 'DripCut, Heatproof, L.A., Cal.' The red one is genuine Fiesta. A pair of shakers found at a rummage sale were made up of syrup bottoms fitted with metal tops, decorated with a painted design and 'Salt' and 'Pepper' lettering. Decades ago a tea company filled syrup bases with tea leaves, added a cork stopper and their label, and unwittingly contributed to the frustration of our time known to collectors who have only a bottom!

Plate 34. Look-alike bottom: $40.00–45.00.

Plate 35. Sweets comport, original colors: $16.00–20.00; red: $28.00–32.00. Syrup, original colors: $75.00–80.00; red: $110.00–120.00. Ash tray, original colors: $20.00–24.00; red, medium green and fifties colors: $24.00–28.00. Mustard, original colors: $45.00–50.00; red: $70.00–80.00. Marmalade, original colors: $60.00–70.00; red: $70.00–80.00.

Plate 36. Large teapot, 8 cups, original colors: $45.00–50.00; red: $60.00–70.00. Medium teapot, 6 cups, medium green: $110.00–125.00; original colors: $35.00–40.00; red and fifties colors: $52.00–56.00.

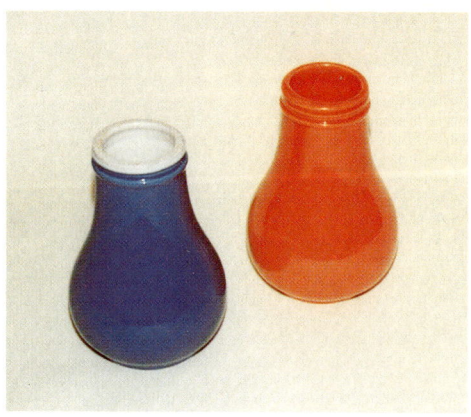

Plate 34

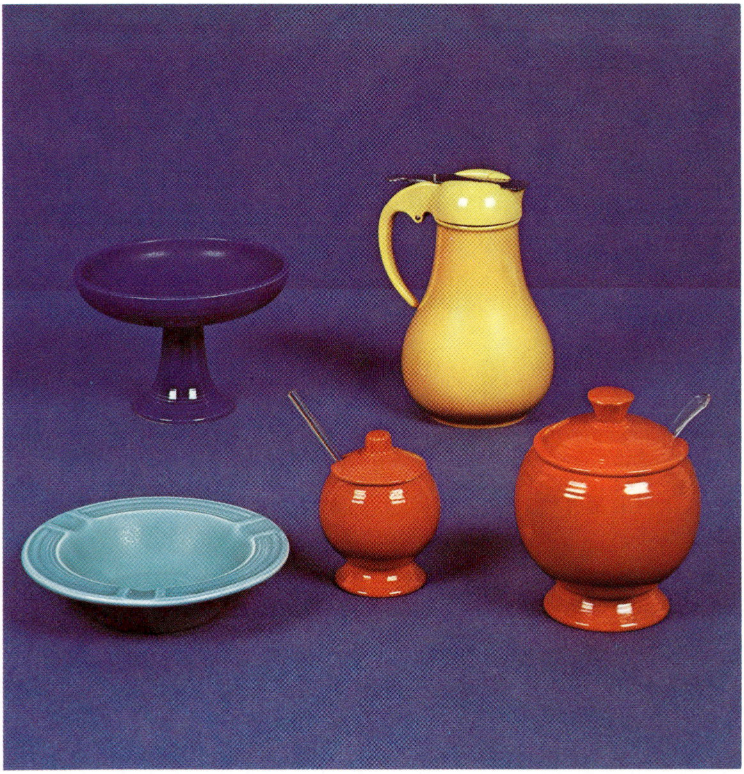

Fiesta

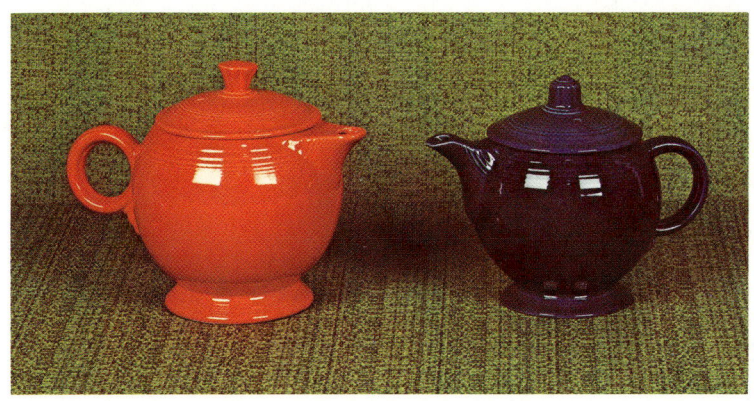

Plate 35

Plate 36

The 10" vase and the bud vase were original, although by August of '36 all four sizes were listed. By 1944, the bud vase and the 8" vase were all that were left in production, and by 1946 even these were gone. All three flower vases are very scarce, especially the 10" size. On the other hand, the bud vases are more readily available. All were produced in the six older colors only. Recently, a collector reported a bud vase in black, a very rare find! He values his vase at $100.00. We have seen a black chop plate, and have heard of black dinner plates. Below, in Plate 38, shown side by side for an interesting comparison is the Fiesta bud vase and a very similar design by Van Briggle.

Tripod candle holders are a fine addition to any collection, but they are among the rarer items in the line. Discontinued around '42 or '43, they were made only in the six original colors. Bulb type candle holders were made for only two years longer than the tripods, but are much easier to find. They are available in the same colors as the tripods, but have also been reported in two unusual colors — bright red and Harlequin yellow.

Plate 37. Bud vase with hand painted florals and gold trim: $40.00–45.00.

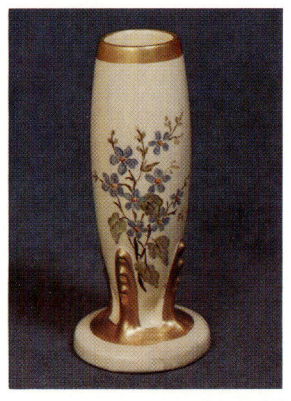
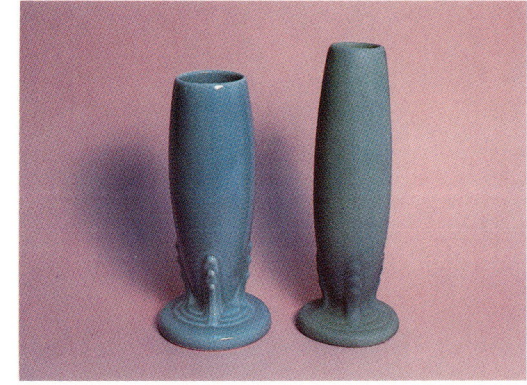

Plate 37   Plate 38

Plate 39. Flower vase, 10", original colors: $150.00–175.00; red: $200.00–225.00. Flower vase, 8", original colors: $130.00–150.00; red: $175.00–200.00. Flower vase, 12", original colors: $165.00–190.00; red: $200.00–250.00. Bud vase, original colors: $20.00–24.00; red: $30.00–35.00.

Plate 40. Tripod candle holders, original colors: $85.00–95.00, pr.; red: $110.00–125.00, pr. Bulb candle holders, original colors: $25.00–30.00, pr.; red: $35.00–40.00, pr.

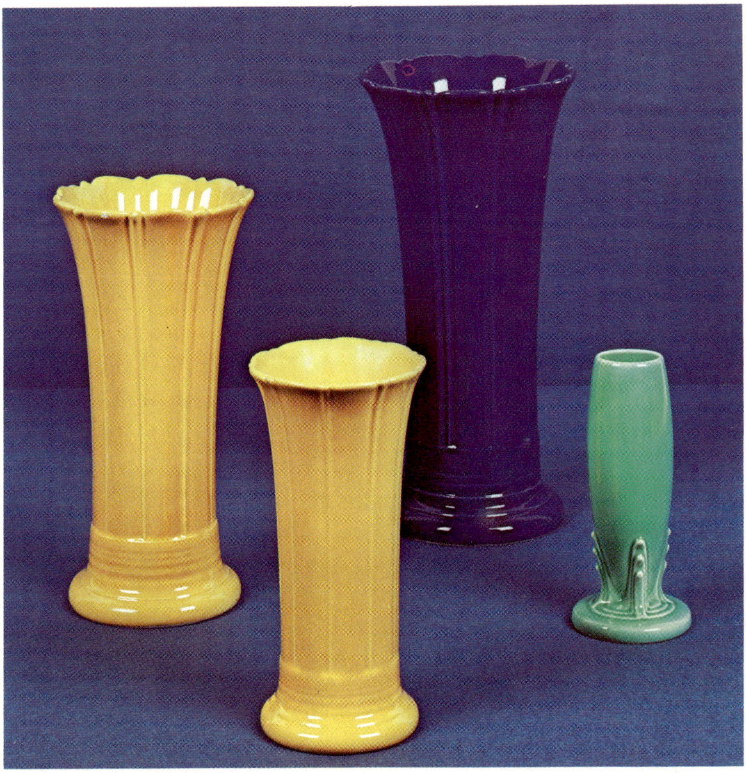

Fiesta

Plate 39

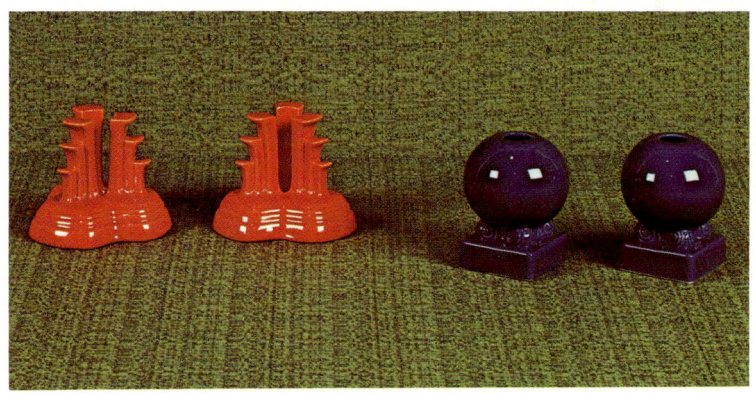

Plate 40

Fiesta

These are four of the eight special campaign items offered by HLC from 1939 to '43. The metal and rattan spring handles have been found in these sizes: 7″, 9″, 10″ (for 10″ plate or relish tray), 13″ and 15″. They are among the few metal accessories that were shipped from HLC. French casseroles are not quite as scarce as we once thought. Virtually all are yellow — only one has ever been reported in dark blue, we've recently heard of one in ivory, and a lid has been found in light green. The individual sugar, creamer and tray set is usually in yellow on a dark blue tray; but occasionally you will find a red creamer, and once in awhile a turquoise or yellow tray. The turquoise creamer shown below is very unusual, and there is at least one sugar known to exist in this color.

Of all the promotional items, the 30 ounce juice pitcher and 5 ounce tumblers are the only ones that are easy to find. 99% of the pitchers are yellow with collectors reporting a high incidence of the use of Harlequin yellow — a slightly lighter shade than Fiesta's. Although one of a kind as far as we know, one pitcher has been reported in light green. Red juice pitchers are rare, but not as rare as the gray ones from the set offered in 1952 with 'green (dark green), yellow and chartreuse' tumblers. Rose juice tumblers, though never mentioned in either promotion, are rather common.

Plate 41. Figure-8 tray, turquoise: $65.00–75.00. Individual creamer, turquoise: $65.00–75.00.

Plate 42. Handled chop plate, handle only: $18.00–22.00. French casserole, yellow: $80.00–100.00; any other color: $165.00–185.00. Figure-8 tray, cobalt: $25.00–30.00; yellow: $75.00–85.00. Individual creamer, yellow: $24.00–27.50; red: $40.00–45.00. Individual sugar, yellow: $30.00–40.00; turquoise: $100.00–125.00.

Plate 43. Juice tumbler, 5 oz., original colors: $11.00–13.50; red and rose: $12.00–15.00. Juice pitcher, 30 oz., red: $80.00–100.00; yellow: $9.00–12.50; gray: $110.00–125.00; any other standard Fiesta color: $150.00–175.00.

Plate 41

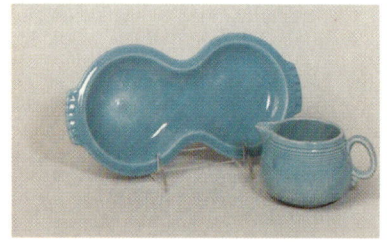

Fiesta

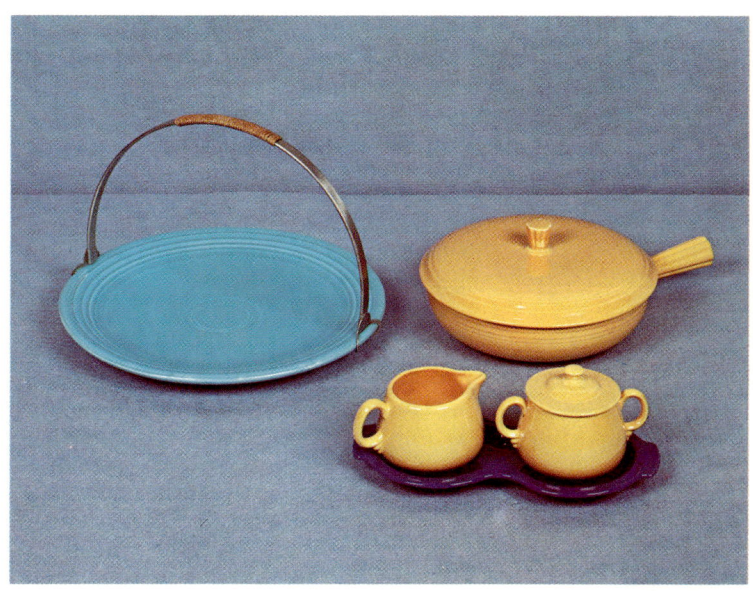

Plate 42

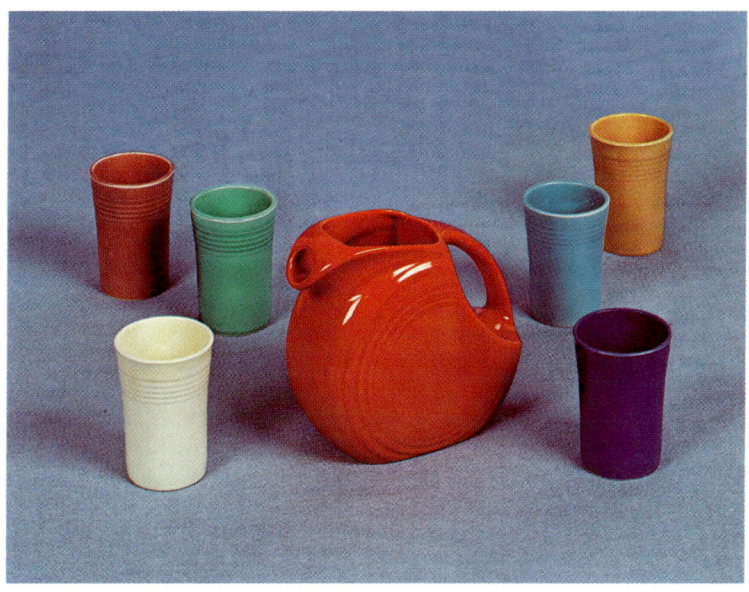

Plate 43

Fiesta

The tiered tidbit trays were not made at HLC, but were drilled and assembled by some other company. Nor were the metal holders for the marmalade, mustard, and salt and pepper shakers ever supplied by Homer Laughlin. Only the metal holders for the Kitchen Kraft casseroles (7½″ size shown), oval platters and pie plates, and the metal handles for the plates were shipped from the factory. The large wooden salad bowl sets on a base banded in Fiesta colors; on the base is a sticker that reads 'G.H. Specialty Co., Fiestawood'. On the following page you will see a large lazy Susan by the same manufacturer. We've heard of some strange things, but none has ever topped this — a kitchen cabinet in ivory trimmed across the top and down each side with red, green, blue, turquoise and yellow bands. Matching wood canisters and a brass plate inscribed 'Fiesta' completed this unlikely cupboard which was offered for the tidy sum of just under $500.00! The pastel juice set, as well as some of the Kitchen Kraft items, was dipped to go with the Jubilee line (see later chapter). These are highly prized by many collectors.

Below is the very rare gray juice pitcher, shown with the chartreuse and dark green juice tumblers from the 1952 promotional campaign. Two tumblers of each color shown plus two of yellow completed the rather drab set. Judging from the rare few available today, they evidently didn't sell in any great volume.

Plate 44. Juice tumbler, dark green or chartreuse: $60.00–75.00. Juice pitcher, gray: $110.00–125.00.

Plate 45. Fiestawood bowl: $40.00–50.00. Metal holders only, for salt, pepper and mustard: $30.00–35.00; for Kitchen Kraft casserole: $12.00–15.00; for marmalade: $25.00–30.00. Juice tumbler, Jubilee pastels: $25.00–30.00. Juice pitcher, Jubilee pastels: $45.00–55.00. Tidbit tray, 3 tier: $30.00–40.00.

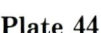

Plate 44

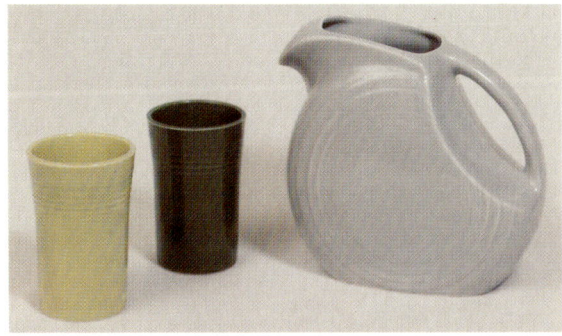

Fiesta

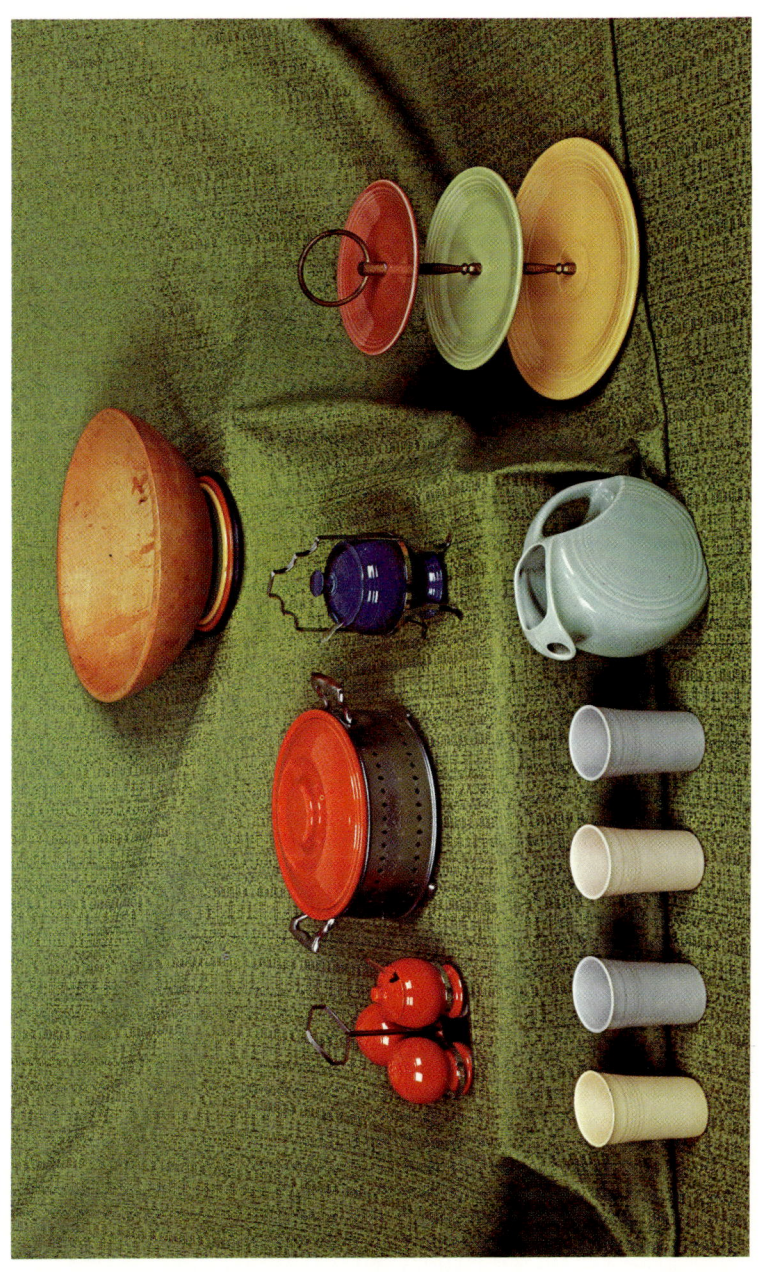

Plate 45

The nappy in the metal holder is the 9½" size. We've found no information on this, but too many have turned up in these holders to be coincidental. The chrome frame for the cream soup converts it very nicely into a jam dish, and the large teapot becomes a dripolator with the addition of the metal assembly (5½" high). These were not from HLC, nor was the wire frame for the juice set — but isn't it nice, and very functional! The Sta-brite flatware, shown center, far right, comes with plastic handles in yellow, red, green and black. It often accompanied Fiesta Ensembles shipped from HLC. The large (20" diameter) lazy Susan is another Fiestawood piece by the G. H. Specialty Co. A similar tray has been found with indentions in the center area to hold a round jug type pitcher and eight tumblers. These items are often marked with this ink stamp:

HOLLYWOOD MERRY-GO-ROUND
Copyright 1936
G. H. SPECIALTY CO. MILWAUKEE, WIS.

Plate 46. Metal holders only, for 9½" nappy: $8.00–10.00; for cream soup/jam set: $25.00–30.00; for juice set: $18.00–22.00. Dripolator insert: $10.00–15.00. Sta-brite flatware, 3 pc. place setting: $7.00–8.50. Fiestawood lazy Susan, 20": $40.00–50.00.

Fiesta

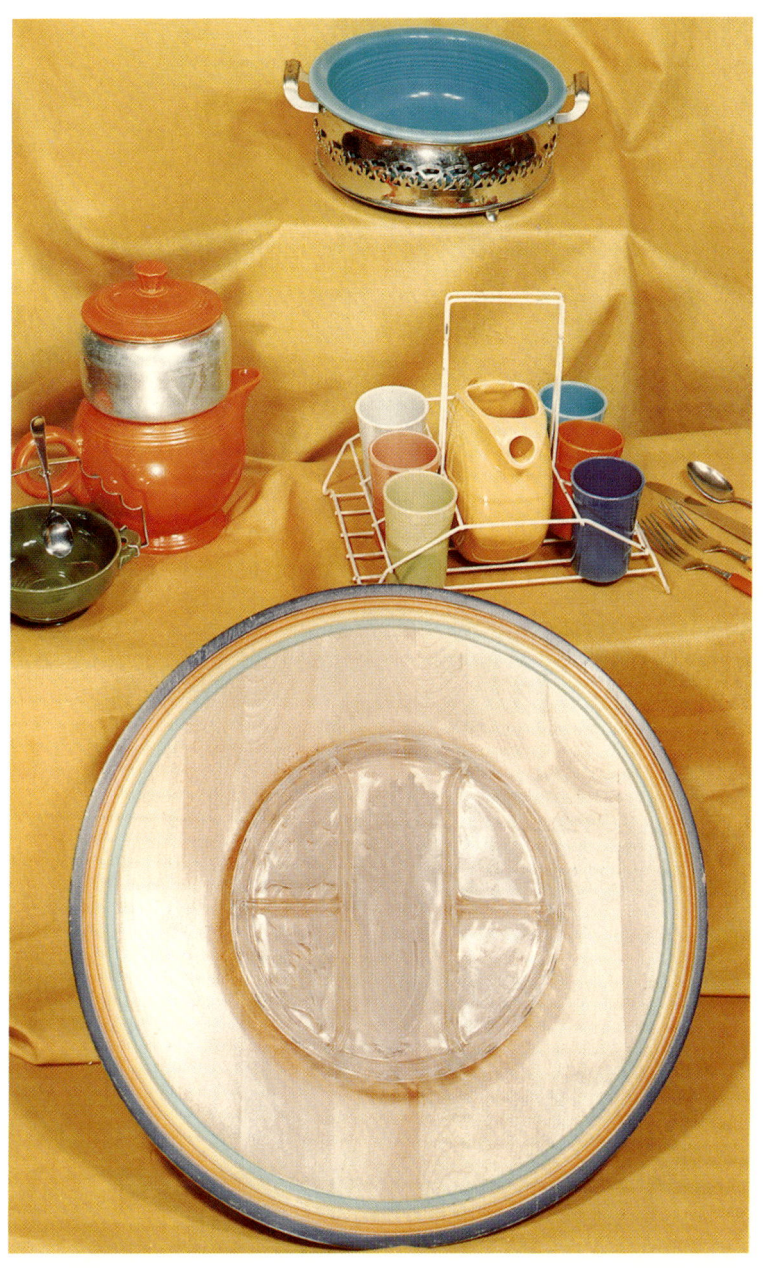

Plate 46

The metal holder for the ice pitcher and six 8 ounce tumblers is attractively styled and completely complimentary to the spherical shape of the jug. Made by an enterprising metal company; not an HLC issue.

This metal frame for the mustard and marmalade is sure to be on the want list of many collectors! The lovely relish tray is accented in gold filigree on the base, and each piece is decorated with an underglaze floral decal. In the background, note the woven tablecloth with matching napkins displayed along the sides of the photo. Linens of this vintage provide a lovely setting for your Fiesta — or, in fact, any of the Mexican patterned dinnerware lines shown later.

Plate 47. Metal holder only: $30.00-35.00.

Plate 48. Metal holder only: $30.00-35.00. Relish tray with floral and gold decoration: $65.00-75.00. Tablecloth and napkins: $30.00-40.00.

Fiesta

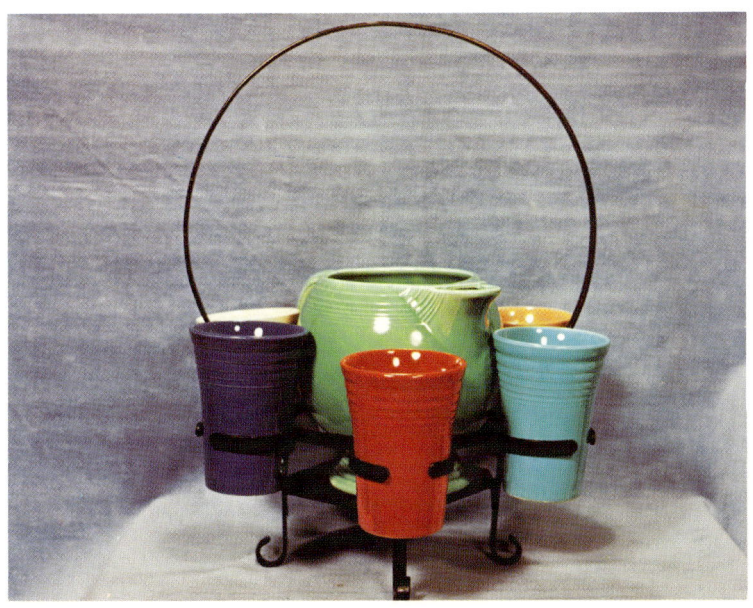

Plate 47

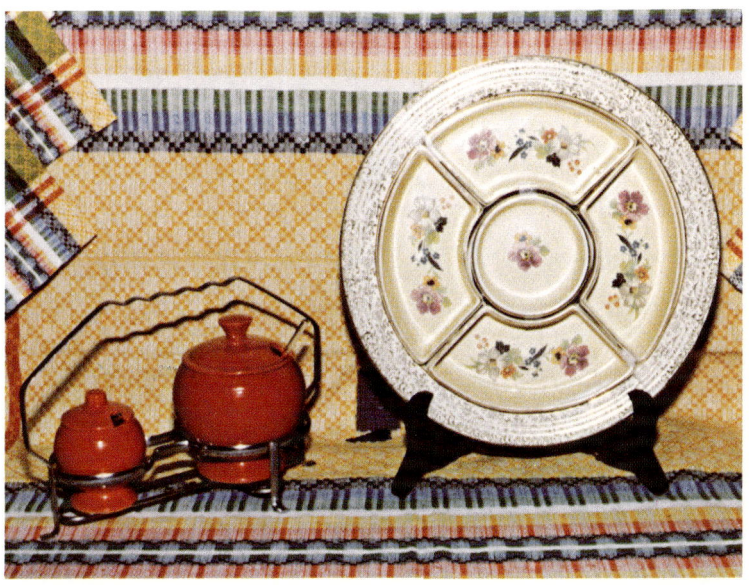

Plate 48

The small teapot is decorated by hand with a fired on pine cone spray. The Fiestawood tray seems to be for hors d'oeuvres since the fish in the center is pierced to hold toothpicks. The border decoration is especially effective — stripes in festive colors punctuated by decals of a snoozing Mexican. On the right, a large Kitchen Kraft covered jar is decorated with a decal of a patio scene, the table set with Fiesta-like dishes. The line is called Sunporch!

The lamp on the left is one of a pair of boudoir lamps made from Fiesta syrup bottoms. A paper label on the back reads 'Decorated by Dunhall'. Another made from a Harlequin syrup with this identical base has also been found!

The Fiesta lamp on the right is actually the fruit of someone's daydreaming — and isn't it attractive! Here casseroles without handles, the stem from a sweets comport, and a base made from a fruit bowl work well together to produce a striking lamp.

Plate 49. Pine cone teapot, medium: $35.00–40.00. Fiestawood hors d'oeuvre tray: $45.00–50.00. Sunporch jar with lid: $55.00–65.00.

Plate 50. Boudoir lamp: $60.00–75.00.

Plate 51. Fiesta lamp, fabricated body: $60.00–75.00.

Fiesta

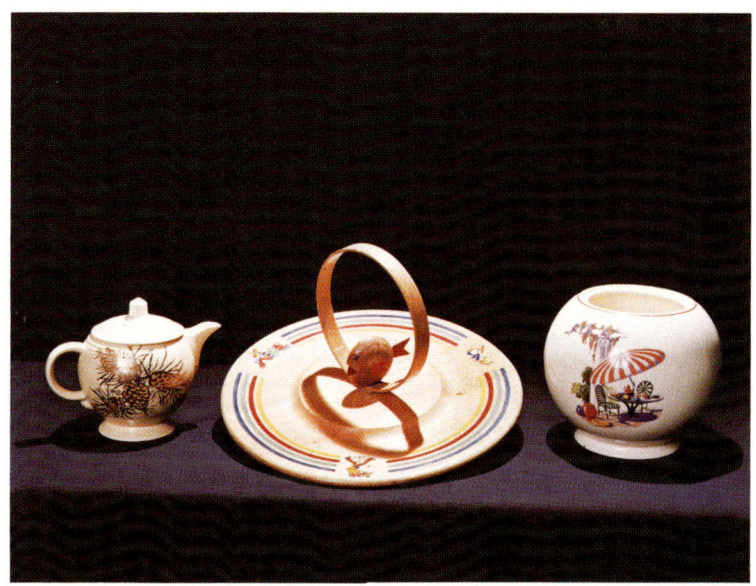

Plate 49

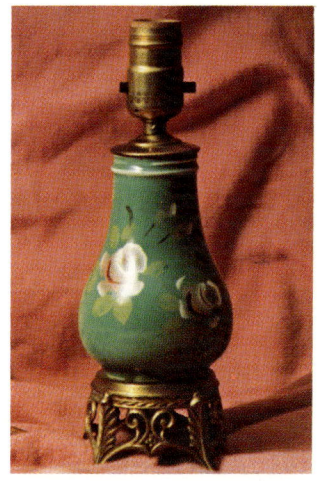

Plate 50

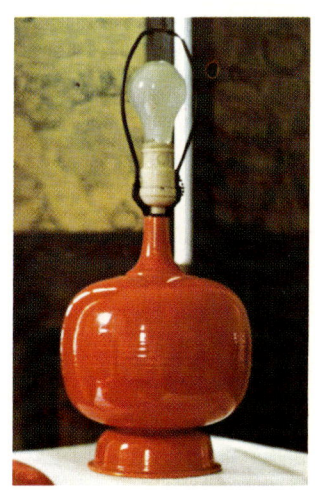

Plate 51

This is the large salad bowl and the Tom and Jerry mugs, with gold bands and lettering. Few complete sets have been located and bowls are harder to find than the mugs.

White, not ivory, is the color of the advertising mugs in Plate 53. Collectors have reported a variety of these — one decorated with a caricature of Lucille Ball, signed 'Love, Lucy', from the Desilu Studios. The Jackson China Co. is producing a line of restaurant ware with a mug identical to HLC's Tom and Jerry — brown with a cream interior. The same company is also making a child's set consisting of a divided plate, a 6" bowl, and the T and J mug in white decorated with a blue stenciled Donald Duck and friends.

Homer Laughlin was quick to deny ever having had anything to do with these striped plates. Can you blame them! As you can see, they are not underglazed, and the stripes are usually very worn.

Plate 52. Tom and Jerry bowl: $65.00–70.00. Tom and Jerry mug: $24.00–28.00.

Plate 53. Advertising mug: $18.00–22.00; blanks, no advertising: $14.00–16.00.

Plate 54. Plate, overglaze stripes, any size: $2.00–3.00.

Fiesta

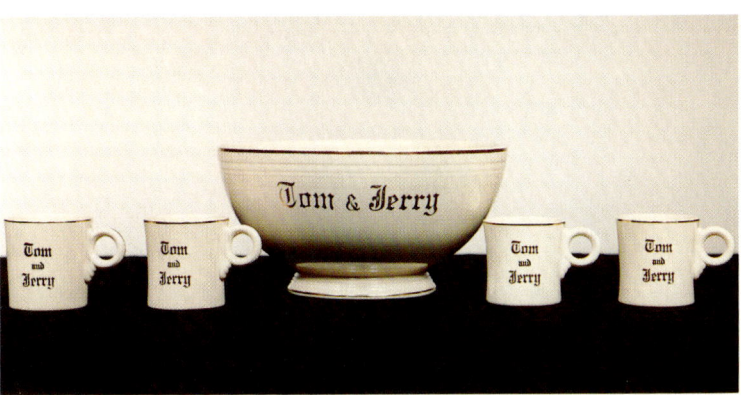

Plate 52

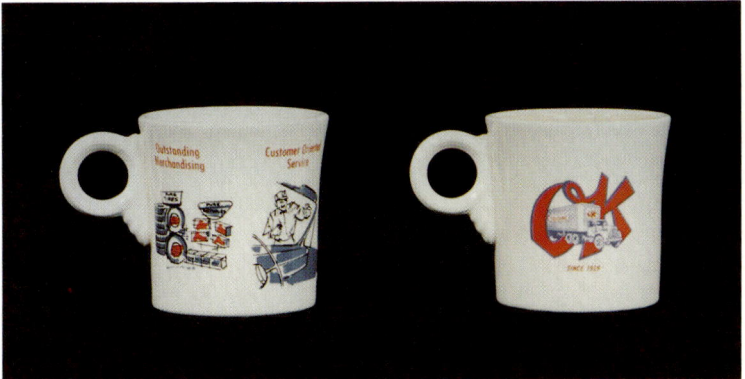

Plate 53

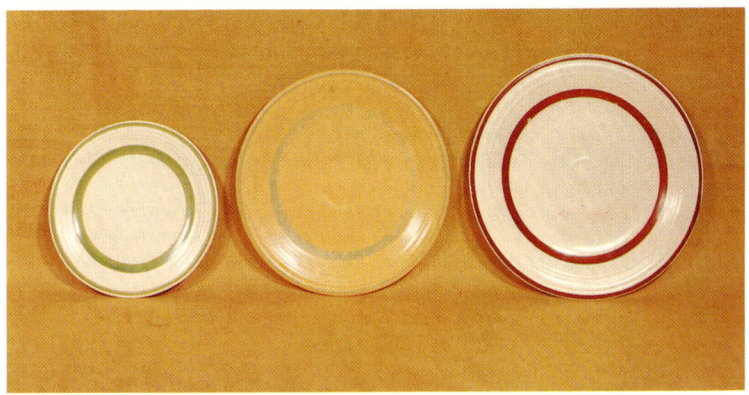

Plate 54

Fiesta

The tall mugs in the top row are from a line of HLC hotel china, but note the Fiesta handle. The Sit 'n Sip set carton contains the advertising mug with a matching coaster, shown on the next row. Nursery characters decorate the mug on the left in Row 2.

In addition to the turquoise and yellow interiors shown, rose, amberstone, and turf green interiors have also been found. The exterior glaze is white, not ivory! These were produced during the late sixties into the early seventies. In the bottom row are four from a series decorated with decals of antique automobiles. There are six in all: 1924 Model '48' Buick, 1904 Model 'B' Buick, 1936 Buick 'Special', 1941 Buick Roadmaster, 1908 Model '10' Buick, 1916 Model 'D' Buick. From 1964 through 1970 these Sit 'n Sip sets were issued for annual meetings of Buick Management and their salaried Retirement Club meetings. The collector that supplied this information also tells us that she has an ash tray dated 1963, Buick Management Meeting, Dec. 11-12. It is 8¾" round, raised in the center with six cigarette rests.

Plate 55. Tall mug, hotel china: $8.00–12.00. Sit 'n Sip, carton only: $6.00–8.50. Tall mug with advertising: $10.00–14.00. Nursery mug: $20.00–25.00. Sit 'n Sip set: $28.00–32.00. Advertising mug in Fiesta colors: $28.00–35.00.

Plate 56. Advertising mug, color inside: $20.00–25.00. Mug with antique car decal: $35.00–40.00. Mug with color inside, blank, no advertising: $16.00–20.00.

Fiesta

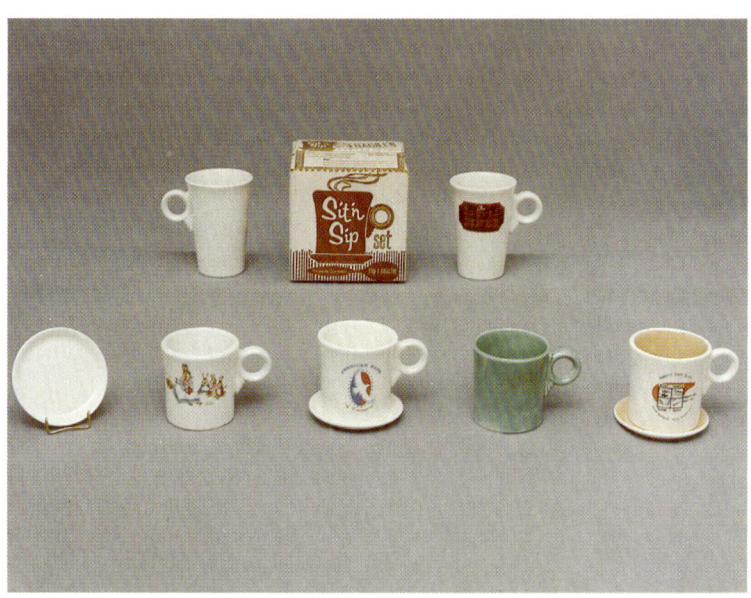

Plate 55

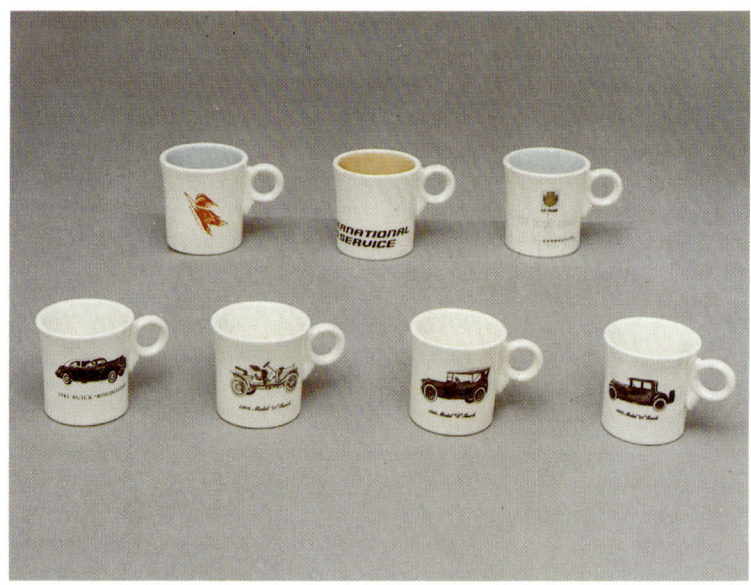

Plate 56

This 15″ chop plate has been decorated by a smaller china company; it's stamped 'Vogue China'. Besides the more familiar Tom and Jerry set on Fiesta shapes, HLC also made this set, and although perhaps not as sought after as the other, it is very nice.

Another Fiestawood piece (remember, not an HLC product!), this large tray measures 16½″ in diameter. The ash tray is one we hunted for several years. On our first trip to HLC in 1972, we saw one on the table in the board room, stamped in gold, as this one is, '1939, East Liverpool, Ohio, Rotary Club'. We advertised for one in local papers while we were there to no avail, and had completely given up ever locating one when a lady from the area wrote, offering this one for trade. The metal lazy Susan stand has a ball bearing section between the disks that allows the top to rotate. The width of that flat rim fits between the rings under some 13″ and 15″ chop plates. The wood and metal handle nicely converts a Fiesta tumbler into a soda fountain mug . . . neither are from HLC.

Plate 57. Chop plate with decal, 15″: $25.00–30.00. Tom and Jerry mug: $6.00–8.00. **Tom and Jerry bowl: $15.00–20.00.**

Plate 58. Fiestawood tray, 16½″: $35.00–40.00. Advertising ash tray: $30.00–35.00. **Metal base only: $18.00–22.00. Wooden handle only:** $7.50–8.50.

Fiesta

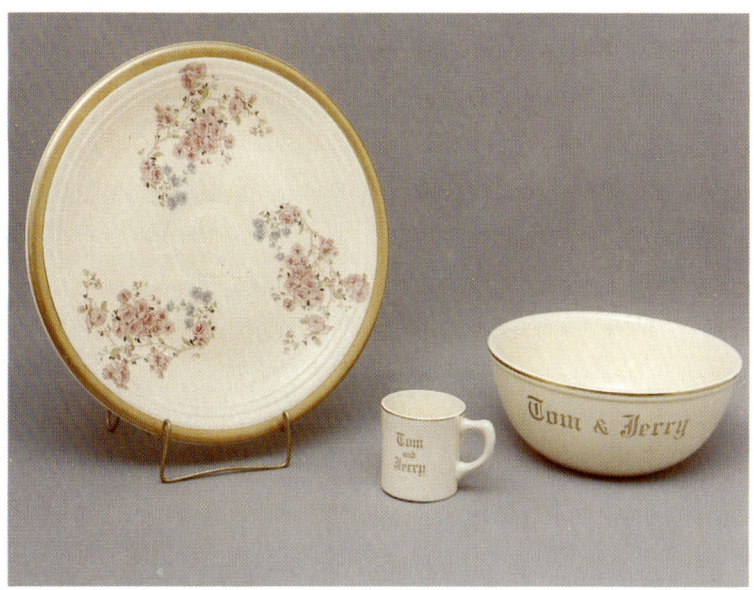

Plate 57

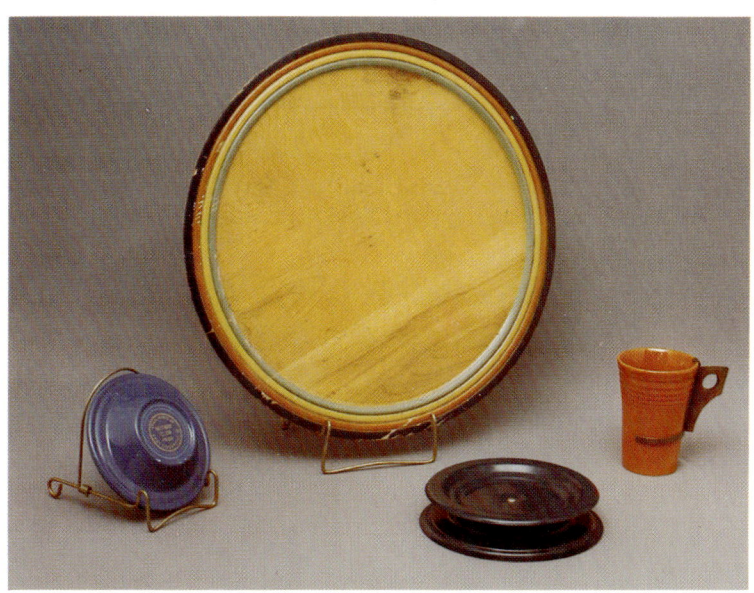

Plate 58

'Colonial Kitchen' is the well chosen name of the dinnerware pattern shown in Plate 59, and 'Swing' is the name of the shape. It is beginning to appear more frequently at dinnerware shows. The child's bowl is decorated with the familiar green and white checks of the Ralston Purina Company — made by HLC as premiums for Ralston customers.

Plate 61 shows the 15" chop plate and a 7" plate each decorated with a multifloral decal in the center and a maroon ring around the rim. They are stamped 'Fiesta' and are quite unusual. The turkey decal is shown here on the 13" chop plate. You may also find it on the 15" size, as well as the dinner plate. This is an underglaze decoration on commercial quality, according to HLC. These are very rare.

The Homer Laughlin China Company issued a calendar plate for a number of years, using whatever blanks were available. In 1954 and 1955, they just happened to use Fiesta. The 9" plate is the rare one; it may be found for either year. The 1954 plate has been found in ivory only, the '55 in green, yellow and ivory.

Plate 59. Colonial Kitchen, dinner plate: $3.00–4.00; **cup and saucer:** $5.00–6.00; **sugar and creamer, pr:** $7.00–8.00; **platter:** $5.00–6.00; **soup bowl:** $3.00–4.00.

Plate 60. Child's bowl, Ralston Purina: $9.00–12.00.

Plate 61. Chop plate with floral decal, 15": $25.00–30.00; **plate, 7":** $5.00–8.00. **Chop plate with turkey, 13":** $60.00–70.00; **15":** $80.00–90.00.

Plate 62. Calendar plate, 1954, 10": $18.00–22.00; **Good Luck, 1955, 9":** $27.00–35.00; **calendar plate, 1955, 10":** $22.00–26.00.

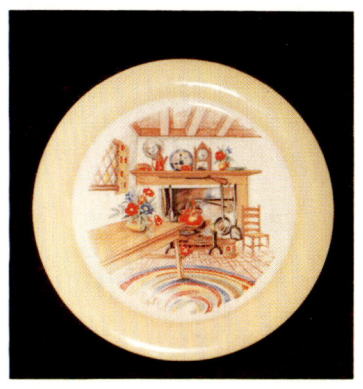
Plate 59

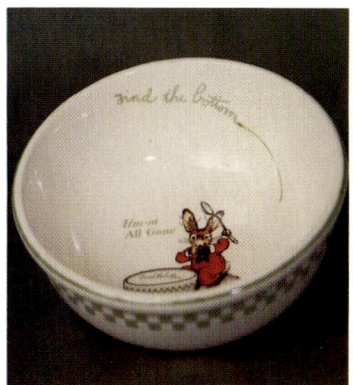
Plate 60

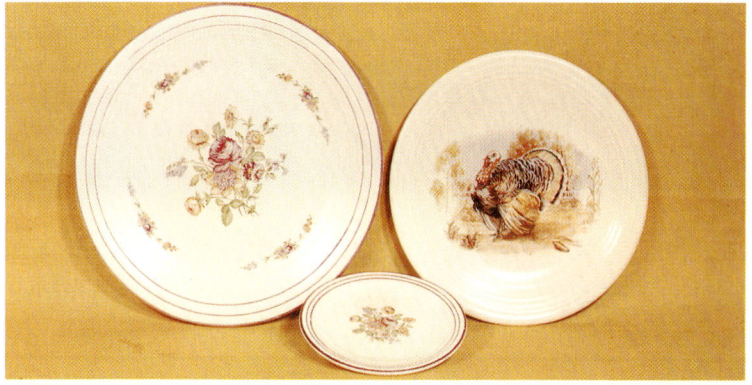
Plate 61

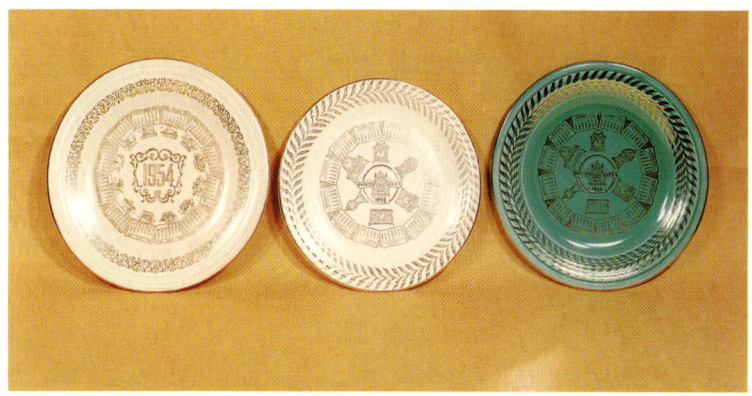
Plate 62

Here are two examples of Fiesta with floral decals. Dinnerware of this type is quite unusual and very rare. It may have been decorated by HLC, but more than likely it was done by a smaller company who specialized in this type of work — there were several in the vicinity.

Plate 63. Plate, 10″: $8.00–12.00; teacup: $13.00–17.00; saucer: $2.00–3.00; fruit, 4¾″: $6.00–9.00.

Plate 64. Creamer: $14.00–18.00; sugar with lid: $18.00–22.00; teacup with saucer: $15.00–20.00.

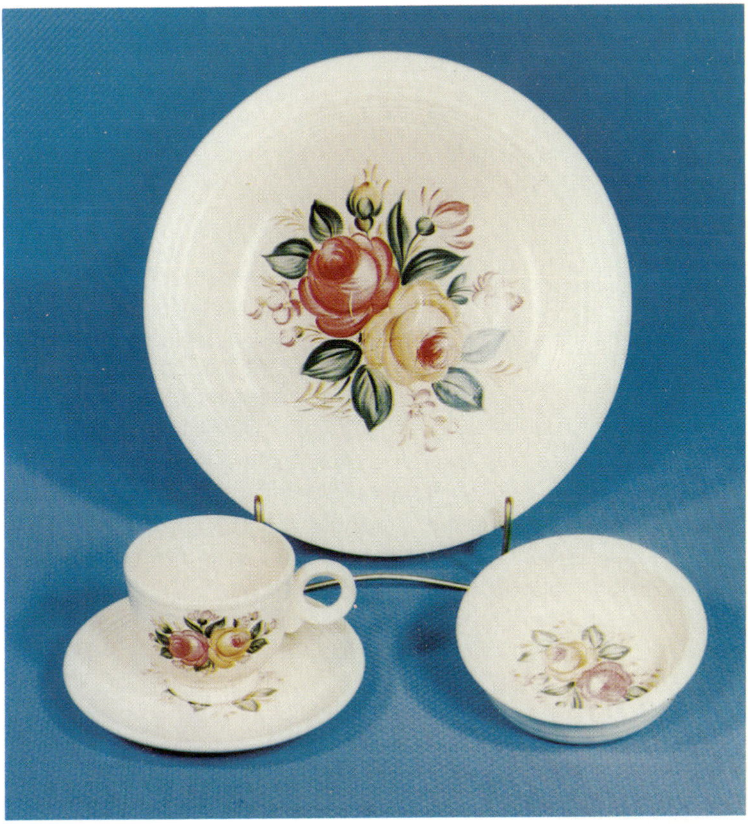

Fiesta

Plate 63

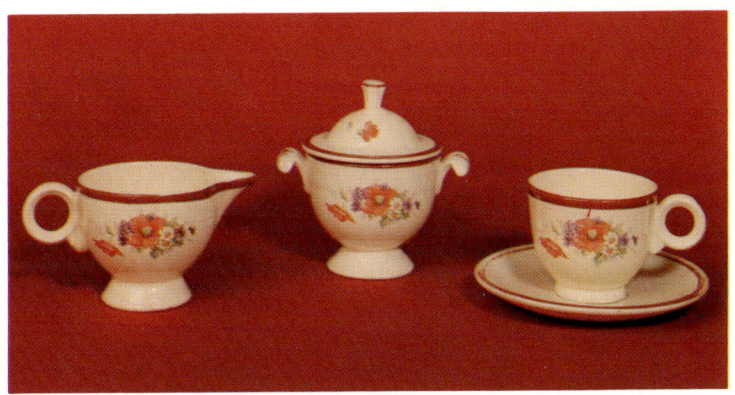

Plate 64

Fiesta

The beautiful fruit comport with overall 22k gold decoration and multifloral decal was decorated by Royal China, according to the backstamp. The relish tray is gold trimmed and decorated with flowers, but there is no indication of the decorating firm. The 8 piece cake set is marked Georgian by Homer Laughlin, but the gold work was done by Royal China. The same decoration has been found on Fiesta chop plates and salad plates, also by Royal China. George and Martha Washington grace the Bicentennial bowl and mug. The bowl is marked 'Rhythm', and on the reverse side of the mug: 'Washington Bicentennial (1732-1932)'.

Plate 65. Fruit comport: $40.00–50.00.

Plate 66. Relish tray: $60.00–70.00.

Plate 67. Cake set, 8-pc.: $30.00–40.00.

Plate 68. Bicentennial bowl: $18.00–22.00; mug: $18.00–22.00.

Fiesta

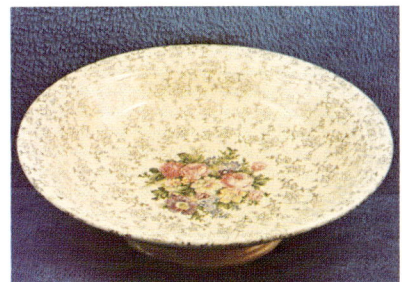

Plate 65

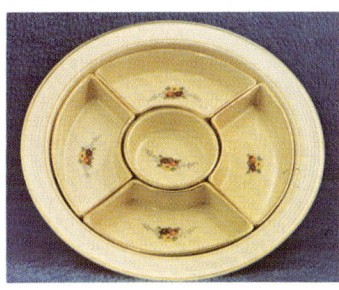

Plate 66

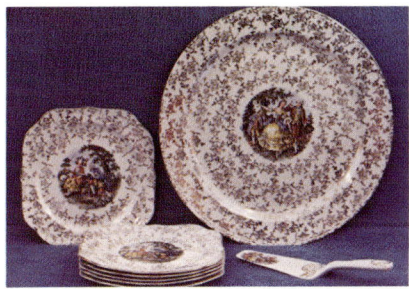

Plate 67

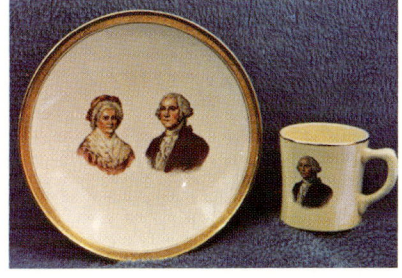

Plate 68

These tin items are decorated with Fiesta-like dinnerware in the style and colors popular through the late thirties and the forties. *The American Home*, Oct., 1938, carried an article called *Pretty Up Your Kitchen* which featured not only Fiesta, but tinware by Owens-Illinois Can Co. decorated in 'Roman stripes in red, blue and green on yellow'. The set consisted of canisters, a bread box, a dust pan, a garbage can, and a kitchen stool. It, too, was called 'Fiesta'.

Plate 69. Bread box: $35.00–45.00. Garbage can: $35.00–45.00.

Plate 70. Canister set, 4-pc.: $35.00–45.00. Napkin holder: $18.00–25.00.

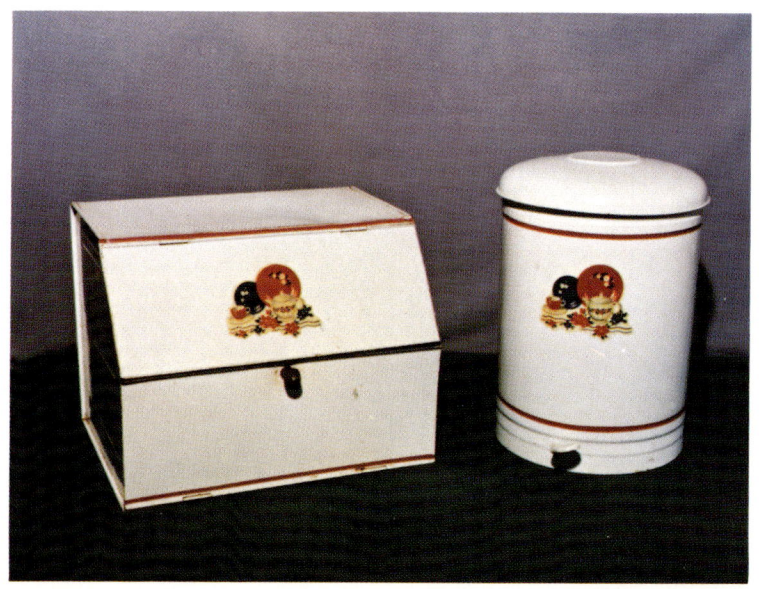

Plate 69

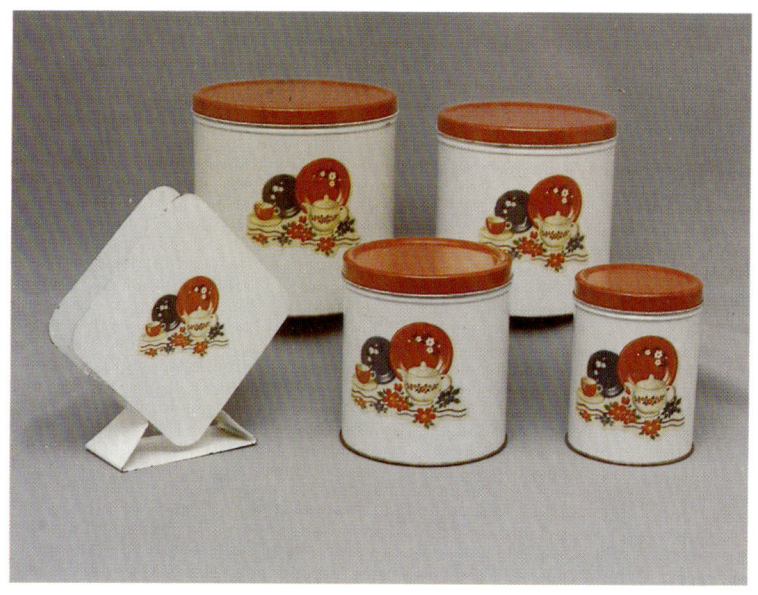

Plate 70

This is a 'Fiesta' popcorn set, marketed during the forties — but not by HLC! These pieces are in tin with baked on enamel. Note the familiar Fiesta rings and colors.

The Quickut Fiesta table set is just another product by an outside firm attempting to capitalize on HLC's success. Fiesta fans seem to approve of the practice and like to add these go-alongs to their collections.

Plate 71. Popcorn set: $40.00–60.00.

Plate 72. Quickut flatware: $35.00–45.00.

Fiesta

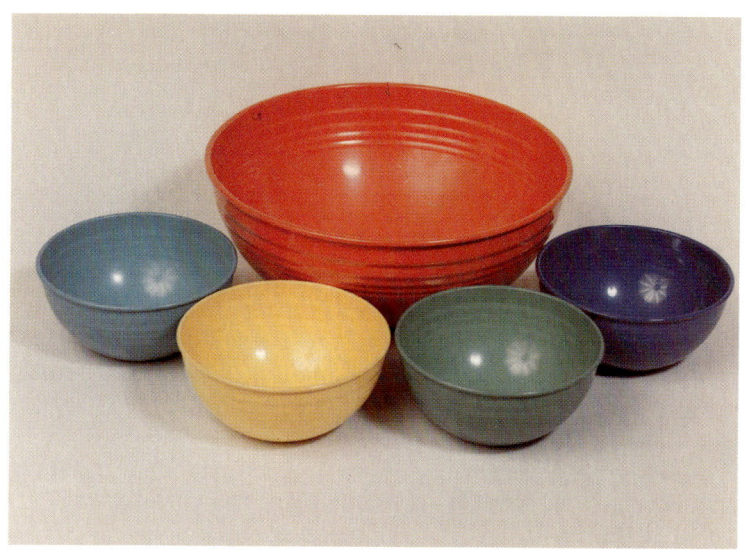

Plate 71

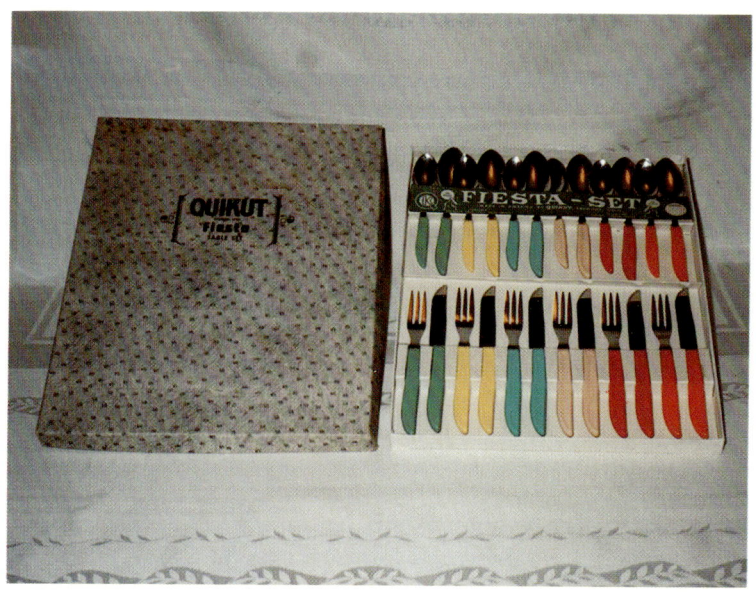

Plate 72

Fiesta

Paper items — especially advertising material — make interesting additions to our collections, and are worthwhile investments! We wanted to show you the cover of this *Saturday Evening Post*, Oct. 10, 1936, so that if the date escapes you, will recognize this issue when you see it. Inside is a beautiful two-page Armstrong floor covering ad with a vintage kitchen-dining room fairly blooming with Fiesta. Another ad featuring Fiesta appeared in *Better Homes and Gardens*, Dec., 1936.

The company's price lists not only contain much information, but are in themselves collectible. The menu and the corn package are examples of the influence of HLC's lines in commercial work. The sheet of decals were produced in 1945 by a company called American Decalcomania of Chicago and New York, and sold for 29¢ per sheet of six designs. The glass decanter shown in two designs has been found, and is marked 'Nolen Austin Co., Feb. 1942, Glasbake, Pat. U.S.A.' You may find tiles in two sizes decorated with these decals. Shelf paper by Betty Brite features Fiesta dishes — it's scarce and very collectible.

The full color display ad in Plate 74 appeared in the *Des Moines Register and Tribune* on March 2, 1939. Only four basic colors were offered, with matching Mexican glassware tumblers. Note the interesting blend of Fiesta and Riviera.

Plate 73. Saturday Evening Post, intact: $15.00–20.00. Fiesta price pamphlet, 1965: $5.00–7.50; 1939: $15.00–20.00. Menu: $5.00–7.00. Sheet of decals: $20.00–25.00. Corn package: $3.00–5.00.

Plate 74. Ad sheet: $90.00–100.00.

Fiesta

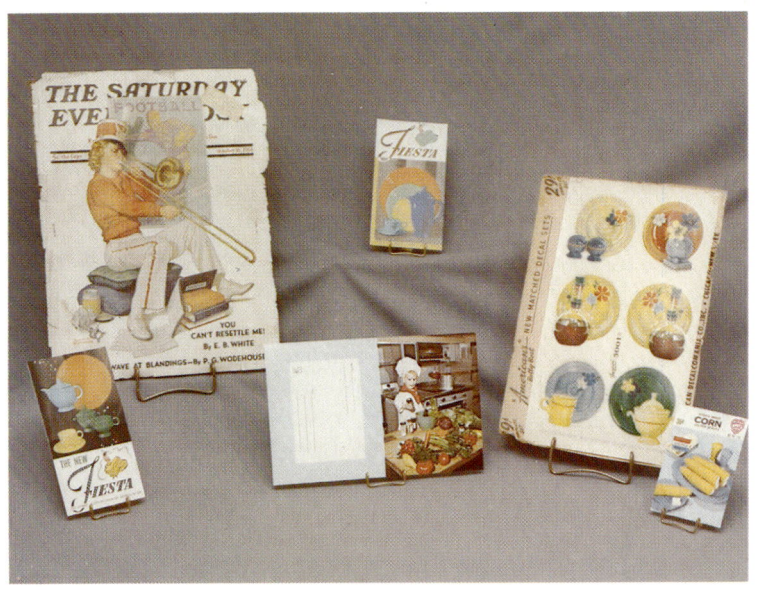

Plate 73

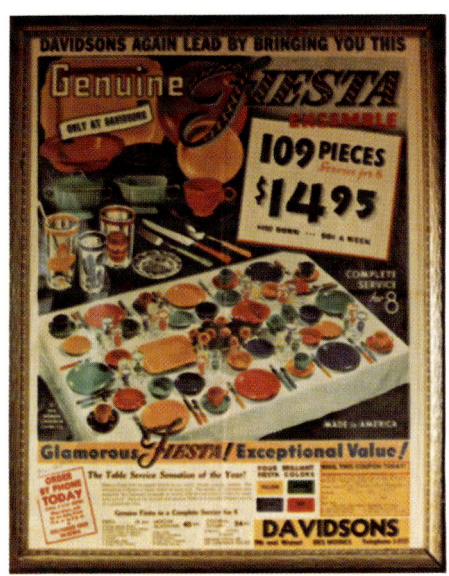

Plate 74

Fiesta

This cardboard store display captures and conveys the festive appeal of Fiesta dinnerware. This particular one never left the HLC pottery, but you may be lucky enough to find one. The recipe file with the familiar graphics was prepared by the Ohio Gas Company — no date, but colors and style would seem to indicate a late thirties to early forties issue.

Recently the Dard Mfg. Co. of Evanston, Ill. produced an item that for awhile caused a bit of excitement in the Fiesta world! In a box marked 'Fiesta Coasters, Tag-Master Line ASI 4850' — exactly the right size to hold the relish tray center — they marketed a set of four plastic advertising coasters. Someone, perhaps less than honest or just misinformed, tried to perpetuate the 'Fiesta Coaster Hoax' by replacing the plastic coasters with the relish center.

Plate 75. Store display, 28": $100.00–150.00.

Plate 76. Recipe file: $8.00–10.00.

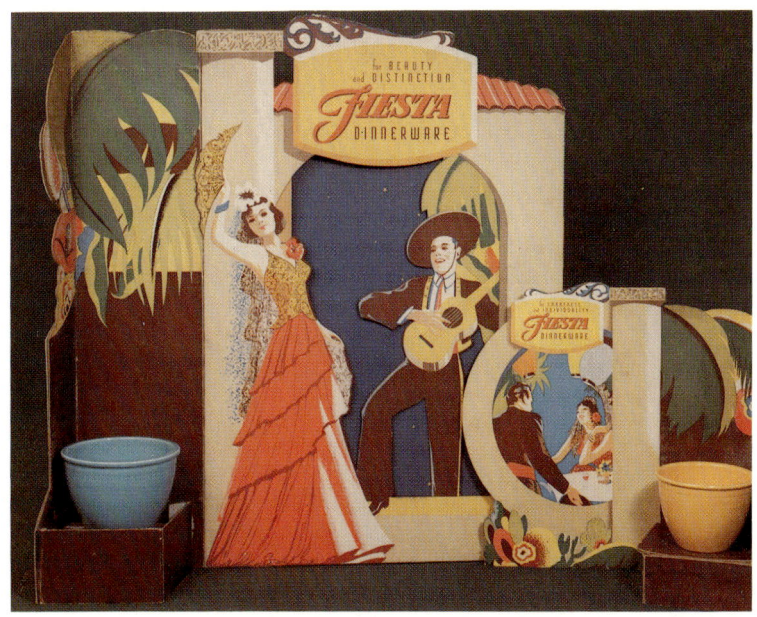

Plate 75

Plate 76

In the early 1940s the Hankscraft Company made and marketed their electric egg cooker in service sets that included the cooker as shown here, 'four vari-colored Fiesta egg cups, (red, yellow, blue and green), ivory (pottery) poaching dish, Fiesta salt and pepper shakers, and maple plywood tray'. They called this set the 'Fiesta Egg Service Set' and sold it for either $9.50 or $13.70, depending upon whose catalog you happened to be using. The set shown at right has not been listed in any of these catalogs, but is the one more often found. Obviously, these are not Fiesta, but are made of the same material as the cooker itself, and are smaller than genuine Fiesta egg cups. Remember, this was a Hankscraft product — another go-along — not made by Homer Laughlin, not genuine Fiesta!

HLC look-alikes! As we've tried to impress on new collectors, examine and study — don't jump to conclusions! The bud vase on the left has an obviously inferior glaze, and is just enough smaller to indicate that it has been cast from a mold made from an original. The disk pitcher is not Fiesta; the cake plate, in Fiesta colors and complete with the band of rings device is Montgomery Modern by Bauer. It has also been reported in maroon and yellow. The donkey may look like its Harlequin double, but sometimes pulls a cart marked 'California'. A 'dead ringer' without rings, the dark blue pitcher looks very much like the Harlequin novelty creamer. Beware!

Plate 77. Egg cooker, complete set with tray: $60.00–70.00. Cooker only: $40.00–45.00. Egg cup only: $8.00–10.00.

Plate 78. Cake stand: $60.00–85.00.

Fiesta

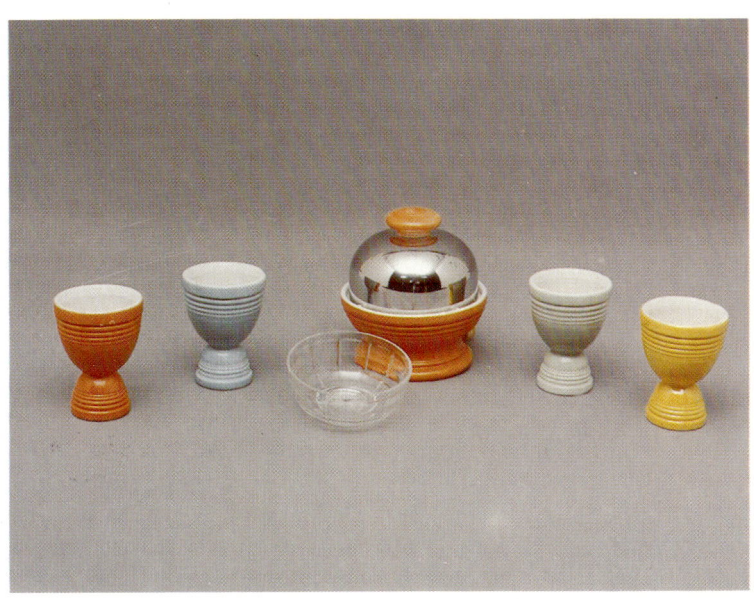

Plate 77

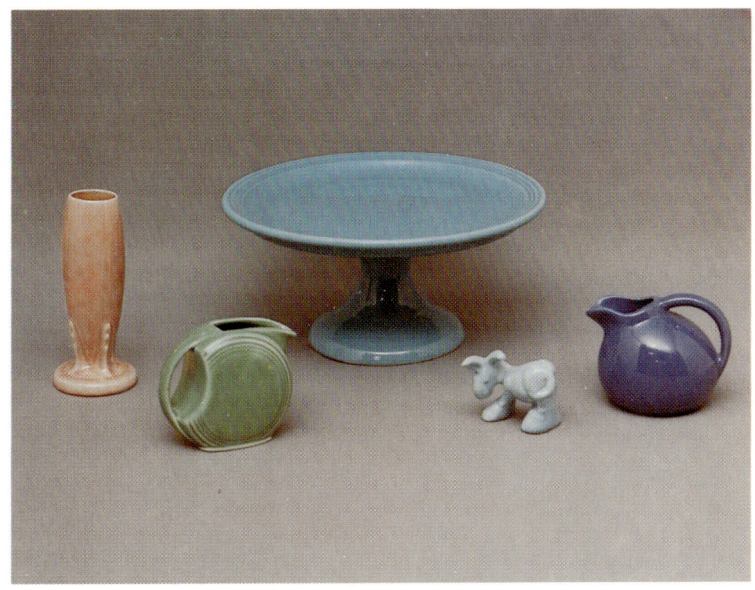

Plate 78

THE FIESTA CASUALS

GENUINE

Fiesta

H. L. Co. USA
CASUAL

There were two designs produced in the beautiful Fiesta Casuals; and although they are both relatively difficult to find, often when they are found the set may be complete, or nearly so. So far, they have not become as popular as we first thought they would. They were introduced in June, 1962, and as sales were only moderately active, they were discontinued around 1968. The Plaid Stamp Company featured both of these designs in their illustrated catalogs during these years.

The Hawaiian 12-Point Daisy design, No. F-108, featured a ½" turquoise band at the rim, and turquoise daisies with brown centers on a white background.

The other design was Yellow Carnation, No. F-107, which featured the yellow flowers with a touch of brown on the white background and yellow piping at the rim. In both lines, only the dinner plates, salad plates, saucers and oval platters were decorated; the cups, fruit dishes, nappies, and sugar and creamers were simply in the matching Fiesta color.

Using a lead mask with the cut out design, the decoration was hand sprayed and overglazed. A complete service consisted of six place settings: dinner plate, salad plate, cup and saucer, and fruit (5½"). A platter, 8½" nappy, and the sugar and creamer were also included.

Plates 79 and 80. Values apply to both patterns. Oval platter: $22.00–26.00; plate, 10": $8.50–11.00; plate, 7": $7.00–8.50; saucer: $5.00–6.50.

The Fiesta Casuals

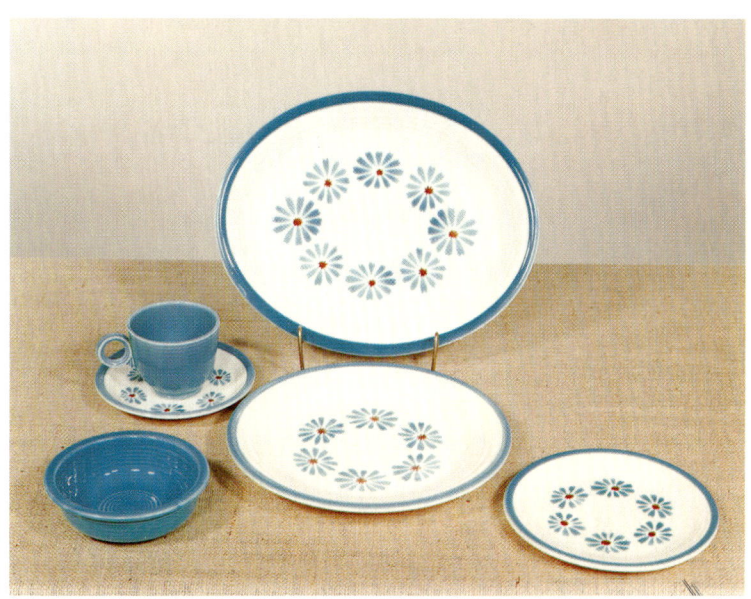

Plate 79

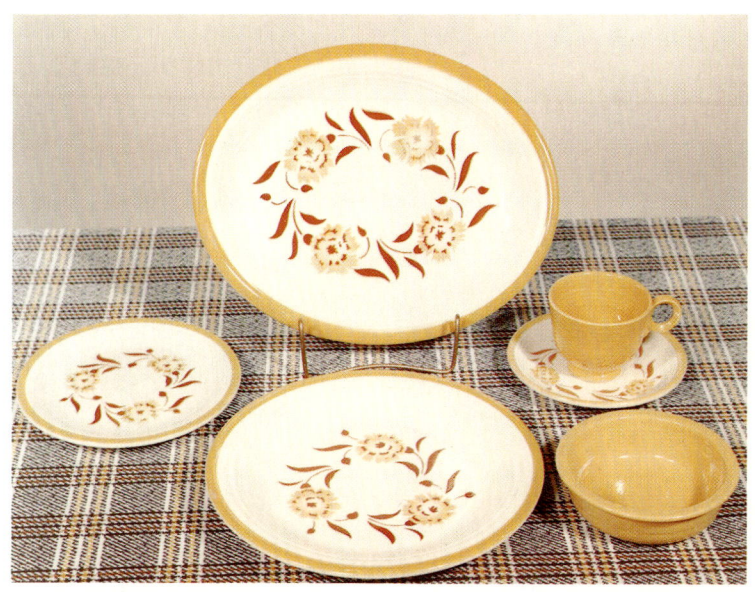

Plate 80

AMBERSTONE

This 'brown Fiesta' seems to have caused quite a stir among our collector friends, and it's easy to see why — especially when some of the hollowware pieces are found with the familiar Fiesta cast-indented trademark!

Amberstone was introduced in 1967, three years before the Fiesta line was restyled; yet the illustration on an old order blank shows that the sugar and creamer, cup, teapot, soup/cereal, casserole and coffee server were from the same molds that were later used for Fiesta Ironstone. Only on the pieces that had relatively flat areas large enough to permit decoration do you find the black, machine stamped underglaze pattern. The remainder were simply solid brown.

Sold under the trade name of Genuine Sheffield dinnerware, it was produced by HLC exclusively for supermarket promotions, and several large grocery chains featured Amberstone as a premium. These items were offered, listed here with current market values. For your information we have indicated those pieces having the design with an asterisk.

Dinner plate*	$4.00-5.50
Dessert dish	$2.00-3.00
Bread and butter plate*	$2.50-3.00
Coffee cup	$5.00-6.00
Saucer*	$1.50-2.00
Vegetable bowl	$6.00-7.50
Covered sugar bowl	$6.50-8.00
Creamer	$4.50-6.00
Oval platter, 13"*	$7.50-10.00
Large soup plate*	$5.00-6.00
Ash tray	$15.00-18.00
Salt & pepper shakers, pr.	$9.00-12.00
Salad plate*	$2.00-2.50
Soup/cereal bowl	$2.50-4.00
Covered casserole	$16.00-20.00
Sauce boat	$12.00-16.00
Relish tray*	$12.00-16.00
Coffee server	$22.00-28.00
Tea server	$15.00-18.00
Covered butter, (stick)*	$28.00-32.00
Round serving platter*	$12.00-15.00
Jumbo salad bowl	$8.00-10.00
Covered jam jar	$24.00-28.00
Serving pitcher (disk)	$18.00-22.00
Jumbo mug	$5.00-7.00
Pie plate*	$22.00-25.00

Amberstone

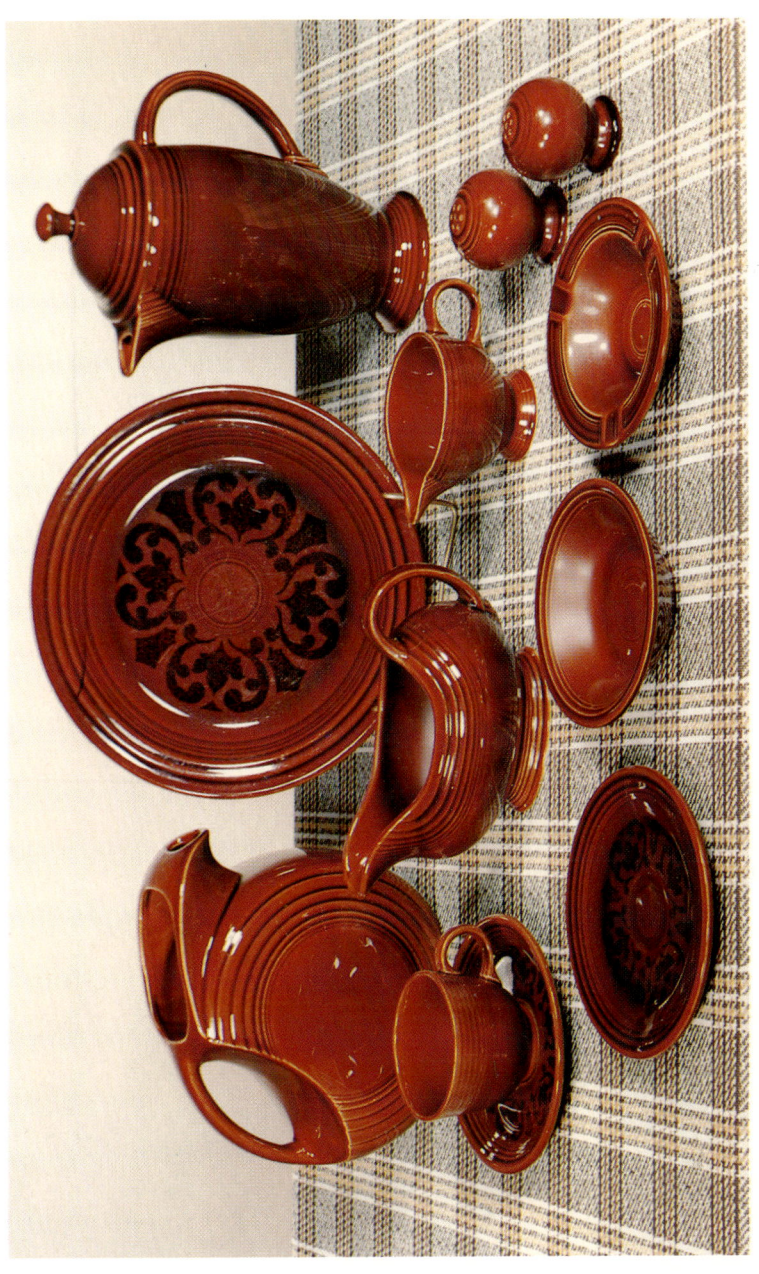

Plate 81

CASUALSTONE

In 1970, Homer Laughlin again produced a line of dinnerware to be sold exclusively through supermarket promotions. This dinnerware was called Casualstone, and was presented under the trade name 'Coventry'. The Antique Gold of the Fiesta Ironstone was decorated with an intricate gold machine stamped design; as with Amberstone, it appeared on only the shallow items.

An old order blank shows that it was less expensive than the Amberstone of three years previous, possibly because a color already in production was used. The following pieces were available; those with the design are indicated by an asterisk. They are listed here with current values.

Covered butter (stick)*	$22.00-28.00
Dinner plate*	$4.00-5.00
Coffee cup	$3.50-4.50
Bread and butter plate*	$1.50-2.00
Covered sugar bowl	$4.00-5.50
Oval platter, 13"	$6.00-8.00
Ash tray	$6.00-8.50
Salad plate*	$1.00-2.00
Covered casserole	$14.00-18.00
Relish tray*	$14.00-18.00
Tea server	$10.00-14.00
Round platter*	$9.00-12.00
Marmalade	$22.00-28.00
Jumbo mugs	$5.00-6.50
Dessert dish	$3.50-4.00
Saucer*	$1.50-2.50
Round vegetable bowl	$6.00-8.00
Creamer	$3.00-4.50
Soup plate*	$3.00-4.00
Salt & pepper shakers, pr.	$5.00-6.50
Soup/cereal bowl	$4.00-4.50
Sauce boat	$7.00-8.50
Coffee server	$14.00-18.00
Jumbo salad bowl, 10"	$9.00-12.00
Pitcher	$15.00-17.50
Pie plate*	$15.00-20.00

Casualstone

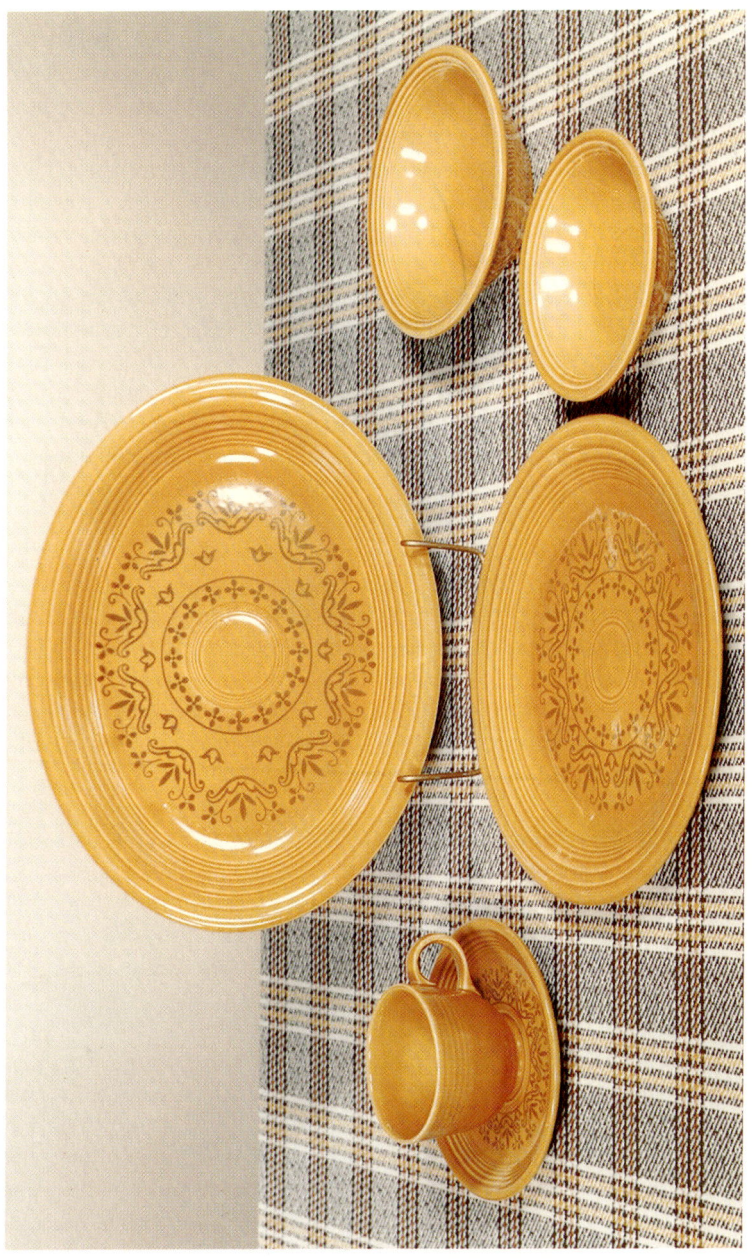

Plate 82

FIESTA IRONSTONE

In 1969, Fiesta was restyled and the line that was offered in February, 1970, was called Fiesta Ironstone. There were many factors that of necessity brought this change about. Labor and production costs had risen sharply. Efforts to hold these costs down resulted in the use of two new colors which were, and still are, standard colors for several other lines of dinnerware produced at HLC, Antique Gold and Turf Green. This eliminated the need of the separate firing that had been necessary for the older Fiesta colors. It was pointed out to us as we toured the factory that since each color required different temperatures in the kiln, orders were running ahead of production on Fiesta as well as their other lines. In order to cut labor costs, all markings were eliminated. (Only very occasionally will you find a marked item; this was never a practice and such pieces must be from the very early transition.)

The restyled pieces had a more contemporary feeling — bowls were flared and the applied handles were only partial rings. The covered casserole had molded, closed handles and the sugar bowl was without handles. The covered coffee server made a return appearance after an absence of several years. Nineteen items were offered in three colors, Antique Gold, Turf Green, and the original red, now called Mango Red. The oval platter was enlarged to 13". Two new items were offered, the sauce boat stand and a 10" salad bowl.

Finally in November, 1972, all production of Fiesta red was discontinued because many of the original technicians who developed this color and maintained control over the complicated manufacturing and firing had retired and modern mass production methods were unsuited to the process. Then at last on January 1, 1973, the famous line of Fiesta dinnerware was discontinued.

Opinions expressed through our recent survey in regard to a question concerning Fiesta Ironstone's collectibility varied from total apathy to 'very collectible'. On the average, enthusiasm is starting to generate. Red mugs and the gravy liner (sauce boat stand) in any color are regarded as good pieces. Red is the most difficult color to find, green is scarce in some pieces and gold is the most available. There have been scattered reports of Ironstone cups with the partial ring handle in Fiesta yellow, medium green and turquoise.

Fiesta Ironstone

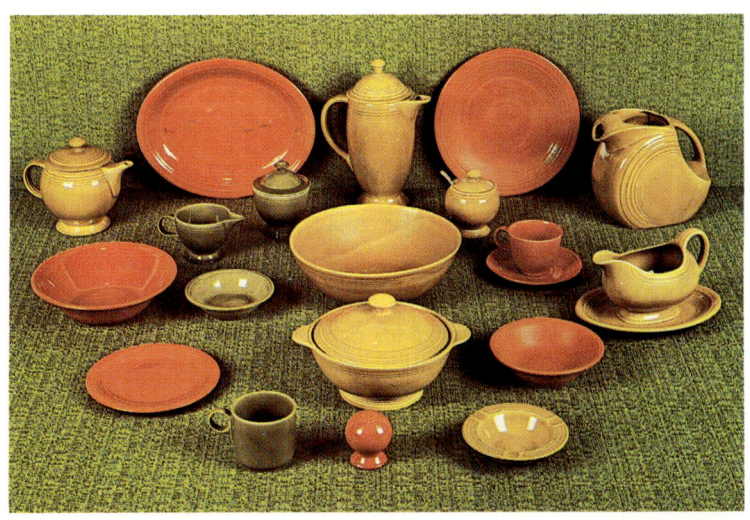

Plate 83

Prices apply to Antique Gold, Turf Green, and all restyled items in red.

Medium tea pot	$8.50–11.00
Oval platter, 13"	$6.00–8.00
Coffee server	$14.00–18.00
Dinner plate, 10"	$3.50–4.50
Disk water pitcher	$15.00–17.50
Sugar with cover	$4.00–5.50
Creamer	$3.00–4.50
Marmalade	$22.00–28.00
Large nappy	$6.00–8.00
Small fruit	$3.50–4.00
Salad bowl, 10"	$9.00–12.00
Teacup	$3.50–4.50
Saucer	$1.00–1.50
Sauce boat	$7.00–8.50
Sauce boat stand	$12.00–15.00
(in red)	$35.00–50.00
Plate, 7"	$1.50–2.00
Coffee mug	$5.00–6.50
Covered casserole	$14.00–18.00
Shakers, pr.	$5.00–6.50
Ash tray	$6.00–8.50

FIESTA KITCHEN KRAFT

Since the early 1930s the Homer Laughlin China Company had been well known as manufacturers of a wide variety of ceramic kitchen wares. In 1939 they introduced a bake and serve line, called Fiesta Kitchen Kraft, as an extension of their already popular genuine Fiesta ware. This they offered in four original Fiesta colors — red, yellow, green and blue. The following pieces (compiled from April, 1941, price list) were available.

Covered jars, small, medium and large
Large covered jug
Mixing bowls — 10", 8", and 6"
Spoon, fork and cake server
Covered casseroles, 8½", 7½" and individual
Refrigerator set, 4 pc.
Pie plate, 10"
Cake plate, 11"
Large salt and pepper shakers
Plates, 6" and 9"

These were chosen from the standard assortment of Kitchen ware items which had been the basis of the many Kitchen Kraft and Oven Serve decaled lines of years previous; none were created especially for Fiesta Kitchen Kraft. This line was in production for a relatively short period — perhaps being discontinued sometime during the Second World War prior to 1945.

Fiesta Kitchen Kraft

In addition to the items listed previously, there are at least three more to add. (These may have been offered in the original assortment and discontinued by the 1941 listing). These are: the oval platter in a chrome holder — shipped as a unit from HLC; a 9" pie plate; and a variation in size of the covered jug. The difference is so slight, even side by side it could go unnoticed. Collectors report as many of one size as the other. If you really want to label yours large or small, check the measurements below.

LARGE   SMALL

LARGE		SMALL
21½"	circumference	20"
5⅛"	base rim	4¾"
3¾"	rim inside of lid	3⅜"
2 ⅜"	diameter of knob	2¼"

The 6" and 9" plates listed on the 1941 illustrated brochure were used as under plates for the casseroles. When we visited the morgue at HLC, we saw an example of these. They were of a thinner guage and seemed to have been taken from one of their other lines, since the style was not typical; they were round and had a moderately wide, slightly flared rim. Although none have been reported in Fiesta KK colors, there are two in ivory with decals shown in later chapters.

If you have been interested at all in the decaled lines, you are probably familiar enough with the Kitchen Kraft molds that you recognize them easily. Several collectors have mentioned finding the stack set, salt and peppers, mixing bowls and other items in an ivory glaze, but as far as we can determine from any information available, ivory was never listed as a Fiesta Kitchen Kraft color, so these are rare. Of the four standard colors, dark blue is most in demand and along with red represents the high side of the price range.

Fiesta Kitchen Kraft

The covered refrigerator jars consist of three flat stacking units and a flat lid, and are usually made up of all four Kitchen Kraft colors. Examples shown here in Plate 85 and Plate 86 are special — one is all red, the other has a unit and the lid (complete with a Kitchen Kraft sticker) in ivory. The red lid in Plate 84 fits these jars perfectly — and that's about all we *do* know about it! It may have been experimental — no others have ever been reported. It may even have been made for some other purpose — a hot plate, for instance, in the regular Fiesta line — the band of rings do seem out of step in Kitchen Kraft. However, the concensus of opinion of those collectors who have had the chance to study it is that it seems to be a variation of the regular refrigerator jar lid.

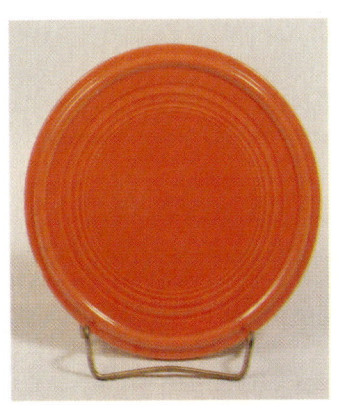

Plate 84

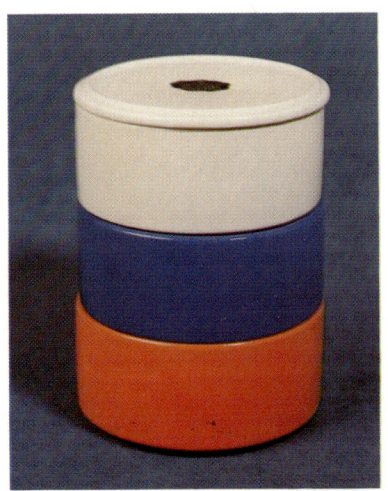

Plate 85

Plate 86. Stacking refrigerator jars, complete: $80.00–90.00; each jar: $20.00–22.50; lid only: $20.00–25.00. Covered jug, either size: $125.00–135.00.

Fiesta Kitchen Kraft

Trademarks:

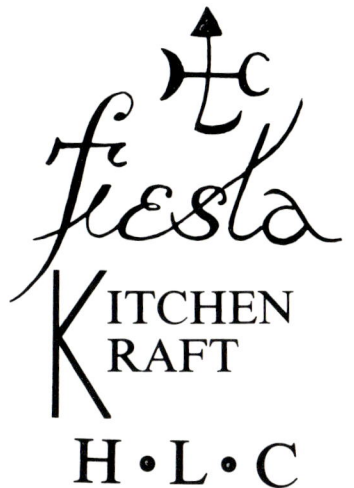

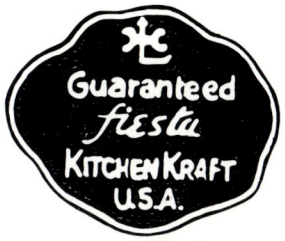

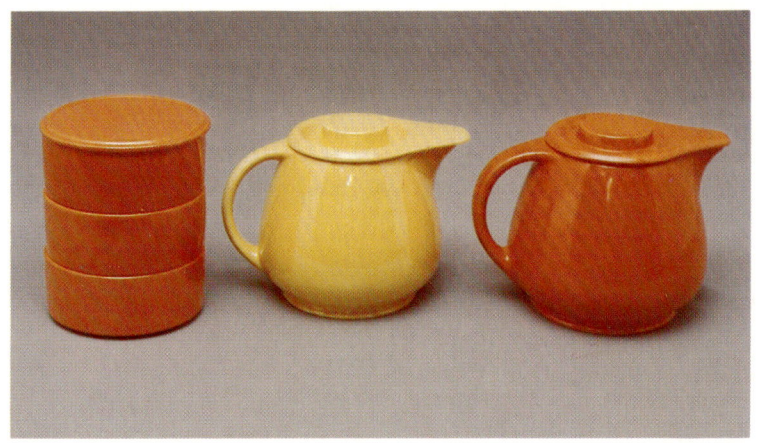

Plate 86

All sizes of the casseroles are scarce; the small one is especially attractive to collectors, and they are usually priced quite high.

To determine the size of your covered jar, measure the circumference. The larger jar is 27½" around, the medium 22", and the small one is 14¼". These make lovely (if unhandy) canisters!

The mixing bowls measure 10", 8" and 6", and have proven to be very difficult to find. Note the original sticker on the large one. They have been found in white as well as Harlequin and Jubilee colors. Such bowls may or may not be signed. Although a Kitchen ware bowl seems an unlikely liquor decanter, the 6" size has been reported with this message in gold under glaze lettering: 'This whiskey is 4 years old, 90 proof Maryland straight rye whiskey, Wm. Jameson, Inc., N.Y., SHOREWOOD, The finest name in rye'.

Plate 87. Casserole, 8½": $60.00-70.00; 7½": $55.00-65.00; individual: $60.00-75.00.

Plate 88. Jar, large: $125.00-135.00; medium: $110.00-130.00; small: $100.00-125.00.

Plate 89. Mixing bowl, 10": $50.00-60.00; 8": $40.00-50.00; 6": $30.00-40.00.

Fiesta Kitchen Kraft

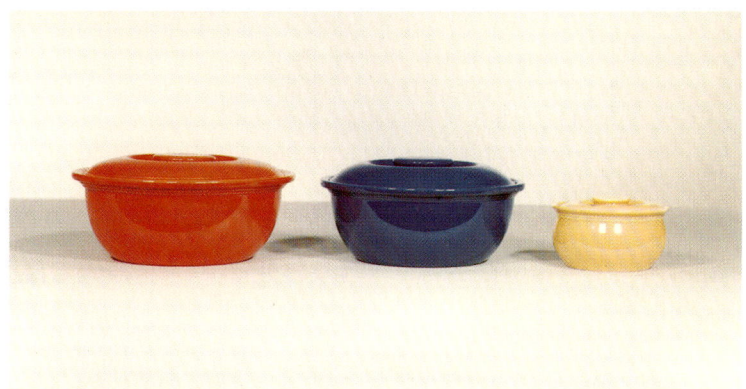

Plate 87

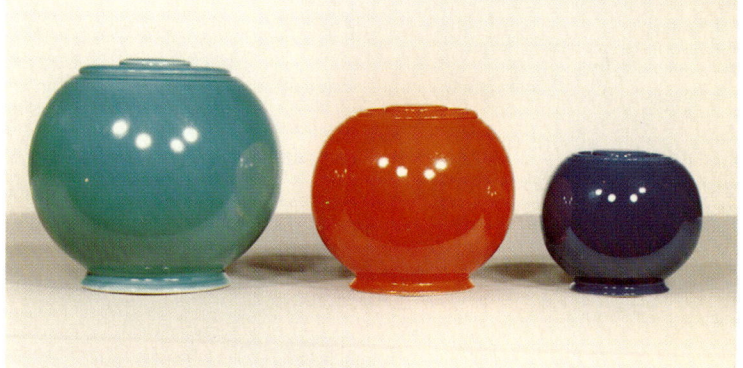

Plate 88

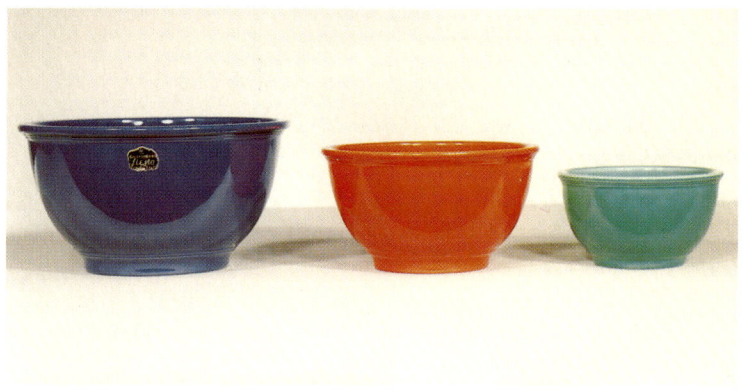

Plate 89

Fiesta Kitchen Kraft

Cake plates may or may not be marked; the only decoration is the narrow band around the edge formed by one inverted ring. The pie plates were produced without rings, either inside or outside, and are unusally not marked, though we have one with a gold Fiesta stamp. The 10″ size has been reported in the maroon and spruce green of the Harlequin line. The small size is very unusual done in the Fiesta colors; this mold is more often found in ivory decorated with decals.

In Plate 92 on the left is the 10″ pie plate in the metal holder. The casserole in the center is the 8½″ size and is shown in the holder as shipped from HLC. On the right is the 13″ oval platter. These are extremely rare, and are probably not marked. Of course, not all were shipped complete with metal holder. A rare few have been found in Harlequin yellow and one in spruce green (shown below).

The spoon, fork and cake server are all rated highly by collectors and are not easily found. The handles are decorated with the same embossed flowers as one of the Oven Serve lines. The salt and pepper shakers are larger replicas of their Fiesta counterpart, although by no means as plentiful. You may find on rare occasions that Harlequin yellow was substituted for the standard Fiesta yellow. The shakers, for instance, have been found in the lighter color of Harlequin.

Plate 90

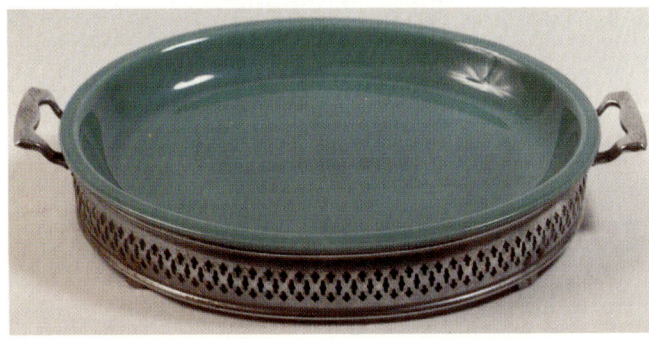

Plate 90. Platter, 13″, in spruce green with holder: $110.00-125.00.
Plate 91. Cake plate, 11″: $25.00-30.00. Pie plate, 10″: $28.00-35.00; 9″: $25.00-32.00.
Plate 92. Metal holders only, for 10″ pie plate: $13.00-16.00; for casserole: $10.00-12.50; for platter: $16.00-20.00. Oval platter without holder, 13″: $42.00-50.00.
Plate 93. Spoon: $32.00-36.00; cake server: $32.00-36.00; fork: $32.00-36.00. Salt and pepper shakers: $38.00-42.00, pr.

Fiesta Kitchen Kraft

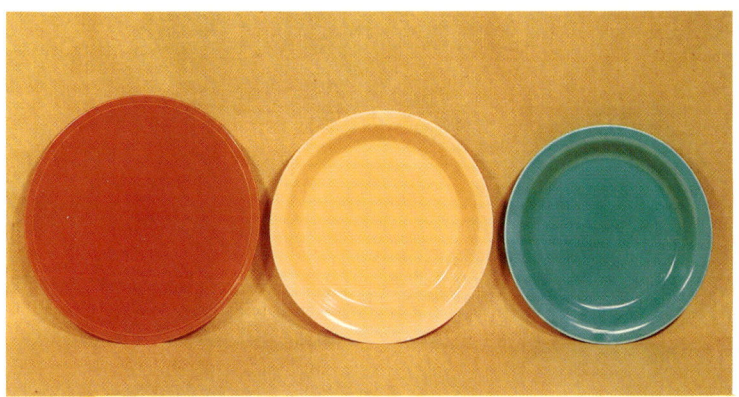

Plate 91

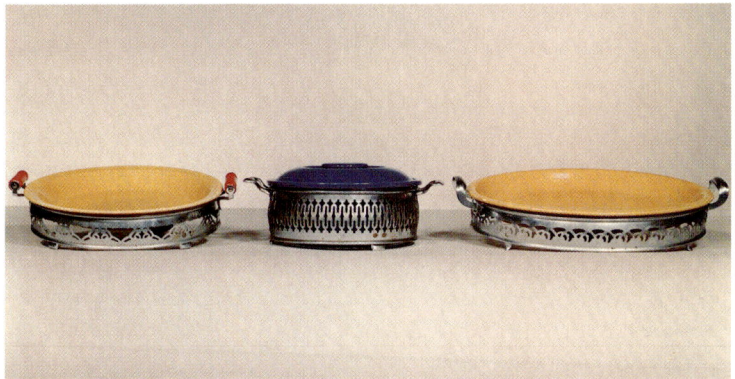

Plate 92

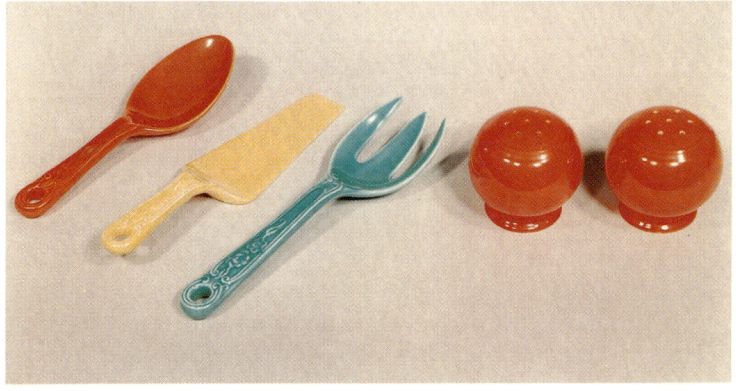

Plate 93

HARLEQUIN

Harlequin was produced by Homer Laughlin in an effort to serve all markets and to fit every budget. It was a less expensive, thinner ware, and was sold without trademark through the F. W. Woolworth Company exclusively. The following is an excerpt from one of the company's original illustrated brochures:

> *The new Harlequin Pottery offers a gift to table gaiety. It brings the magic of bright, exciting color to the table, dresses the festive board with pleasantness and personality, makes of every meal a cheerful and companionable occasion.*
>
> *The new ware comes in four lovely colors . . . Yellow, Green, Red, and Blue . . . and offers the hostess endless possibilities for creating interesting and appealing color effects on her table. All the colors are brilliant and eye-catching . . . designed to go together effectively in any combination the hostess may desire. To set a table with Harlequin is an adventure in decoration. Plates are of one color, cups of another, saucers and platters of another . . . you can give free range to your artistic instincts.*
>
> *And it is very easy to build up a comprehensive set of Harlequin in whatever items and colors you desire, because it may be bought by the piece at extremely reasonable prices.*
>
> *Sold Exclusively by*
> *F.W. WOOLWORTH CO. STORES*

Although it was first listed on company records as early as 1936, Harlequin was not actively introduced to the public until 1938.

It was designed by Fredrick Rhead and like Fiesta the style was pure Art Deco. Rhead again used the band of rings device as its only ornamentation, but this time chose to space the rings well away from the rim. Flat pieces were round and concave with the center areas left plain. Hollowware pieces were cone shaped; bowls were flared. Handles were applied with small ornaments at their bases, and with few exceptions were extremely angular.

Over the years the color assortment grew to include nearly all of Fiesta's lovely colors, except ivory and dark blue. The original colors (those mentioned in the brochure quoted above), however, were developed just for Harlequin. Harlequin yellow was a lighter and brighter tint than Fiesta yellow, the green was a spruce green, and the blue tended toward a mauve shade. It is interesting to note that the color the company referred to as 'red' is actually maroon. To avoid confusion, today's collectors reserve 'red' for the orange-red color of Fiesta red.

It seems logical here to conclude that because Harlequin was not extensively promoted until 1938, that it would have been then or soon after that the line was expanded and new colors added. The new colors of the forties were red (orange-red like Fiesta's, called tangerine by the company); rose (though records show a color called salmon that preceeded rose, if indeed these are two individual shades the difference is so slight it is of no significance to today's collectors); turquoise; and light green. (Light green was possibly added in the mid-forties since it is rare or non-existent in several pieces which, though not original, were listed as discontinued by 1952).

Gray, chartreuse and forest (dark) green were new in the fifties. Harlequin yellow, turquoise and rose continued to be produced. By 1959, the color assortment was reduced to four colors again — red (coinciding with the resumed production of Fiesta red), turquoise, Harlequin yellow, and the last new color, medium green.

The original line consisted of these items:

10″ plate	Teacup and saucer
9″ plate	Creamer, regular
8″ soup plate	Sugar bowl
7″ plate	11″ platter
6″ plate	5½″ fruit
9″ nappy	Double egg cup
Salt and pepper shakers	4½″ tumbler
Covered casserole	

To the original line these pieces were soon added: cream soup cup, sauce boat, after dinner cup and saucer, novelty creamer, 13″ platter, teapot, syrup*, service water jug, 36s bowl, ash tray (both styles), 36s oatmeal, individual salad bowl, 22 oz. jug, 4½″ tumbler, ash tray saucer*, basketweave nut dish*, relish tray with inserts*, individual egg cup*, individual creamer, candle holders*, marmalade*, butter dish with cover, tankard and 9″ baker. Of the assortment, those items marked with an asterisk (indicating them to be rare or non-existent in light green) were probably the first to be discontinued. Knowing that the Fiesta line suffered a severe pruning during 1944-45, it would certainly follow that the same fate would befall Harlequin.

The dated material from May, 1952, indicates that even more pieces had by then been dropped: the 9″ baker, the covered butter, the individual creamer and the tankard.

Harlequin proved to be quite popular and sold very well into the late fifties when sales began to diminish. Records show that the final piece was actually manufactured in 1964.

In 1939, the Hamilton Ross Co. offered a Harlequin look-alike which they called Sevilla. It came in assorted solid colors, eight in all, with the same angular handles, similar style and decoration. The round platter was distinctive — it featured closed handles formed by the band of rings device which was allowed to sweep gradually outward to just past mid-point; no doubt you have seen an occasional piece.

In 1979, the Homer Laughlin Co. announced that they had been approached and would comply with a request from the F. W. Woolworth Company to reissue the Harlequin line, one of that company's all time best sellers, as a part of their 100th Anniversary celebration. The Harlequin Ironstone dinnerware they produced was a very limited line and is easily recognized. It was made in three original colors — medium green, yellow, turquoise, and a new shade, coral. The sugar was restyled with closed handles and a solid finial. A round platter (the original was oval) in coral was included in the 45 pc. set, which was comprised of only plates, salad plates, cereal/soups, cups and saucers, yellow sugar and turquoise creamer, and one round green vegetable bowl. The plates were backstamped Homer Laughlin (the old ones are not marked) and even the pieces made from authentic molds are easy to distinguish from the old Harlequin. Considering the many lovely colors of the original line and that virtually none of its unique accessory pieces were reproduced, this late line should cause little if any concern to the many collectors who love Harlequin dinnerware. In fact, in a recent poll, 90% of the collectors we contacted feel that the reissue did nothing to hurt the collectibility or the market value of the old line.

A letter from the company dated April, 1983, advised that Woolworth's, as well as a few other dealers throughout the country, had again began to feature the new Harlequin. It stated that a few round platters and vegetable bowls had been made in yellow by mistake, and that some of these were backstamped 'through error in the Dipping Department'. The letter closed by saying that 'at this time, we are unable to estimate it's current life span'.

Plate 94. Harlequin Ironstone brochure.

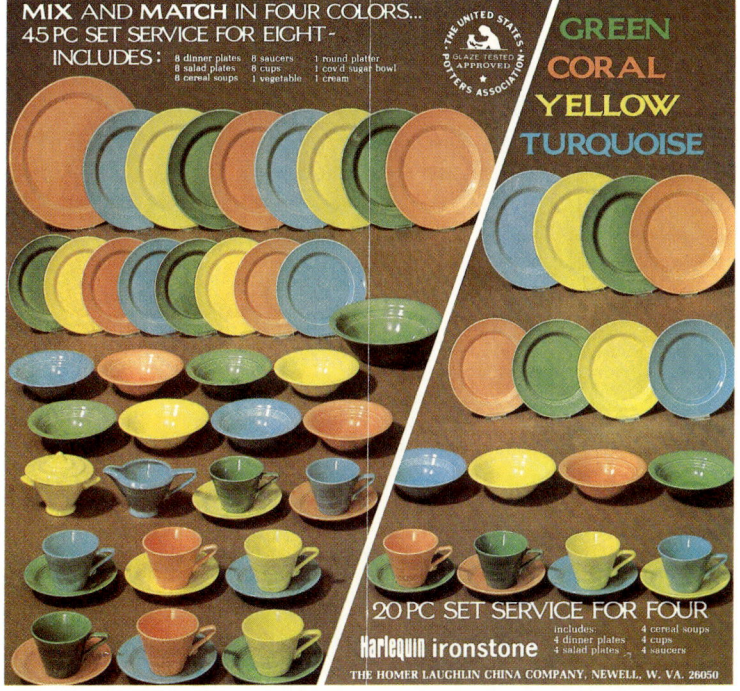

Plate 94

Harlequin

The higher side of the range of suggested values applies to these colors: maroon, spruce green, red, medium green and the fifties colors.

The 10" dinner plate is becoming very hard to find; the 9" and 7" have each been reported in ivory, not a standard Harlequin color. The 5½" fruit at the bottom of the page has been found in a slightly larger variation that measures 6" across, in maroon, blue, spruce and yellow.

Plate 95. Plate, 10": $5.50–7.00; 9": $4.50–5.50; 7": $3.00–4.00; 6": $2.50–3.00.

Plate 96. Platter, 13": $9.00–12.00; 11": $5.00–7.00.

Plate 97. Soup plate (deep plate), 8": $8.00–10.00. 36s oatmeal, 6½": $4.00–5.50. Fruit, 5½": $3.50–4.50. Cream soup: $5.50–7.00.

Harlequin

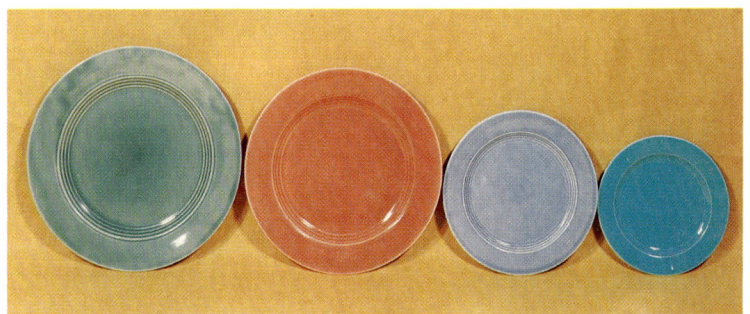

Plate 95

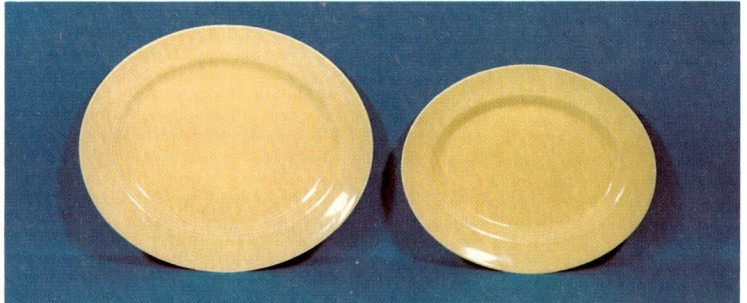

Plate 96

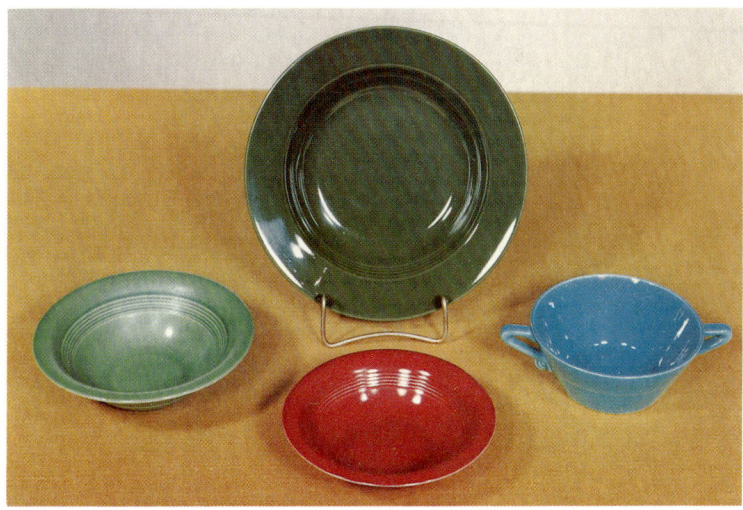

Plate 97

The oval baker, discontinued before the fifties, is found in the first eight colors only. The 36s bowl, as well as the individual salad, has not proven to be particularly rare in the fifties colors, but instead seems to be most difficult to find in red, maroon and spruce green. As a general rule, you will find less medium green, chartreuse, gray and dark green in Harlequin than in Fiesta.

Plate 98. Nappy, 9″: $8.00–10.00. 36s bowl: $8.00–10.00. Casserole w/lid: $24.00–28.00. Oval baker, 9″: $6.50–7.50. Individual salad bowl, 7″: $7.00–8.50.

Harlequin

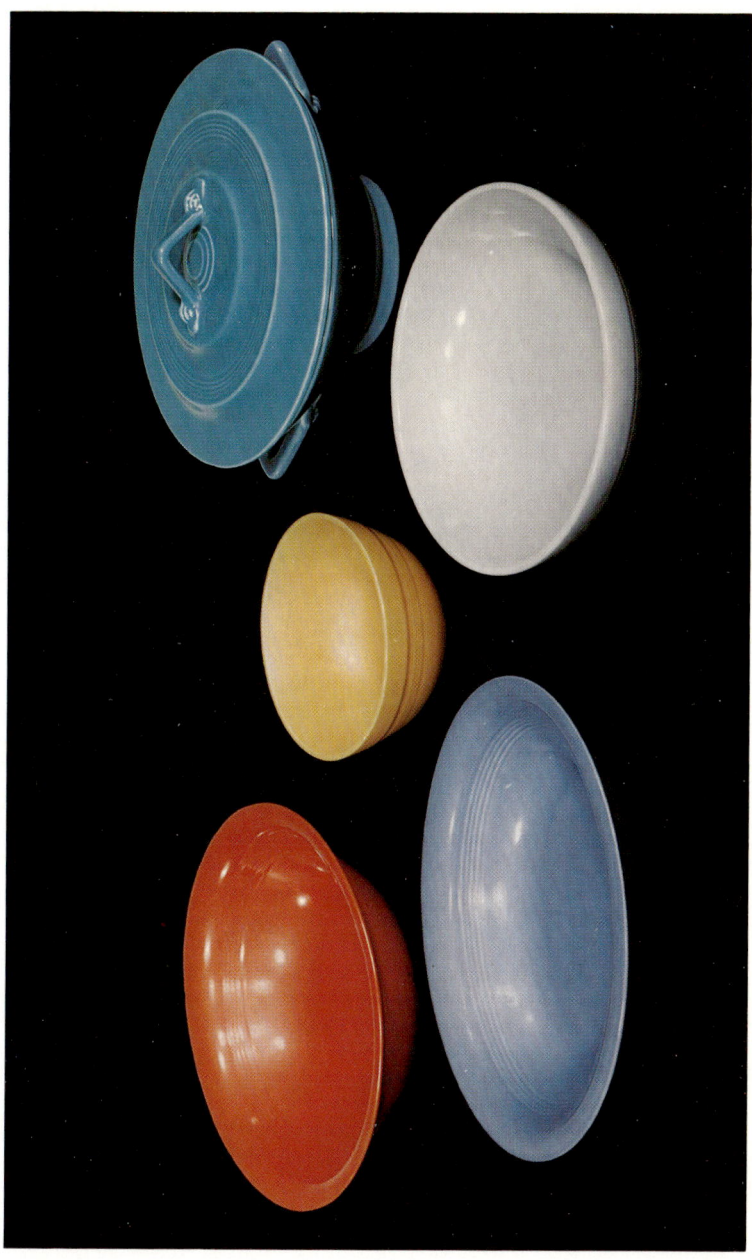

Plate 98

Harlequin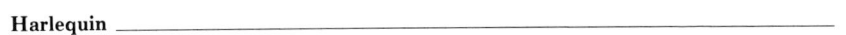

Look for the Fiesta-like band of rings near the base on the water jug. This will help you identify the Harlequin jug from several look-alikes by other companies. Since the fourth edition, a few of these have been reported in gray, chartreuse, and dark and medium green. The tumblers, however, are found in the first eight colors only.

Plate 99. Service water jug: $15.00–17.50; in gray, chartreuse, dark and medium green: $25.00–30.00. Tumbler: $18.00–22.00.

Plate 100. Teapot: $20.00–24.00. Teacup: $4.50–5.00; saucer: $1.00–1.50.

Harlequin

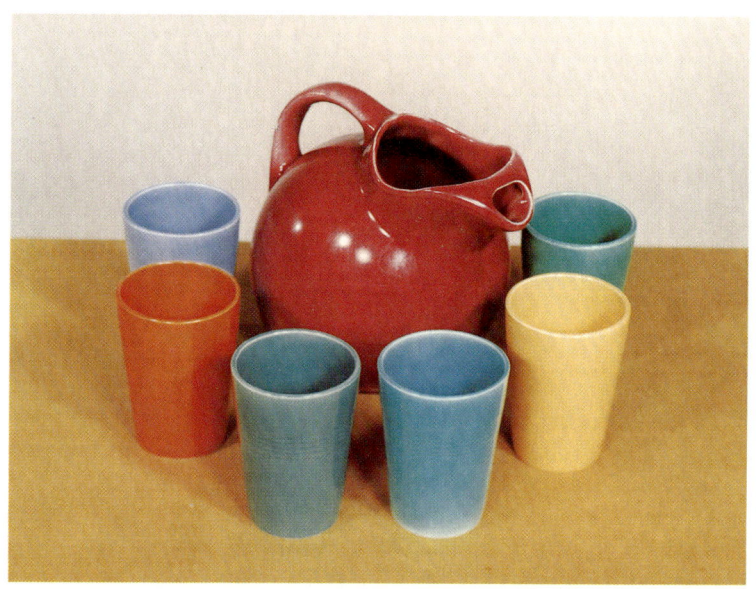

Plate 99

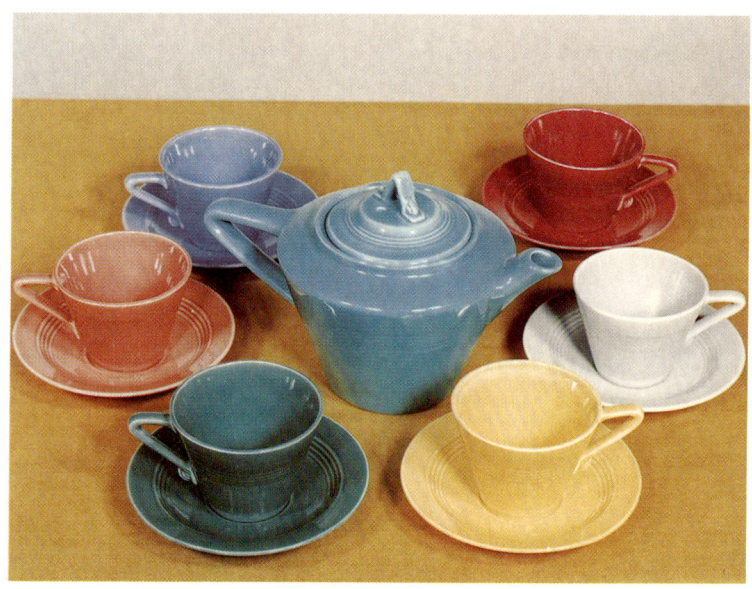

Plate 100

One collector reports that upon comparing sugar bowls of various colors in his collection, he suspects that those with the inside rings were earlier, and that these rings were eliminated sometime during the forties. The 'high-lip' creamer is found in the four original colors only. Note the difference in the length of the lips on the two shown (far left); this is due to the fact that they were trimmed off by hand. These are very hard to find. Marmalades are found in the first eight colors only — light green is very rare. In Plate 102, the tumbler with the decal of the antique car is one of a set of 6, decorated by Pearl China.

Plate 101. Sugar bowl with lid: $5.00–7.00. Creamer, regular: $4.00–5.00. Creamer, high-lip: $18.00–20.00. Salt and pepper shakers: $6.00–7.50, pr. Marmalade: $38.00–42.00. Novelty creamer: $8.00–10.00.

Plate 102. Sauce boat: $6.00–8.00. Tumbler with car decal: $22.00–25.00. 22 oz. jug: $15.00–17.00; in gray, chartreuse, dark and medium green: $20.00–25.00.

Harlequin

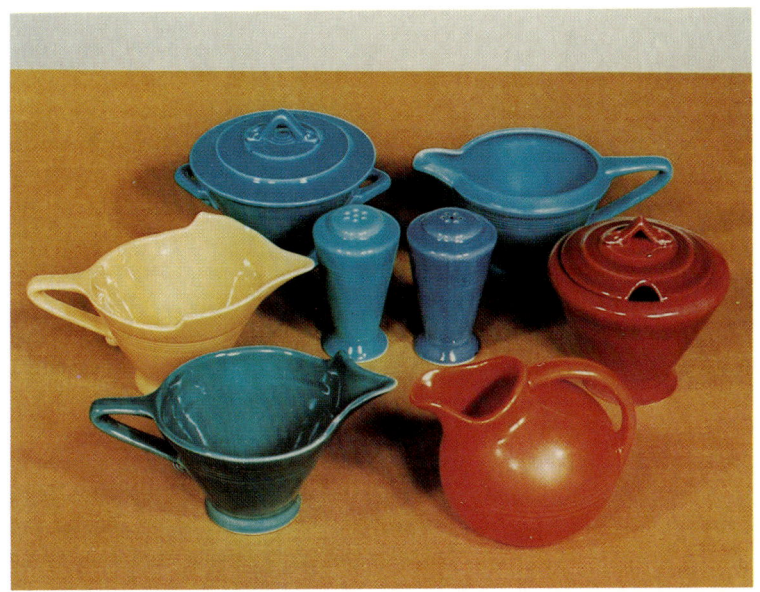

Plate 101

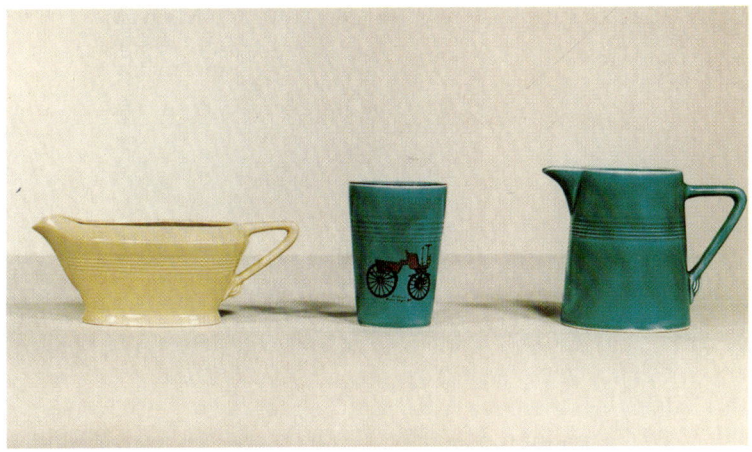

Plate 102

Harlequin

The ash tray saucer on the far left in Plate 104 and the one below, Plate 103, have been reported in maroon, spruce green, yellow, red, and turquoise. In ivory it is extremely rare. It has been found in medium green, and the fifties colors of dark green and chartreuse. Yellow, turquoise and rose also exist. Company records list the tankard as discontinued by 1952. Notice that though it has the typically angular handle, it lacks the band of rings design. The small basketweave nut dishes are found in the first eight colors — light green is quite rare. Syrups are scarce and have been reported in red, yellow, mauve blue, spruce green . . . and one in turquoise. The plain ash tray comes in the first eight colors only, while the basketweave version was made in all twelve, including medium green. The ½ pound butter dish was originally a piece from the Century line that was later dipped in Harlequin and Riviera colors to be sold with these lines. They have been found in these colors: cobalt blue, rose, mauve blue, spruce green, light green, maroon, turquoise, red, ivory, and Fiesta and Harlequin yellow. The tiny perfume bottle (not actually Harlequin) was a special order for a cosmetic company. They're very rare, but a couple have been found in light green.

As strange as it seems, the true Harlequin relish tray base is found only in turquoise; when these pie wedge inserts are occasionally found in bases of another color, they have been Fiesta bases! The inserts are found in only seven of the first eight colors — no light green. To the right (Plate 105) is an example of a common practice: some enterprising company has turned a 36s bowl into a nut dish with the addition of a little chrome and a glass knob!

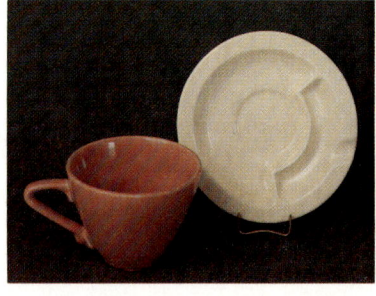

Plate 103

Plate 103. Ash tray saucer in ivory: $35.00–40.00. Tankard: $35.00–40.00.

Plate 104. Basketweave nut dish: $5.00–6.50. Syrup: $80.00–85.00. Tankard: $35.00–40.00. Ash tray saucer: $22.00–25.00. Plain ash tray: $15.00–18.00. Basketweave ash tray: $17.50–20.00. ½ lb. butter dish: $32.00–35.00. Perfume bottle: $40.00–45.00.

Plate 105. Relish tray, 5 pc.: $42.00–48.00. Nut dish: $20.00–25.00.

Harlequin

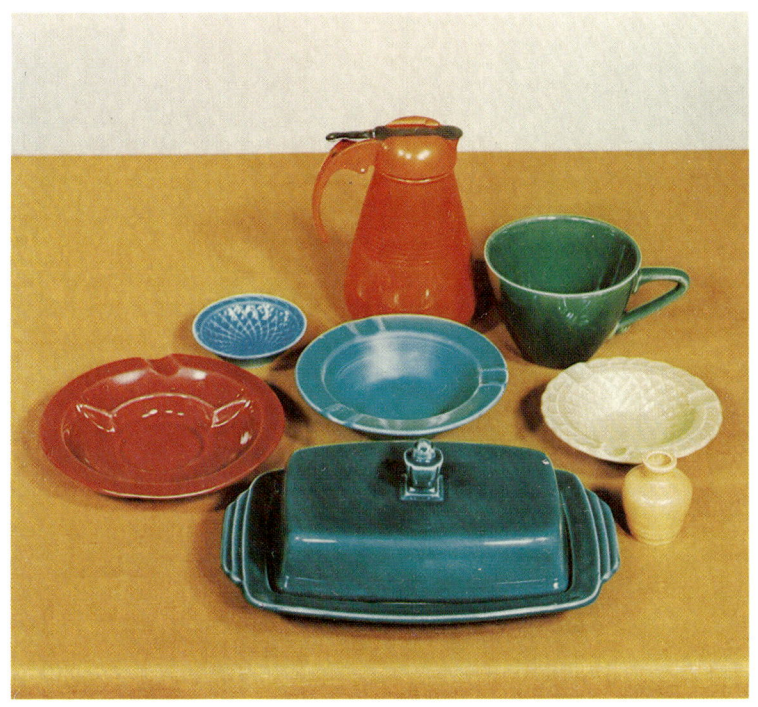

Plate 104

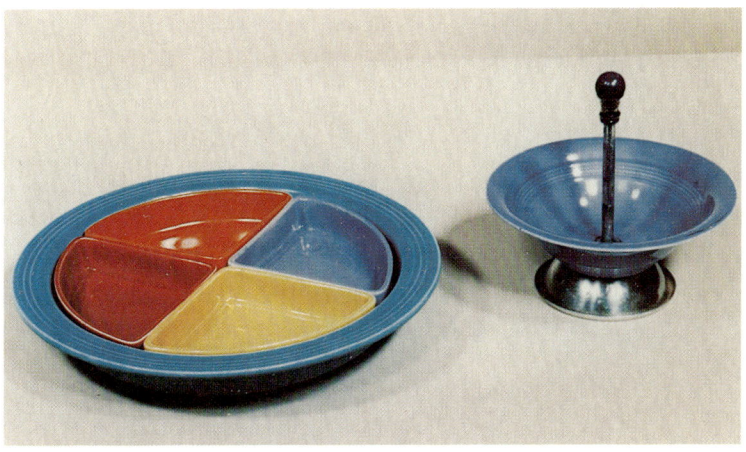

Plate 105

Double egg cups have been found in eleven colors, but no medium green has been reported, and they were not included in the 1959 listing. The individual egg cups were discontinued before the advent of light green, due the fact, no doubt, that they were tedious and costly to make since the stems were hand turned and trimmed. They are among the few pieces of Harlequin devoid of rings. So far, the candle holders have not been found in light green, just seven of the first eight colors. Styled to scale to match the teacups, the A.D. cups are becoming scarce in the fifties colors, and are perhaps non-existent in medium green. They do not appear on the 1959 listing (when medium green was introduced), and collectors are doubtfull that they were produced in that color.

Shown in Plate 107, the wandering spoon rest has at long last arrived at home! In the eight years since it was discovered, it was first thought to be Fiesta (eight years ago anything of exceptional merit was assumed to be Fiesta); then, when this one was found with the Harlequin label intact, we naturally revised our thinking. Only within the past year or two during a newsletter interview with the man who designed this piece was the full truth revealed! Don Schreckengost, HLC designer in the fifties, told the reporter the spoon rest was part of his Rhythm line. (For more information, see the chapter on Rhythm.) But since turquoise was not a Rhythm color and this label is undoubtedly authentic, obviously these were also sold with Harlequin. They have been reported in forest green, yellow and turquoise to date. The second one has an advertising message. You will also find these in white with colorful decals.

Plate 106. Candle holders: $30.00–34.00, pr. Double egg cup: $6.50–7.50. Single egg cup: $9.00–11.00. Demitasse cup: $15.00–20.00; in fifties colors: $34.00–38.00; demitasse saucer: $3.00–5.00; fifties colors, $6.00–8.00.

Plate 107. Spoon rest, 8¼″ x 6¼″: $100.00–135.00; with original label, add $25.00. Advertising spoon rest: $65.00–75.00.

Harlequin

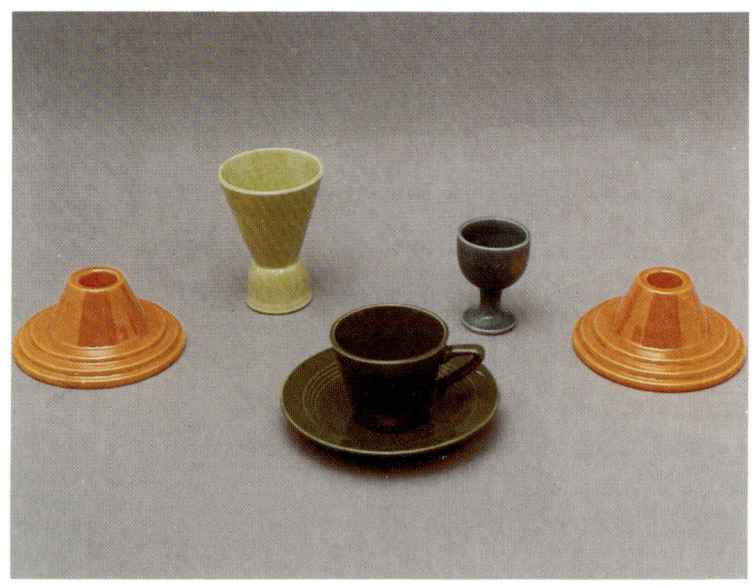

Plate 106

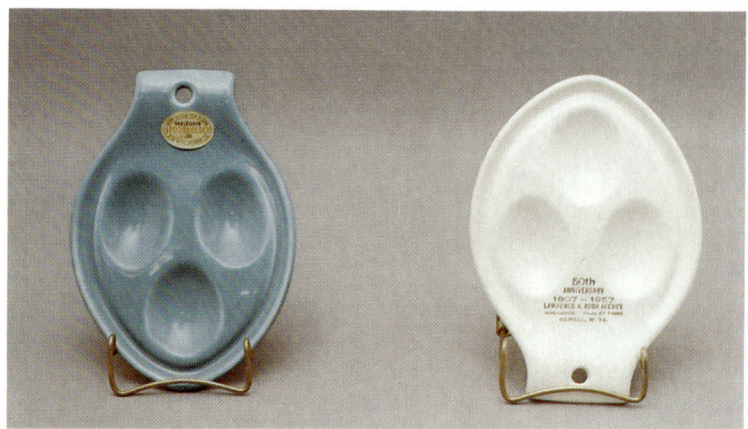

Plate 107

Harlequin

The Kitchen Kraft style mixing bowl set below may be Harlequin, or it may be Rhythm — these are not marked. A pastel set in gray, blue gray and pink also exists as part of the Jubilee line. These may or may not carry the Jubilee backstamp. Shown in Plate 109, the wire frame donkey and the metal holder for the tumbler are not of HLC origin, but accessories such as these are popular with today's collectors. You'll find the individual creamer only in the first eight colors.

The cup in Plate 110 is the rare tankard while the saucer, though considerably oversized (7"), is the standard Rhythm shape. Probably one of a kind, the lamp in the center has the base of a large Fiesta comport, a body made of two Harlequin casseroles, and the neck is a small Fiesta comport stem. The Harlequin pamphlet introduces the new line, but lists no prices or assortment. It does name the original colors, yellow, green (spruce), red (maroon), and blue (mauve blue). Although today we all seem to prefer matching our cups and saucers, the pamphlet suggests the buyers be more adventurous... it recommends 'cups of one color, saucers of another'.

Plate 108. Mixing bowls in colors shown, or gray, blue gray and pink, any size: $45.00-55.00.

Plate 109. Donkey frame only: $10.00-13.00. Individual creamer: $5.00-7.00. Metal holder for tumbler: $10.00-12.00.

Plate 110. Tankard and saucer: $50.00-55.00. Lamp base: $75.00-90.00. Harlequin pamphlet: $12.00-15.00.

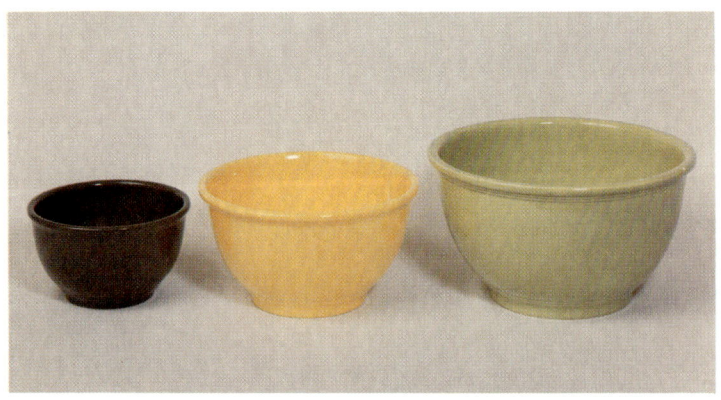

Plate 108

Harlequin

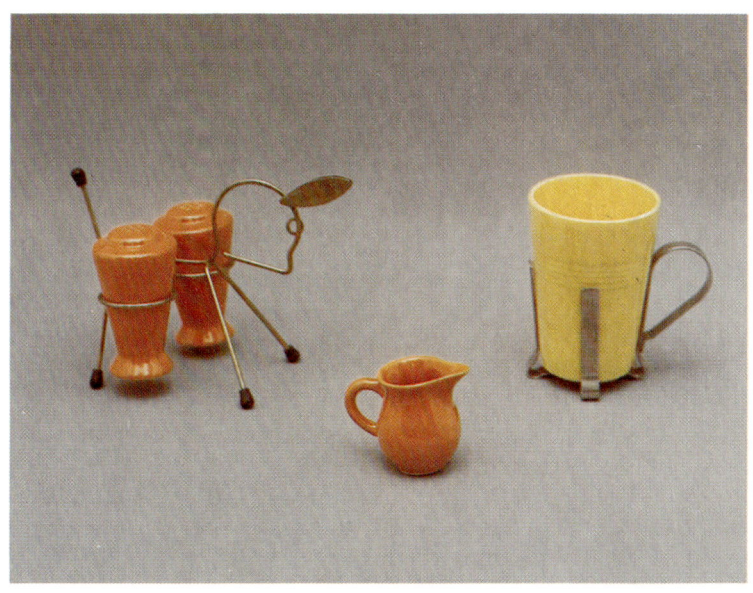

Plate 109

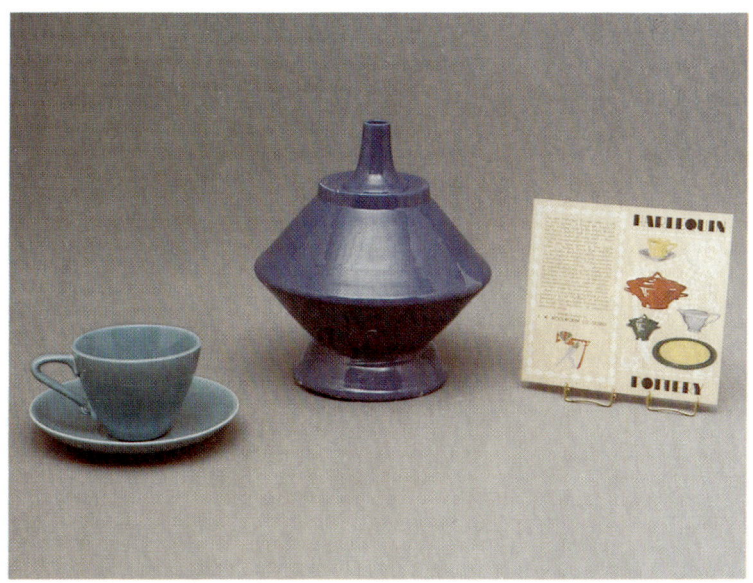

Plate 110

HARLEQUIN ANIMALS

This menagerie of darling animals is part of the Harlequin line. They were sold through F. W. Woolworth Co. Stores during the late thirties and early forties when miniatures such as these were enjoying a hey-day. For photography session, a whole herd arrived — each of the six represented in all four colors — maroon, spruce, mauve blue and yellow — plus gold, and white with gold trim!

In the top photo are the original HLC Harlequin animals in authentic glazes. There are no others, although this wee clique has been besieged by hordes of little deer, elephants, other ducks — even a cart — trying to squirm into line. True, the duck has a double, a perpetually hungry little gander, his head bent into a permanent feeding position, but he was made by the Brush Pottery Company! And though several collectors were almost sure their 2½" elephant was a 'charter member', HLC disowned him! The cart we mentioned is pulled by a donkey 'lookalike' but a second look shows an uncharacteristic lack of sharp detail and has been found to occasionally bear a 'California' mark!

The second photo displays the 'Maverick' animals . . . a most appropriate term adopted by collectors to indicate animals that have been glazed by someone outside the Homer Laughlin China Company. Those in the double row at the bottom are the same size as the original animals. In some cases, the gold finish has been applied over a Harlequin color. One company involved in decorating the animals was Kaulware, of Chicago, who utilized an iridescent glaze and gold hand painted trim. On the top row are examples of salt and pepper shakers of a slightly smaller size, indicating that they were cast from molds made from the original animals . . . in fact, one of the penguins is a bit smaller than the other.

Though probably not a production run, there are a few red cats being found, as well as one red duck. Photo 114 shows turquoise, light green and cobalt blue animals borrowed from HLC for their portrait photo.

Plate 111. Any animal: $40.00–45.00.

Plate 112. Mavericks: $24.00–28.00.

Plate 113. Red cat: $90.00–100.00.

Harlequin Animals

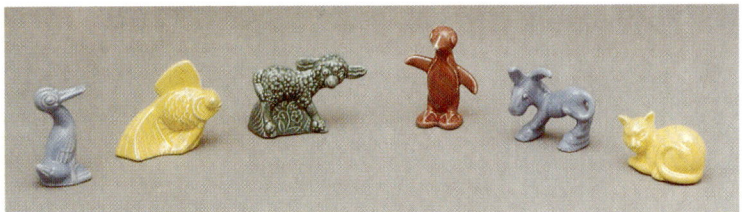

Plate 111

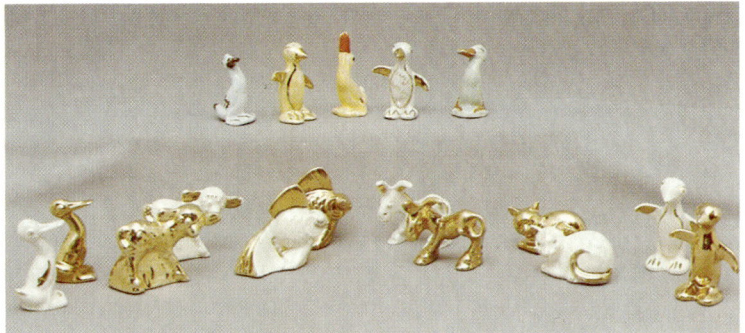

Plate 112

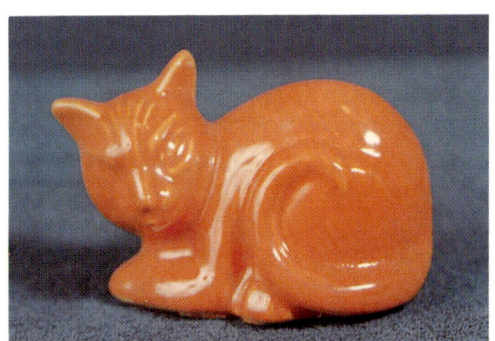

Plate 113

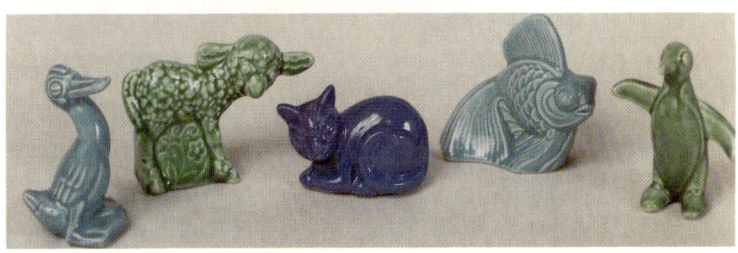

Plate 114

RIVIERA

Riviera was introduced by HLC in 1938 and was sold exclusively by the Murphy Co. In contrast to Fiesta and Harlequin, the line was quite limited. It was unmarked, lighter in weight, and therefore less expensive. Only rarely, a piece may be found with the Homer Laughlin gold ink stamp.

Of the three colored dinnerware lines, Riviera has the rather dubious distinction of being the only one which was not originally created as such. Its forerunner was a line called Century — an ivory line with a vellum glaze. Century shapes were also decorated with a wide variety of decals and were the basis of many lines, such as Mexicana and Hacienda. The butter dish was used in the Virginia Rose line. An enterprising designer (Rhead, no doubt) applied the popular colored glazes to these shapes, and Riviera was born! Even the shakers were from another line. They were originally designed as Tango — which accounts for the six section design in contrast to the square Riviera shape.

Riviera is in very short supply, and much to the chagrin of Riviera collectors everywhere, mint condition pieces are very few indeed. Especially bad to chip were the flat pieces — plates, platters, saucers, and undersides of lids. Still, when it is found with no chips, the glaze is nearly always in beautiful condition.

Colors are mauve blue, red, yellow, light green and ivory. On rare occasions, dark blue pieces are found, evidently made for special color effects. Ivory pieces are technically Century (the old price lists we've seen never show but four colors) and you will find a more diversified assortment in ivory than in the colored glazes. However, collectors appreciate the effect of the ivory with their Riviera and value these items as worthwhile additions to their collections.

Riviera

Records for this line are especially scanty; but as accurately and completely as possible, here is a listing of the items in the line as it was first introduced. Sizes have been translated from the English measurements listed by the company and in our previous editions to actual sizes to the nearest inch.

    11" dish (platter)
    13" dish (platter)
    10" plate
    9" plate
    6" plate
    Teacups and saucers
    Fruit
    9" baker (oval vegetable bowl)
    Salt and pepper shakers
    Covered casserole
    8" deep plate
    8" nappy
    6" oatmeal
    Tumblers (with handle)
    Open jug (also found with lid)
    Teapot
    Sauce boat
    Creamer
    Covered sugar

We have also found 15" platters, a covered syrup pitcher and two sizes of butter dishes . . . a half pound and a quarter pound. In addition, there is a juice set. The juice jugs are standard though scarce in yellow, unusual in red, and extremely rare in mauve blue.

Although it is uncertain just when Riviera was discontinued, it was sometime prior to 1950. Riviera is a challenge to collect, but you can be sure the effort will be worthwhile!

The 10″ dinner plates are very hard to find! The 7″ plate is not uncommon in cobalt, and collectors report this size in Fiesta yellow as well. Perhaps as one reader suggests, they were dipped in these colors to go with a Riviera/Fiesta ensemble such as shown in the ad in the color plates of the Fiesta section. This hypothesis may also explain the cobalt platter with the square well (bottom, right). The 13¼″ platter has been found with an oval well, and a large 15″ platter, also with an oval well, has been reported.

Plate 115. Plate, 10″: $6.00–7.00. Plate, 9″: $4.50–5.50. Plate, 7″: $3.00–3.50. Plate, 6″ $2.00–2.50.

Plate 116. Platter, 11½″: $7.50–9.00. Platter, closed handles, 11¼″: $8.00–9.50.

Plate 117. Platter, 13¼″: $10.00–11.50. Platter, 12″: $9.00–10.50.

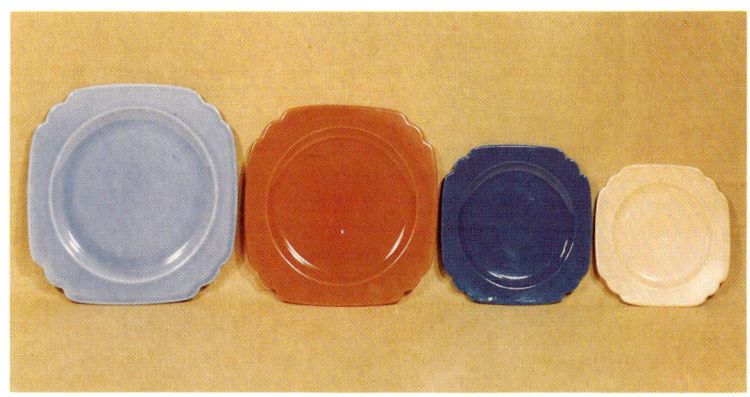

Plate 115

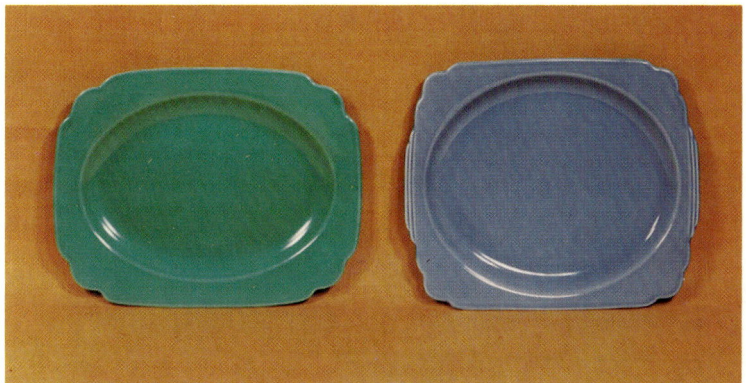

Plate 116

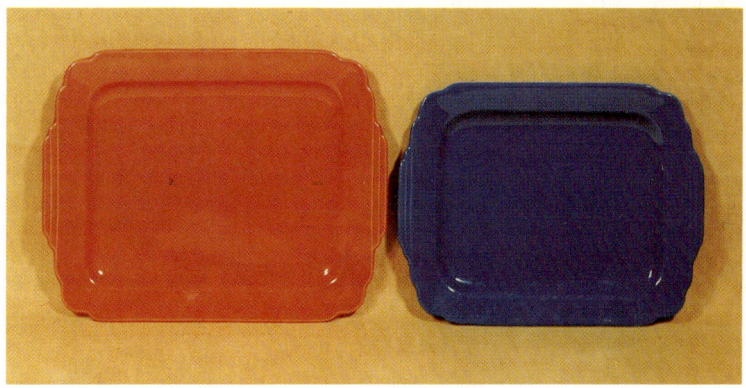

Plate 117

Below is a comparison photo showing the 5½" fruit and the deeper 6" oatmeal, which seems to be rather scarce. The ivory piece is a cream soup with liner; these are also scarce — don't expect to find these in the colored glazes.

Plate 118. Oatmeal, 6": $6.00-10.00. Fruit, 5½": $3.50-4.50. Cream soup with liner: $32.00-36.00.

Plate 119. Teapot: $35.00-45.00. Cup: $3.50-5.00. Saucer: $1.50-2.00.

Plate 120. Fruit, 5½": $3.50-4.50. Baker, 9", either style: $6.00-7.00. Deep plate, 8": $6.00-7.50. Nappy, 9¼": $7.50-8.50.

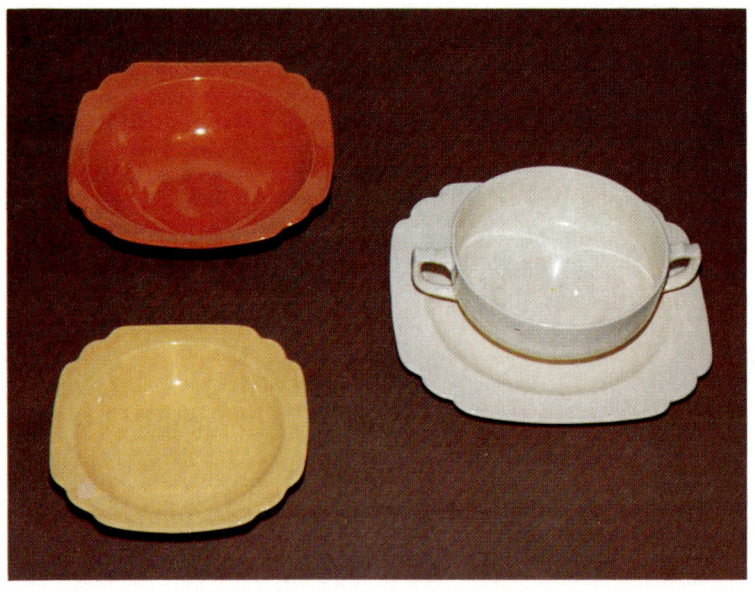

Plate 118

Riviera

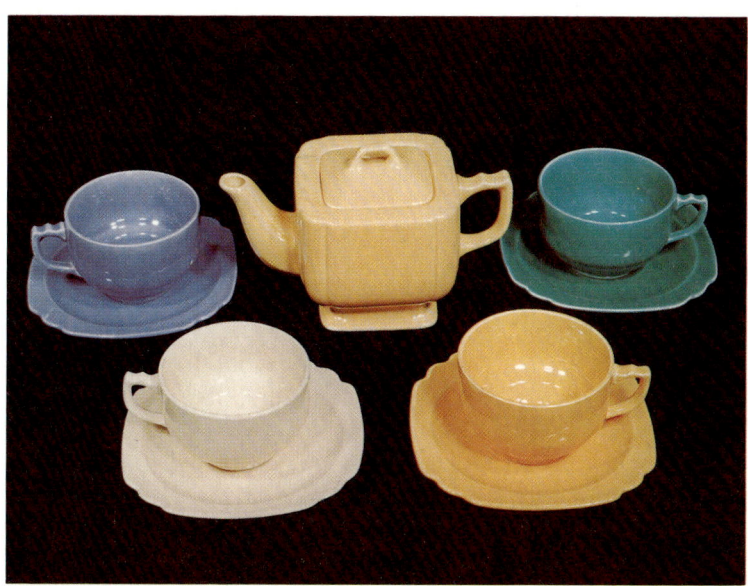

Plate 119

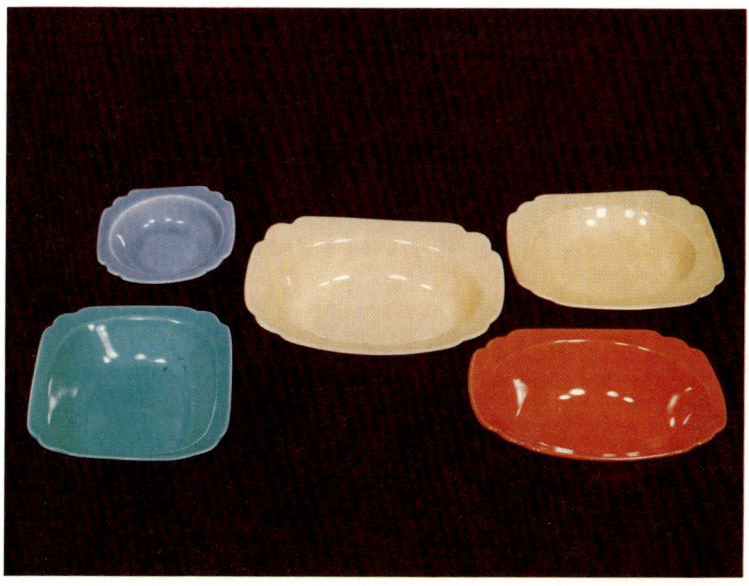

Plate 120

Scarce in any color but standard in yellow, the juice pitcher in red or mauve blue is rare indeed. Juice tumblers are also hard to find items. In the original sets, the tumblers were turquoise, mauve blue, red, yellow, light green and ivory.

The covered casserole is a very nice piece, one you may find difficult to locate for your collection.

Plate 121. Juice pitcher, yellow: $40.00-45.00; in mauve blue: $85.00-100.00. Juice tumbler: $20.00-24.00.

Plate 122. Sauce boat: $6.50-8.00.

Plate 123. Casserole with lid: $35.00-40.00.

Riviera

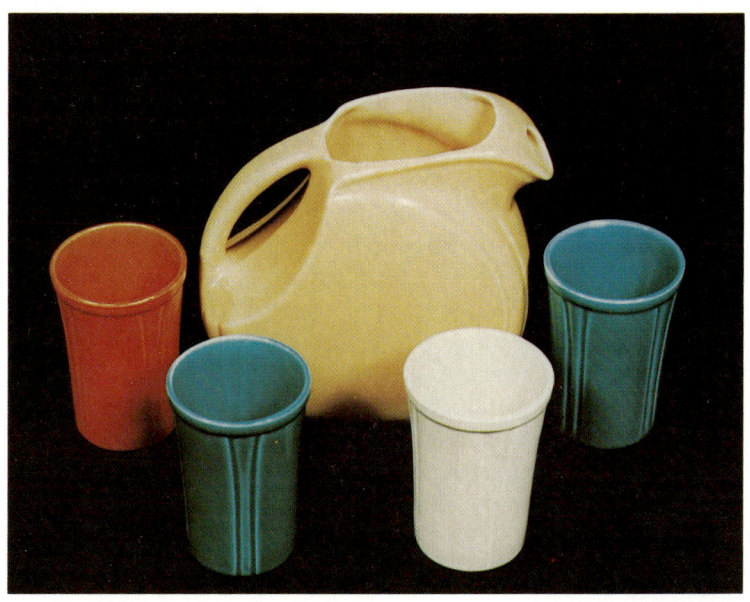

Plate 121

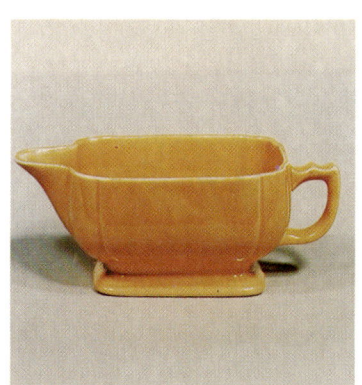

Plate 122

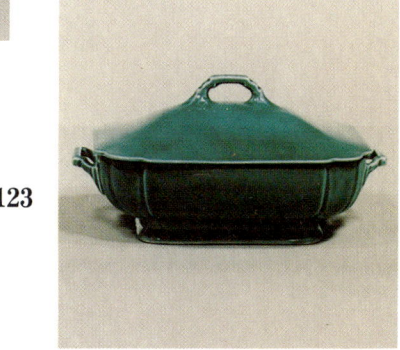

Plate 123

Shown here is the covered jug, surrounded by four colors of the handled tumblers. Jugs are really quite hard to find and have been found with the cover in only light green and ivory. Ivory tumblers are very scarce and often command high prices. As you can see, there are six orange-like segments that make up the design of the salt and pepper shakers. These were borrowed from the Tango line, so expect to find them in Tango colors, too. Two pairs have been found in a true red glaze . . . origin unconfirmed. Near the center of the picture are the butter dishes. The large one holds a half pound, and they are much easier to find than the smaller quarter pound size. The larger is available in mauve blue, rose, spruce green, light green, turquoise, maroon, cobalt blue, red, ivory, and in both Fiesta and Harlequin yellow. The quarter pound size is very rare in turquoise and cobalt blue, both shown below. The covered syrup pitcher is a darling piece, and rather hard to find.

Plate 124. Butter dish, quarter pound, cobalt or turquoise: $100.00–125.00.

Plate 125. Handled tumbler: $38.00–42.00. Covered jug: $42.00–48.00. Quarter pound butter dish: $38.00–42.00. Syrup with cover: $48.00–52.00. Salt and pepper shakers, $5.00–6.00, pr. Half pound butter dish: $45.00–55.00. Creamer, regular: $4.50–5.50. Sugar with lid: $6.00–7.00.

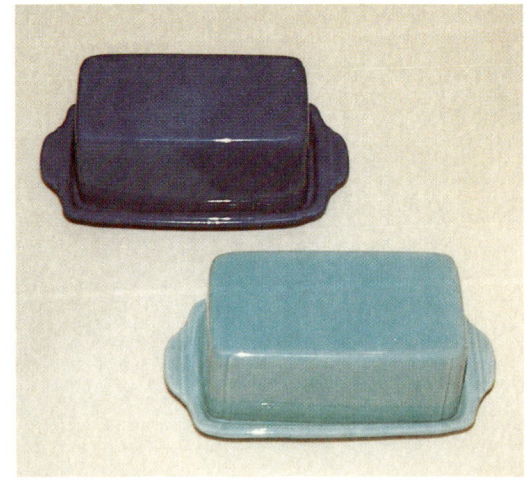

Plate 124

Riviera

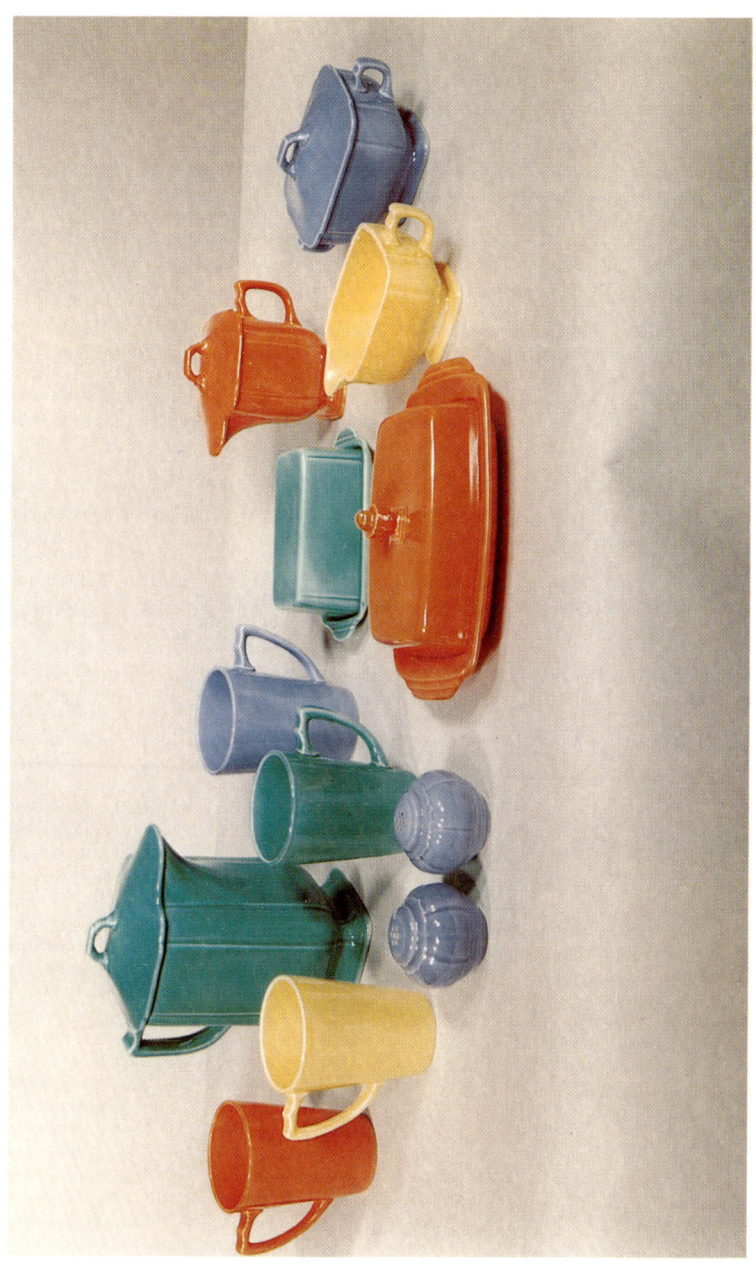

Plate 125

The batter set, complete with tray in cobalt, covered syrup pitcher and the tall covered jug — used for mixing, storing and pouring the batter for pancakes. These complete sets are quite unique, since they utilize one of the rare cobalt blue pieces and the cover for the tall jug — another hard to find item. In fact, the little covered syrup is also scarce.

The tumblers in Plate 127 are 4" and 5¼" tall and feature a band of Riviera mauve blue. A collector has reported similar glassware styled with vertically paneled sides trimmed with one band of color (light green, mauve blue, yellow or red) at the rim. Bought at auction with a set of Riviera, the glassware was still in the original box marked 'Juanita Beverage Set, Rosenthal and Ruben, Inc., Binghampton, N.Y., 1938'. There were two each of the four colors in four different sizes of tumblers: 3", 3½", 4" and 5¼". Matching swizzle sticks completed the 40 piece set. The demitasse cup and saucer is from the Century line, the forerunner of Riviera. So far, they have been reported only in ivory, and on occasion with the Mexicana decal. Egg cups and 8" plates may also be found in the ivory glaze.

Plate 126. Batter set, complete: $115.00–125.00.

Plate 127. Tumblers: $4.00–5.00. Riviera pamphlet: $12.00–15.00. Demitasse cup and saucer: $28.00–32.00

Riviera

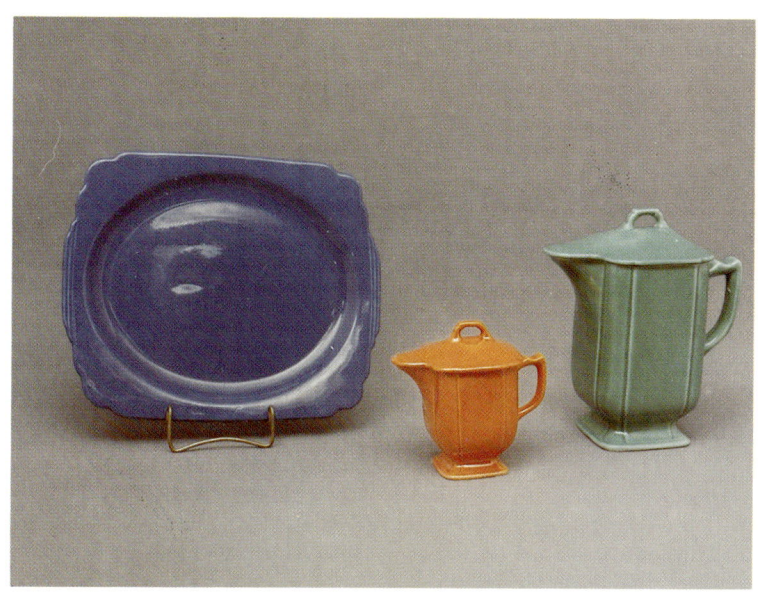

Plate 126

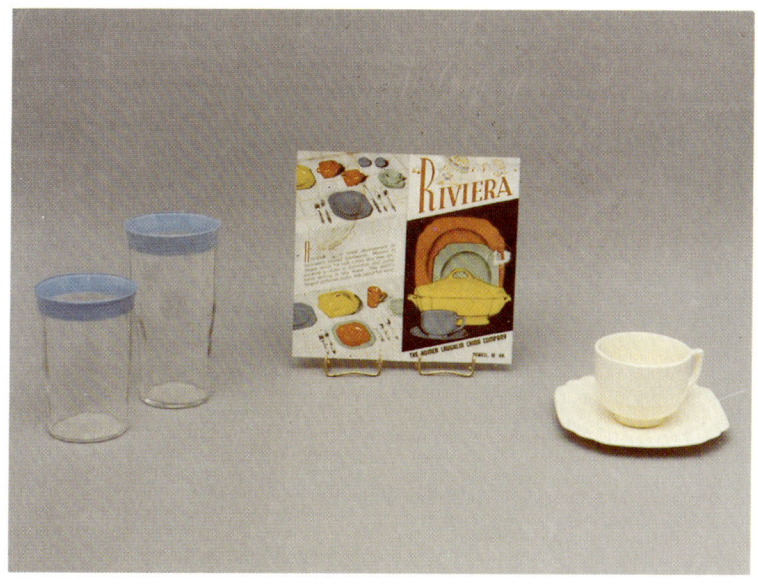

Plate 127

Shown opposite is the rare red juice pitcher and a Harlequin/Riviera handled tumbler that may well be one of a kind. Batter sets in ivory with various decals such as this one are not too easy to come by and are quite collectible.

Plate 128. Juice pitcher in red: $100.00–125.00

Plate 129. Handled tumbler, no established value.

Plate 130. Batter set with decals: $80.00–100.00.

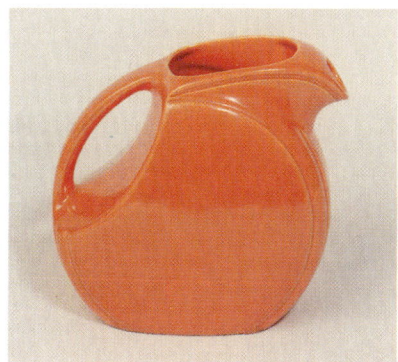

Plate 128

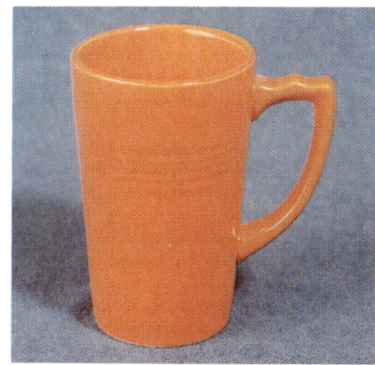

Plate 129

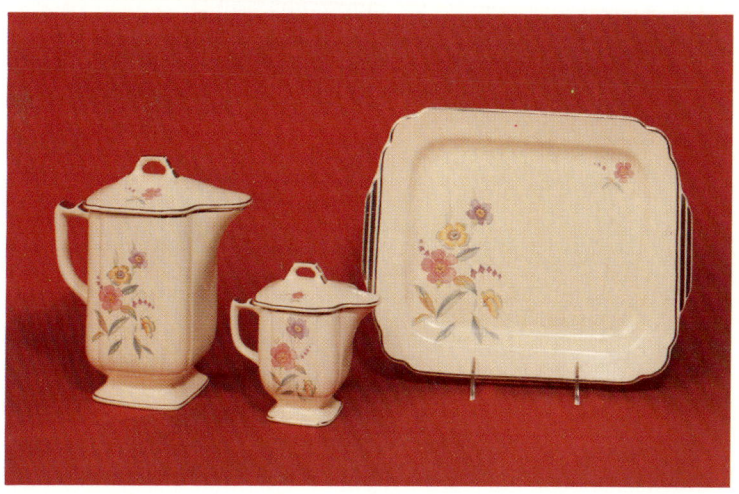

Plate 130

Children's Sets

Borrowing a Century plate, this Dick Tracy child's set is rare and very collectible. According to the backstamp, it was made in 1950.

Sure to become a 'must' on everyone's 'want list', the HLC child's set in Plate 132 is beautifully done in colorful detailed decals on ivory. This set and many other items often carry an ink stamped series of letters and numbers. For help in deciphering these codes, see section called *Dating Codes and English Measurements*.

Plate 131. Dick Tracy child's set: $110.00–135.00.

Plate 132. Animal characters child's set: $100.00–125.00.

Children's Sets

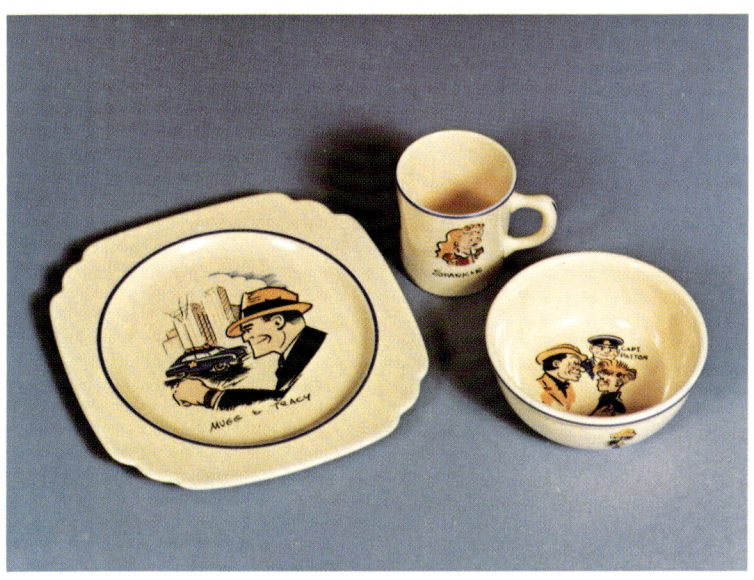

Plate 131

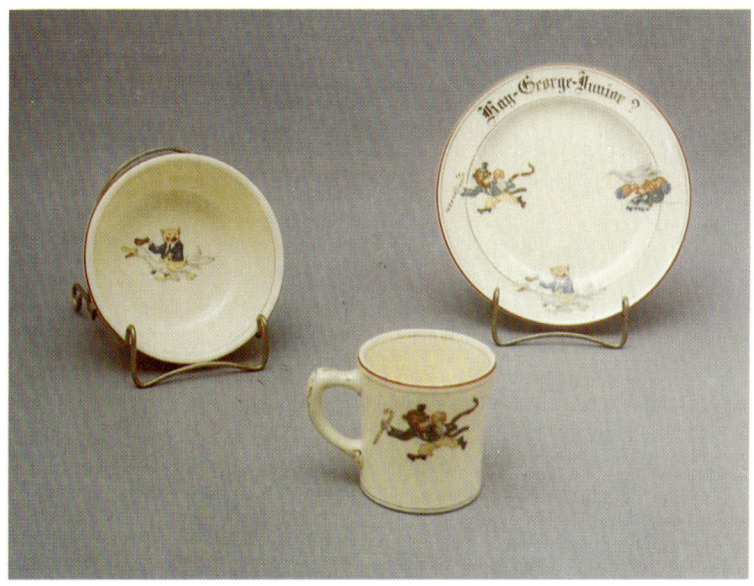

Plate 132

Children's Sets

'Tom Thumb and the Butterfly' — a darling HLC child's set! On the front of the cereal bowl, Tom is chased by a dragonfly; on the back, Tom is talking with a turtle. What a shame these are so rare. Every collector should have a set!

Shown in Plate 134 is only one place setting from a service for four — a gift to us from collector-friends here in our 'Hoosier' state. The shapes are 'Rhythm by Homer Laughlin' and each piece is so marked, except for the cups. According to the dating code, they were made in 1945.

Plate 133. Tom Thumb and the Butterfly child's set: $100.00–125.00.

Plate 134. Child's Western dinnerware, cup and saucer: $10.00–12.00; plate, 9":$6.00–7.00; fruit: $10.00–12.00. Service for 4: $100.00–125.00 .

Children's Sets

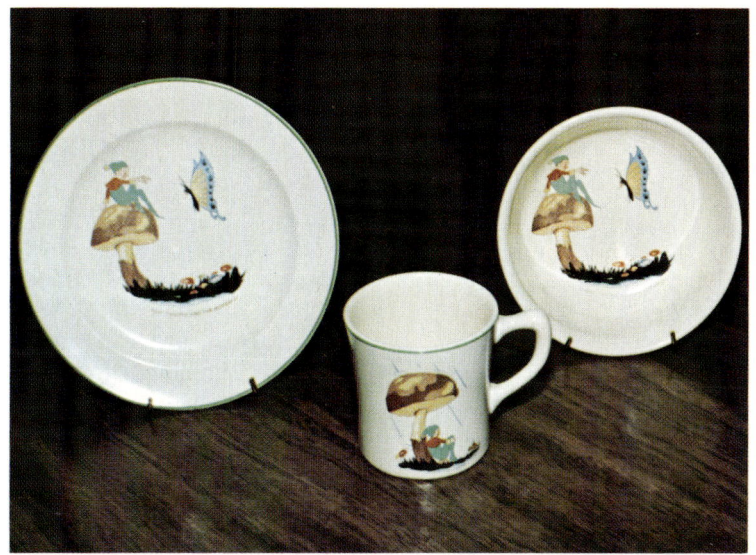

Plate 133

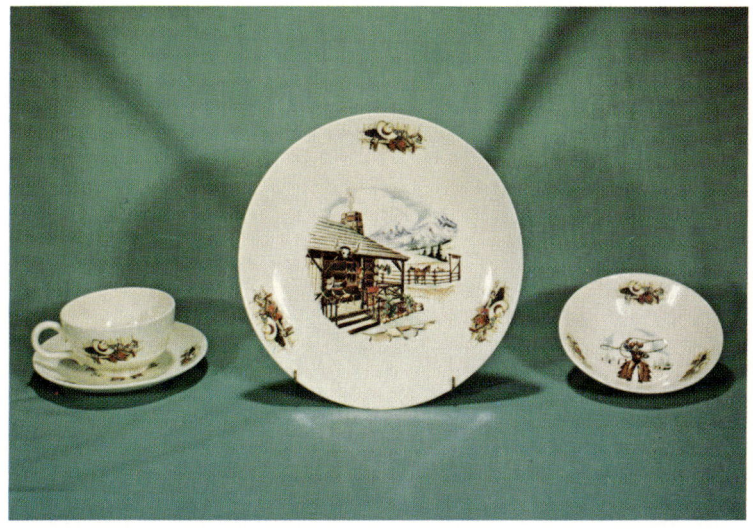

Plate 134

DECALED CENTURY

These are only a few examples of the many different decal decorations applied to Century shapes by Homer Laughlin. Many carry the particular name of the line on the back, and the year of manufacture is often represented by a dating code. Some of the more attractive and accessible lines are being reassembled by today's collectors.

In Plate 137, the advertising platter with a beautiful rose decal is stamped 'L. Linsenberg; Meats, Groceries, Bakers; 217 E. Main St.; Morristown, Pa.' It measures 12″. In the center is a scarce 15½″ platter with a square well; its backstamp indicates a 1933 manufacture. The 10½″ platter with an oval well is very rare.

Plate 135. Plate, 9″, any pattern: $3.00–4.00.

Plate 136. Platter, gold decal, 13″: $4.50–5.50. Platter, Petitpoint, 11″: $4.50–5.50.

Plate 137. Platter with advertising, 12″: $12.00–15.00. Platter with square well, 15½″: $10.00–12.00. Platter with oval well, 10½″: $6.00–8.00.

Decaled Century

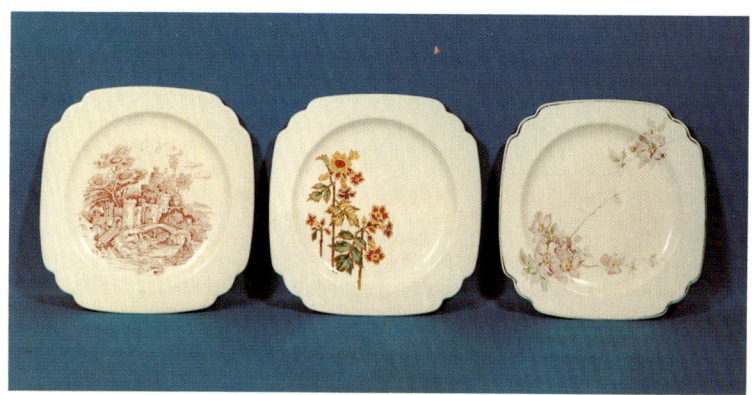

Plate 135

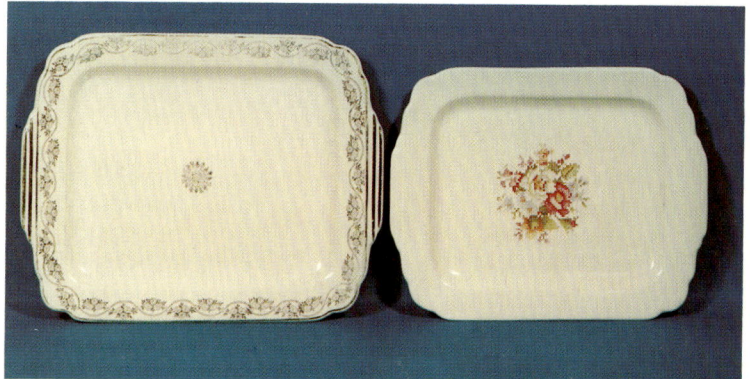

Plate 136

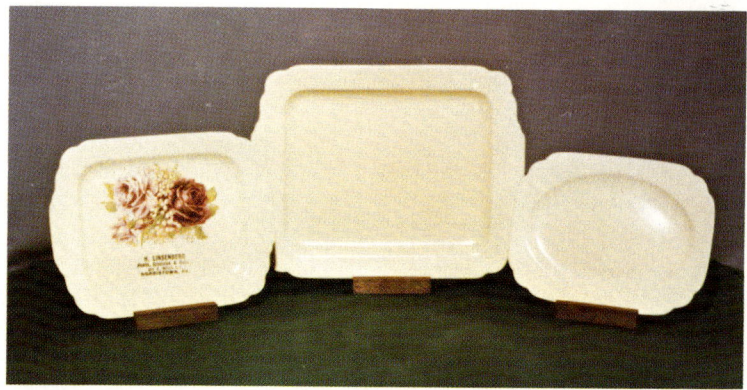

Plate 137

VIRGINIA ROSE

Virginia Rose was the name given a line of standard HLC shapes which from 1929 until the early 1970s was used as the basis for more than a dozen patterns of decaled dinnerware. It was one of the most popular shapes ever produced. Even after it was discontinued for use in the home, the shape was adopted by the hotel china division at HLC, and became a best seller in the field of hotel and institutional ware. Shown here is only a sampling of the floral pattern most collectors refer to as Virginia Rose. You may find other pieces.

Plate 138

11½" platter	$5.00–7.50
10½" dinner plate	$4.50–6.00
10½" platter	$4.50–6.00
8½" vegetable bowl	$4.50–6.00
9" plate	$3.50–4.50
10½" covered casserole	$18.00–25.00
7½" vegetable bowl	$3.50–4.50
9½" platter	$4.50–6.00
8" plate	$2.50–4.00
Deep plate	$4.00–6.00

Plate 139

7" plate	$2.00–3.00
5" milk pitcher	$8.00–10.00
Double egg cup	$5.00–7.00
6" plate	$1.00–2.00
Sauce boat	$10.00–12.00
Half pound butter dish	$32.00–35.00
Covered sugar	$5.50–6.60
Creamer	$4.50–5.50
Mug	$8.00–10.00
Deep bowl	$4.50–6.00

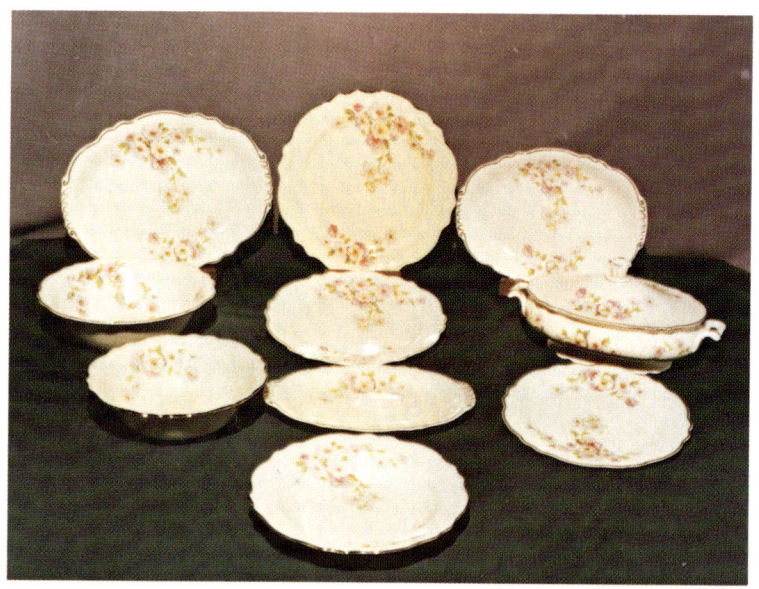

Plate 138

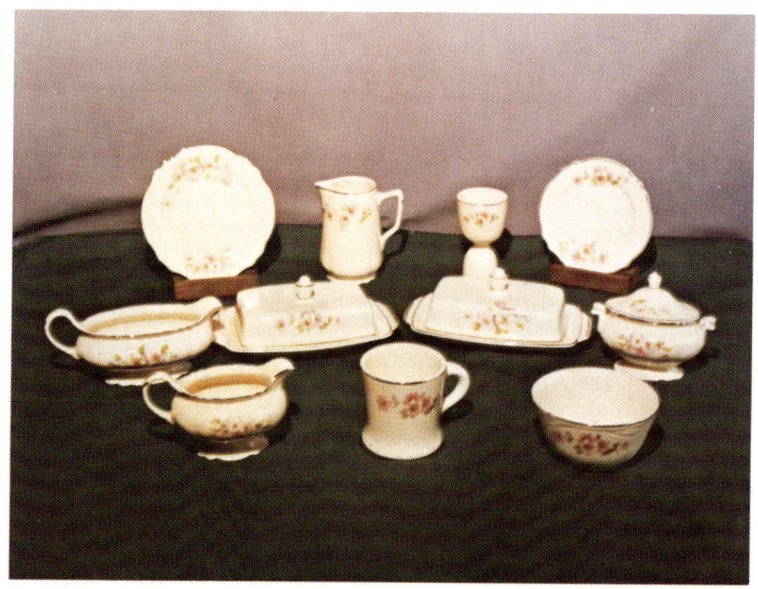

Plate 139

Virginia Rose

We thought these nested mixing bowls were especially nice. The orange tree pattern is similar to the one used by Fenton, and very typical of Rhead's work. They're marked with the HLCo mark, and have also been found in yellow.

Plate 140

11½" platter	$5.00–7.50
15½" platter	$6.00–8.50
Nested bowl, large	$12.00–15.00
Nested bowl, medium	$10.00–12.00
Nested bowl, small	$8.00–10.00
Kitchen Kraft casserole	$12.00–15.00
9½" pie plate	$10.00–15.00
8" oval vegetable	$3.50–4.50
5" fruit	$2.00–3.00
9" vegetable	$4.50–6.00
Salt and pepper shakers, pr.	$5.00–7.00
Cup and saucer	$4.50–6.50
6" oatmeal	$2.50–4.00

Plate 141

Nested bowl set, 5", 6", 7", 8", 9½" $22.00–28.00

Virginia Rose

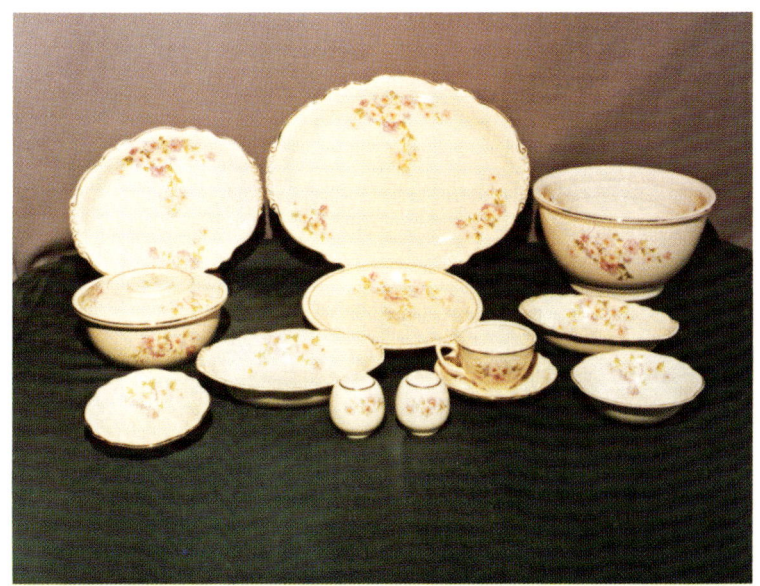

Plate 140

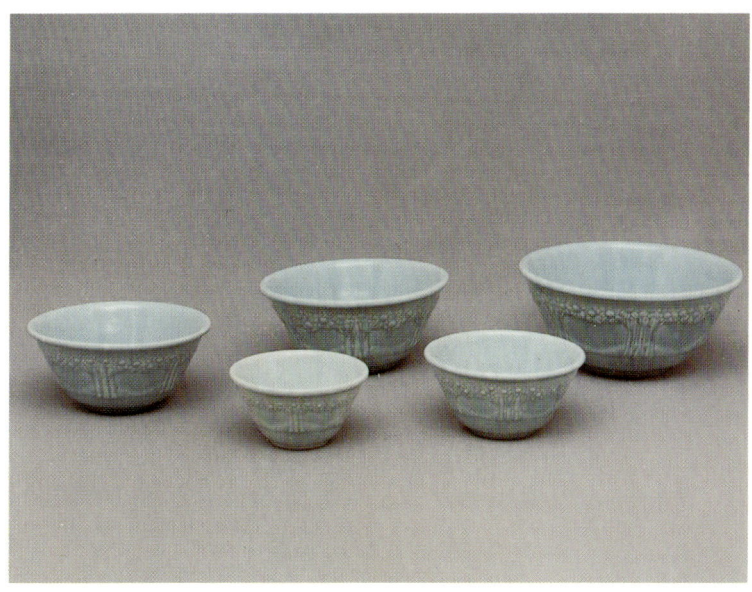

Plate 141

RHYTHM ROSE

Rhythm Rose — beautiful rose decoration usually on standard Rhythm shapes, though some items are 'borrowed' from other HLC lines. It was produced from the mid-forties through the mid-fifties, and is marked with the gold stamp: Household Institute, Rhythm Rose.

Not shown are cups and saucers, fruits, oatmeals, and vegetable bowls. No doubt you will find other items. Considered a 'real prize' and understandably so by its owners — a 'Rhythm' spoon rest with the Rose decal!

Plate 142

9" dinner plate	$3.00–4.00
10½" cake plate	$7.00–8.50
9" Kitchen Kraft under plate	$8.00–12.00
Kitchen Kraft jug pitcher	$10.00–12.00
8" deep plate	$4.50–5.50
8½" Kitchen Kraft casserole	$12.00–16.50
After dinner cup and saucer	$8.00–10.00
9½" Kitchen Kraft pie plate	$10.00–12.00
Sauce boat	$5.00–7.00
Cake server	$7.00–10.00

Plate 143

6" plate	$1.50–2.00
Kitchen Kraft coffee pot	$18.00–25.00
Nested bowl, large	$12.50–15.00
Nested bowl, medium	$10.00–12.00
Nested bowl, small	$8.00–10.00
Kitchen Kraft coffee pot	$18.00–25.00
6" Kitchen Kraft under plate	$7.00–10.00
Teapot	$18.00–25.00
13" platter	$6.00–7.50
Covered sugar	$5.00–6.50
Creamer	$4.00–5.00

Rhythm Rose

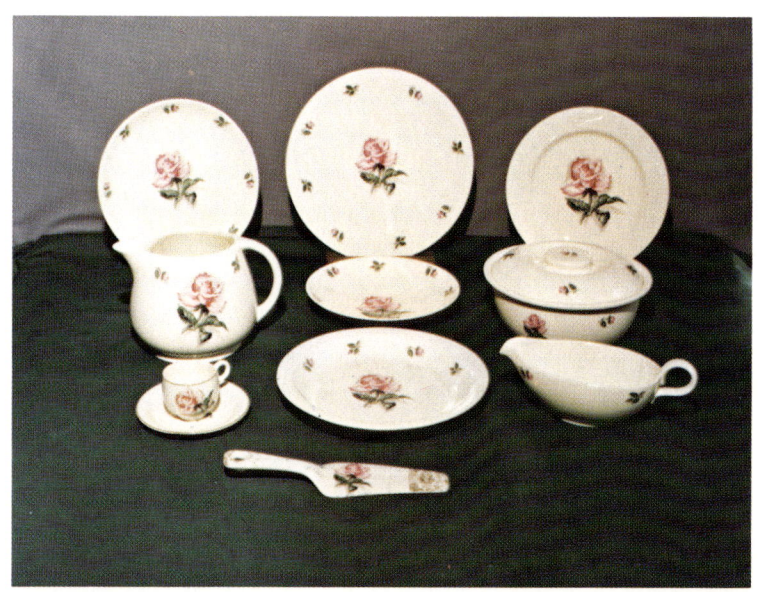

Plate 142

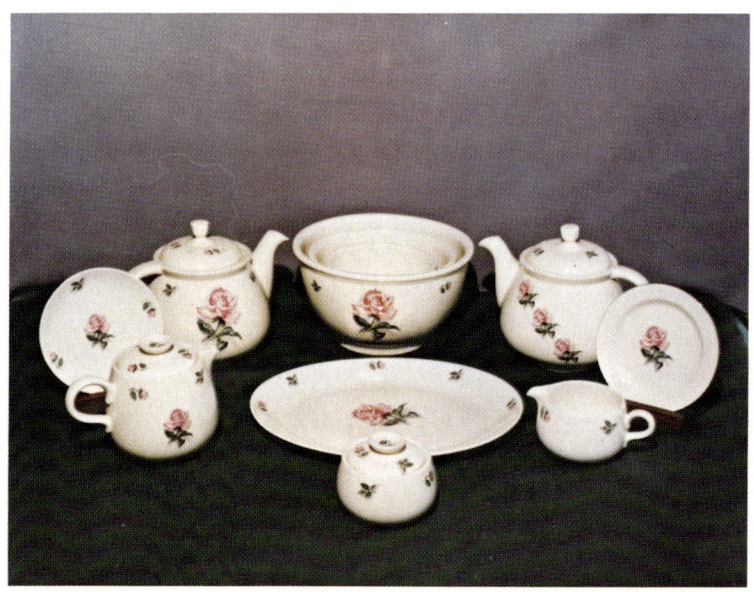

Plate 143

PRISCILLA PATTERN DINNERWARE

This is only one of the many beautiful patterns of dinnerware fast becoming very collectible. As the photo indicates, this lovely line was offered with a wide assortment of serving pieces.

Plate 144

Coffee pot	$18.00–23.00
Fruit bowl, 9½"	$10.00–14.00
Sugar	$5.00–8.00
Creamer	$4.00–6.00
Gravy boat	$6.00–7.50
Cup and saucer	$5.00–6.00
Oval vegetable, 9"	$4.00–5.50
Soup plate, 8½"	$4.00–5.50
Platter, 13½"	$5.00–8.00
Dinner plate, 9"	$4.00–6.00
Luncheon plate, 8"	$3.00–4.00
Dessert plate, 6"	$2.00–3.00
Fruit, 5"	$3.00–4.00

DOGWOOD

Dogwood is an especially lovely line of HLC dinnerware produced in the early 1960s. It is decorated with delicate sprigs of flowering dogwood.

Plate 145

Plate, 9"	$3.00–4.00
Fruit, 5½"	$2.50–3.50
Dessert plate, 6½"	$2.00–3.00

Priscilla Pattern Dinnerware; Dogwood

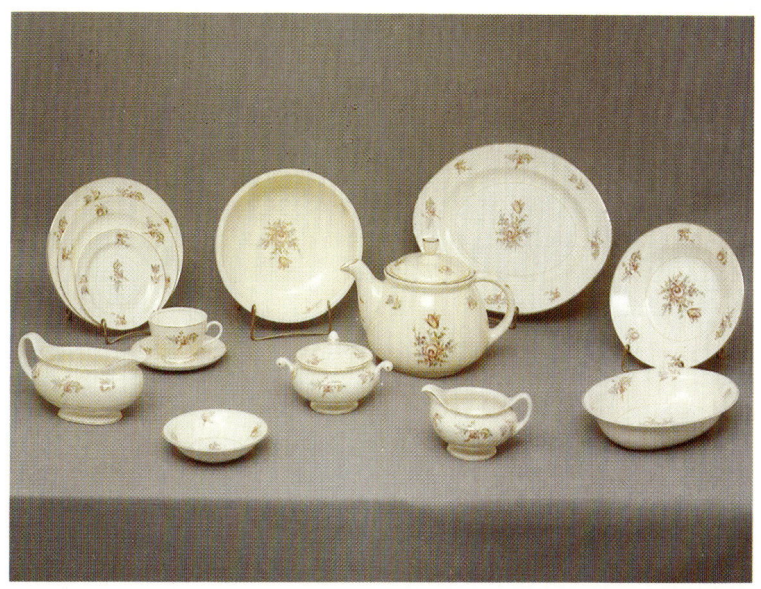

Plate 144

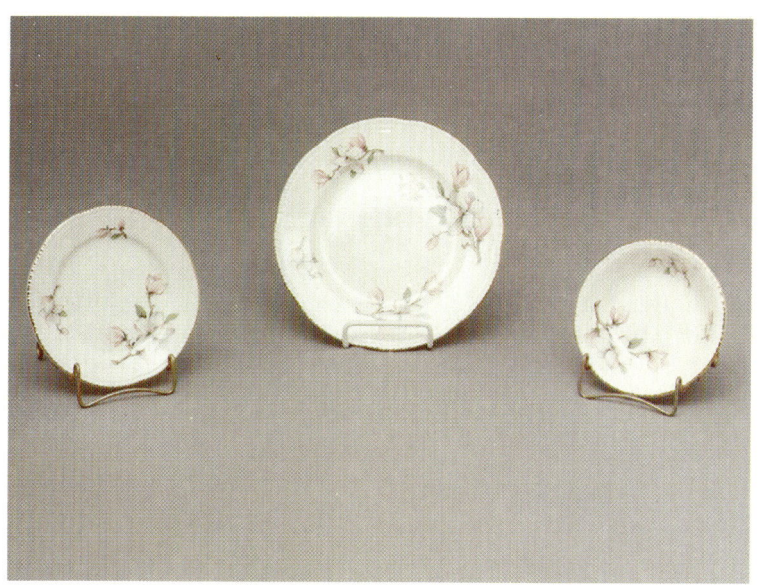

Plate 145

SERENADE

Serenade was a pastel dinnerware line that was produced for only about three years in the early forties. It was offered in four lovely pastel shades — yellow, green, pink and blue. Although not well accepted by the public when it was introduced, today's collectors find its soft delicate hues and dainty contours appealing. There is growing interest in this elusive pattern, but prices are still relatively moderate.

Lug soups and teapots are rare; so are 10" plates. You may also find deep plates, 7" plates, 6" fruits and 9" nappies to be scarce. Sugar bowls are harder to find than creamers, and the lid for the casserole (the only Kitchen Kraft piece dipped in Serenade colors) has never been reported found.

Plate 146. Cup and saucer: $5.00-8.00. Coffee pot, 6 cup, 7½": $25.00-35.00. Plate, 10": $6.00-8.00. Plate, 9": $5.00-6.00. Plate, 7": $3.00-4.00. Plate, 6": $2.00-3.00.

Plate 147. Chop plate, 13": $15.00-18.00. Kitchen Kraft casserole bottom, marked Serenade in mold: $15.00-18.00. Lid (not shown): $12.00-15.00. Platter, 12½": $10.00-12.00. Covered casserole: $25.00-30.00.

Plate 148. Deep plate: $5.00-8.00. Creamer: $6.00-8.00. Fruit: $3.00-5.00. Sauce boat: $8.00-10.00. Nappy, 9": $6.00-8.00. Listed but not shown, lug soup: $9.00-12.00; Teapot: $30.00-40.00.

Serenade

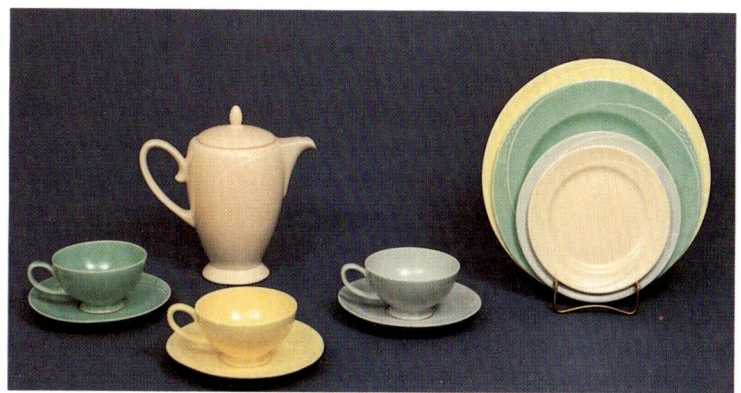

Plate 146

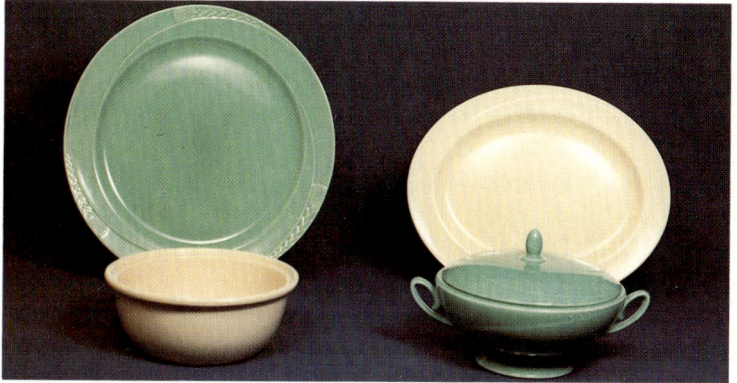

Plate 147

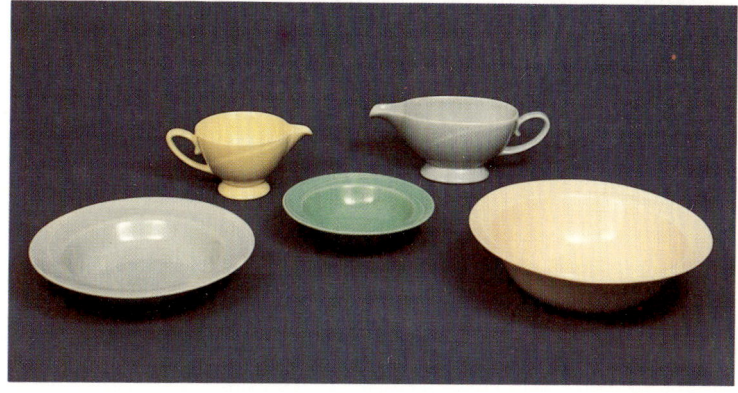

Plate 148

TANGO

Tango was introduced in the late 1930s, made for promotion through Newberry's and the McLellan Stores Company, N.Y. City. For some reason, it was not a good seller — perhaps its rather Colonial design seemed a bit incongruous alongside other styles of colored dinnerware. Standard colors were spruce green, mauve blue, yellow and maroon, but as you can see in the color plate, a few pieces may also be found in Fiesta red.

The salt and pepper shakers should be very familiar to Riviera collectors — they were original with this line, but since their shape was compatible they were borrowed for use with Riviera.

Plate 149. Nappy 8¾": $5.00-6.00. Platter, 11¾": $5.00-6.00. Plate, 9¼": $2.50-3.00. Creamer: $3.50-4.00. Sugar: $5.00-6.00. Salt and pepper shakers: $5.00-6.00, pr. Plate, 6": $1.50-2.00. Fruit, 5¾": $2.50-3.00. Cup and saucer: $5.00-6.00. Listed but not shown, oval baker, 9": $5.00-6.00. Casserole with lid: $12.00-15.00. Deep plate: $3.50-4.00. Plate, 10": $3.50-4.50. Plate, 7": $2.00-2.50.

Tango

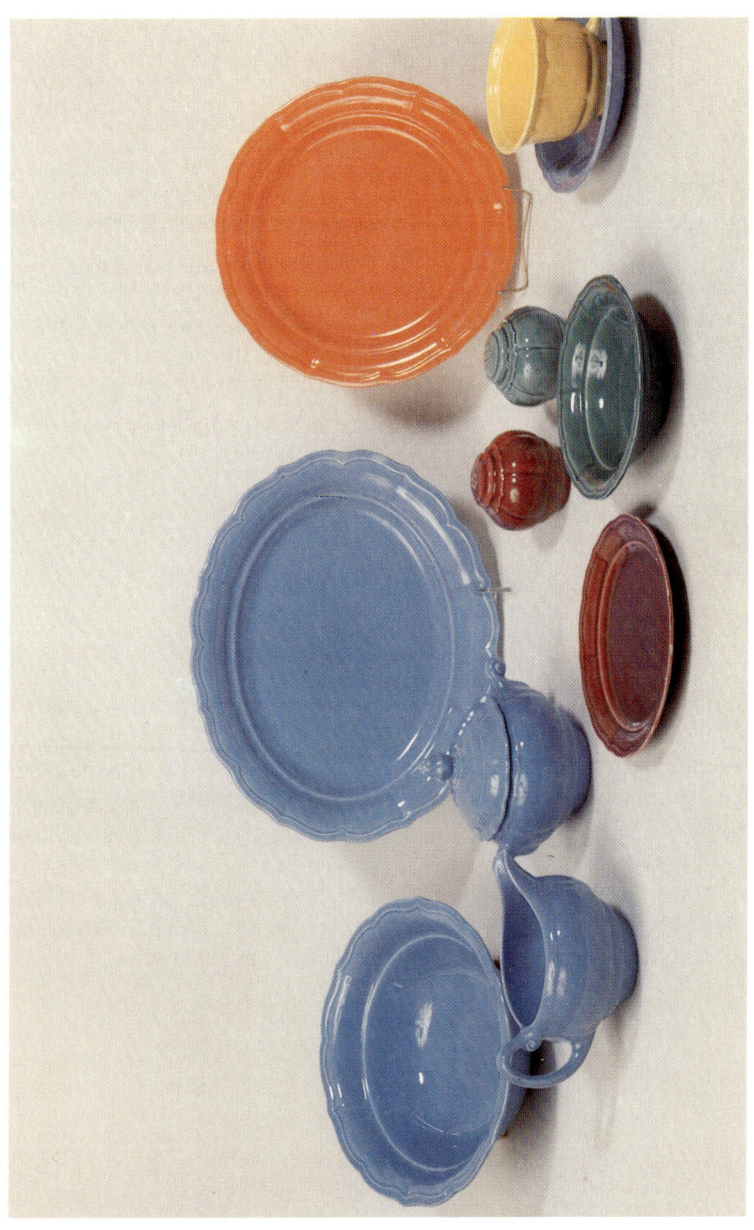

Plate 149

JUBILEE

Jubilee was presented by Homer Laughlin in 1948, in celebration of their 75th year of ceramic leadership. Shapes were simple and contemporary. It was offered in four colors: Celadon Green (blue-gray); Shell Pink; Mist Gray (lighter than Fiesta gray); and Cream Beige. The pastel juice set utilizing Fiesta molds is reported by collectors of this line to match the Jubilee glazes rather than those of Serenade. Kitchen Kraft bowls have been found in pink, blue-gray, and gray. Some are marked; others are not.

Jubilee shapes were also used as the basis for other lines. Skytone is a very attractive example, in pastel blue with white handles and lid finials.

Plate 150 (price list). Plate, 6": $1.00-1.25. Plate, 7": $1.50-2.00. Plate, 9": $2.00-2.50. Plate, 10": $3.00-3.50. Chop plate, 15": $4.00-5.00. Fruit: $2.00-2.25. Cereal soup: $2.00-2.50. Nappy, 8½": $3.00-4.00. Casserole: $8.00-10.00. Sauce boat: $5.00-6.00. Platter, 13": $3.50-4.00. Teacup and saucer: $3.00-3.50. A.D. coffee cup and saucer: $4.00-5.00. Creamer: $2.50-3.00. Sugar: $3.00-3.50. Platter, 11": $2.50-3.00. Egg cup: $3.50-4.00. Salt and peppers shakers: $3.50-4.00, pr. Teapot: $10.00-12.00. Coffee pot: $10.00-12.00. Not shown, Kitchen Kraft bowls, any size: $45.00-55.00. Calendar plates, 10": $6.00-8.00.

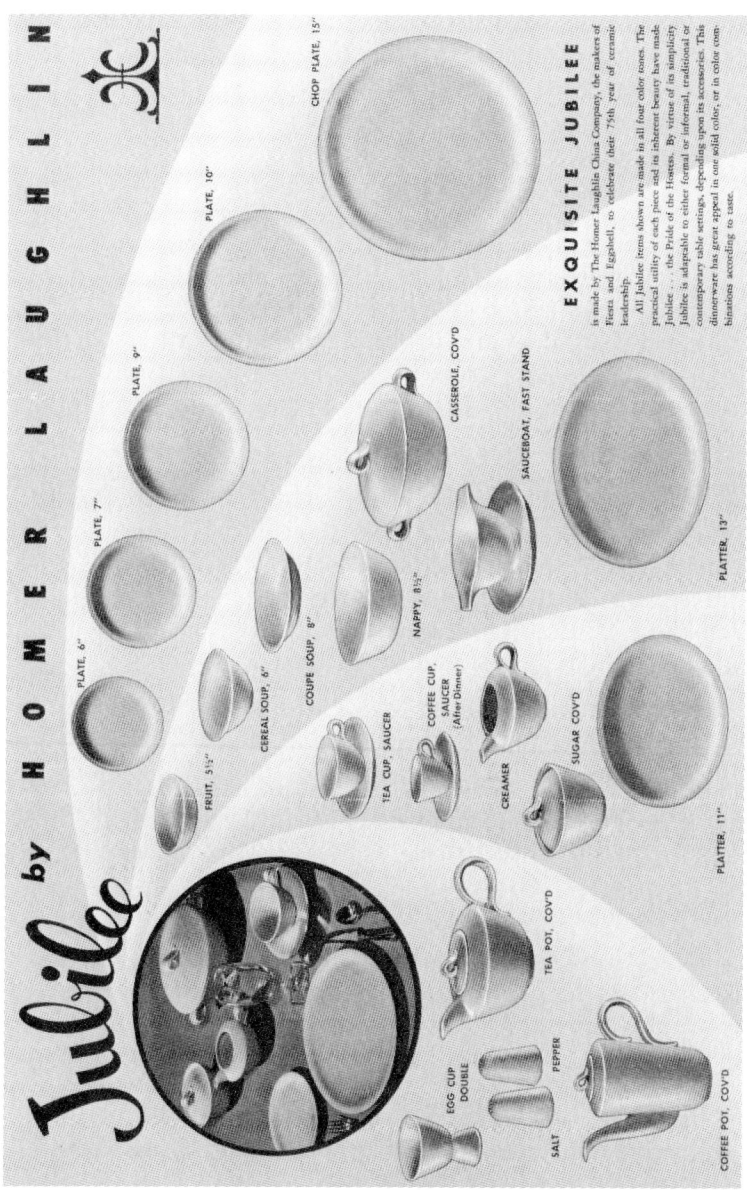

Plate 150

RHYTHM

With Rhythm steadily emerging from its 'sleeper' state, more accurate information than we had in the beginning is being pieced together by its dedicated fans. Those with large collections report backstamps with dates indicating a span of production from 1951 to 1958. It was made in Harlequin yellow, chartreuse, gray, green and burgandy (collectors call it maroon). Only one piece, a sauce boat, has been found in turquoise.

Rhythm shapes are simple and streamlined with a 'designer' look. Don Schreckengost was that designer, who early in 1982 was interviewed by a newsletter which was at that time being published in the East. In that interview, Mr. Schreckengost revealed that the spoon rest, which we thought to be Harlequin, was, in fact, a piece he had originated for the Rhythm line.

Several lines featuring decals on a white glaze were manufactured during the fifties utilizing Rhythm shapes. You will find several examples of these in the color plates. The spoon rests are often found with decals — Rhythm Rose and American Primitive are the most common.

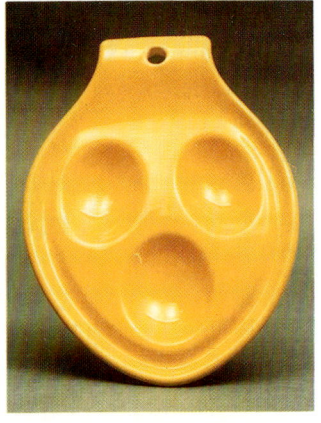

Plate 151

Plate 151. Spoon rest: $100.00–135.00.

Plate 152. Casserole (rare), 3½" x 9": $30.00–35.00. Platter, 13½": $10.00–12.00. Creamer, 2¾": $3.00–5.00. Sugar: $4.00–6.00. 3-tier tray: $25.00–30.00. Creamer, 3¼": $3.00–5.00. Platter, 11½": $5.00–6.00. Sauce boat stand, 8½": $3.00–5.00. Teapot, 5½": $18.00–22.00.

Plate 153. Salt and pepper shakers: $4.00–6.00. Soup, 8¼": $5.00–7.00. Cup and saucer: $5.00–7.00. Plate, 6": $1.50–2.00. Plate, 7" (scarce): $3.00–4.00. Plate, 9": $3.00–4.00. Plate, 10": $6.00–8.00. Snack plate (no maroon), 10¼": $10.00–12.00. Sauce boat: $5.00–6.00. Footed cereal/chowder, 5½": $3.00–4.00. Nappy, 9": $6.00–8.00. Fruit, 5¼": $2.00–3.00. Listed but not shown, platter, 15": $12.00–15.00.

Rhythm

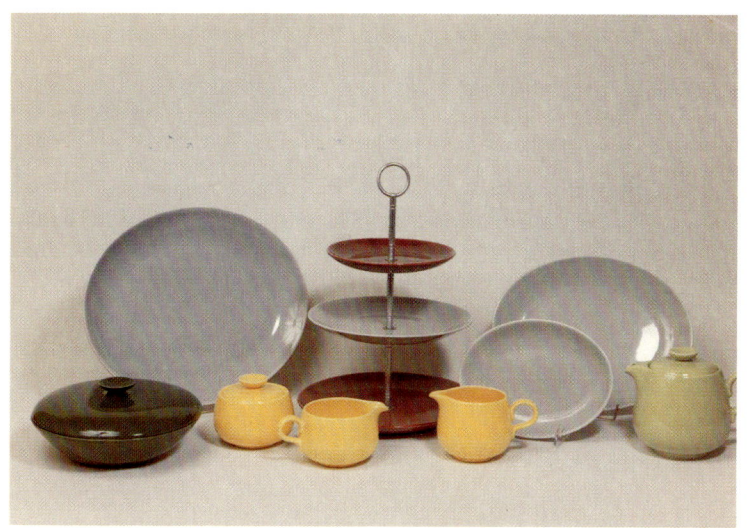

Plate 152

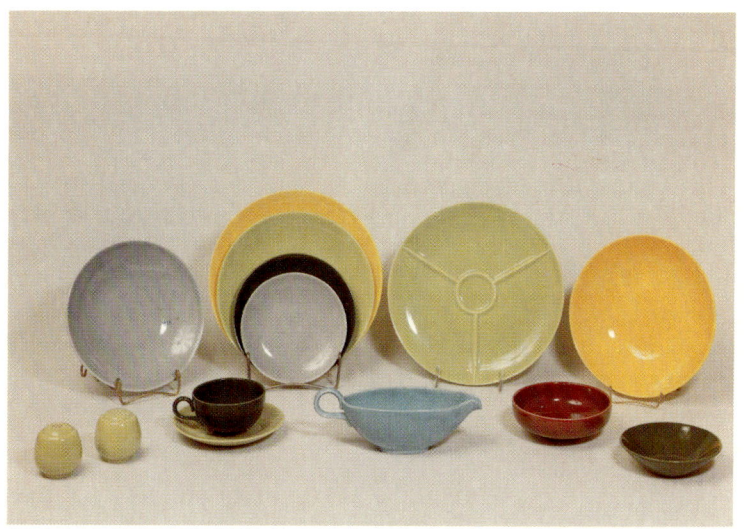

Plate 153

WELLS ART GLAZE

If you like a real challenge, here's one for you! This line was produced from 1930 at least until 1935 in the colors shown — rust, peach, green and yellow. It's a lovely design, and records list an extensive assortment. But because of its limited availability on today's market, values are still low. Since this is the first time we've shown this pattern, it may have just been overlooked. Let us hear from you if you're a successfull Wells Art Glaze collector!

Teacup and saucer	$3.50–4.00
Coffee cup, 4¾"	$4.00–5.00
A.D. coffee cup and saucer	$4.00–5.00
Cream soup	$2.50–3.50
Cream soup stand	$2.00–3.00
Plate, 10"	$3.00–3.50
Plate, 9"	$2.00–2.50
Plate, 7"	$1.00–1.50
Plate, 6"	$ .75–1.00
Fruit, 5"	$1.50–2.00
Oatmeal 36s	$2.00–2.50
Double egg cup	$4.00–5.00
Chop plate with handle, 10"	$4.00–5.00
Creamer	$1.50–2.00
Sugar with lid	$2.00–3.00
Teapot	$10.00–12.00
Oval baker, 9"	$3.00–4.00
Covered jug (center), 9"	$10.00–12.00
Nappy, 8"	$3.00–4.00
Sauce boat	$5.00–7.00
Sauce boat, fast-stand	$7.00–8.50
Individual coffee pot	$8.00–10.00
Covered muffin	$12.00–15.00
Individual sugar, open	$2.00–3.00
Individual creamer	$2.00–3.00
Pickle with handle	$3.00–4.00
Deep plate	$3.00–4.00
Casserole	$12.00–15.00
Square plate, 6"	$1.50–2.00

Wells Art Glaze

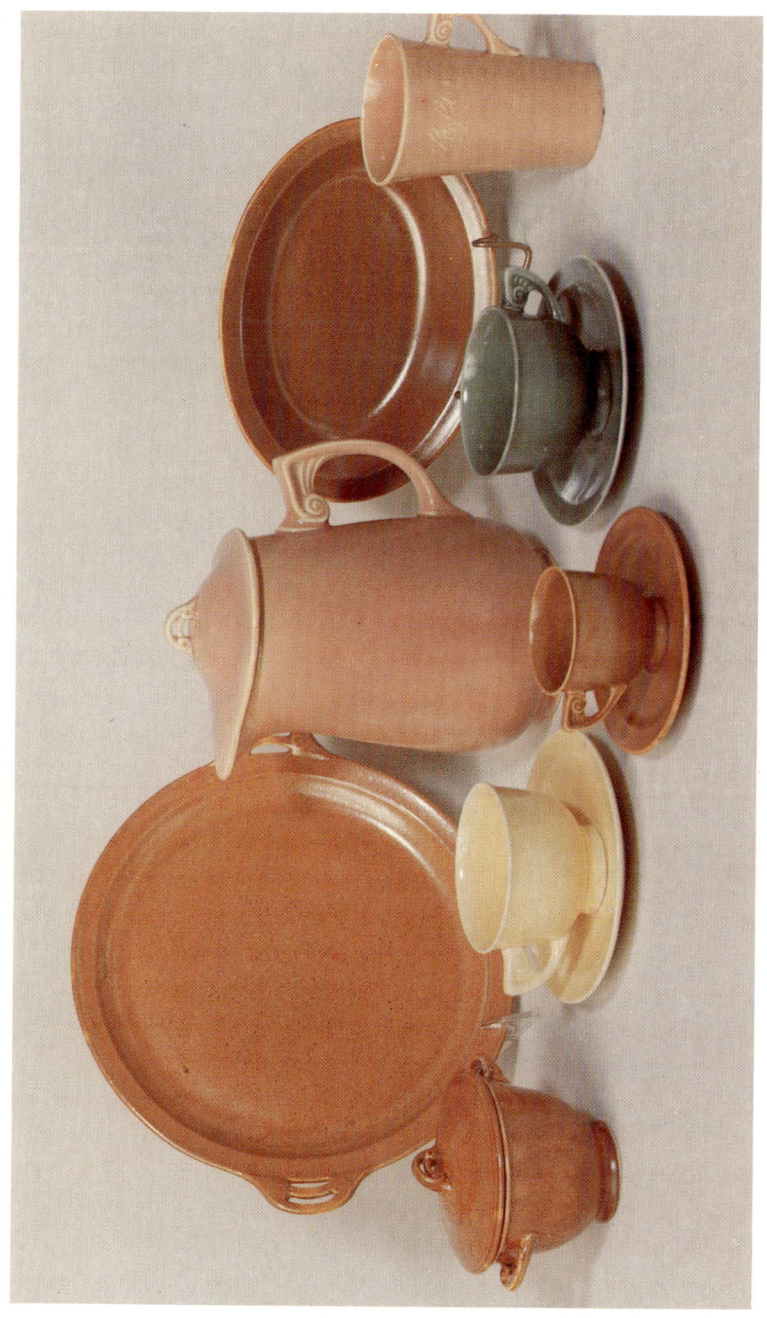

Plate 154

CARNIVAL

Carnival was made exclusively for the Quaker Oats Company who gave it away to their customers, one piece packed in each box of oatmeal. While no records exist to verify the year it was first produced, we must assume it was in the late thirties or early forties, by reason of the color assortment. Harlequin yellow and turquoise (both new in 1938), light green, and Fiesta red were evidently the original colors. The only mention of Carnival in company files was dated 1952 and lists these glazes: dark green, turquoise, gray and Harlequin yellow. The same record itemized the pieces in production at that time. These we have listed here with suggested values. A company representative recalled that coupons were also included in the boxes, redeemable for the larger pieces. What these might have been or when they were made, we have no way of knowing. Perhaps there were larger plates, bowls, and platters — if so, they may one day turn up to answer our questions.

Teacup and saucer	$2.50–3.00
Small fruit	$1.50–2.00
Oatmeal 35s	$1.50–2.00
Plate, 6½″	$1.00–1.50

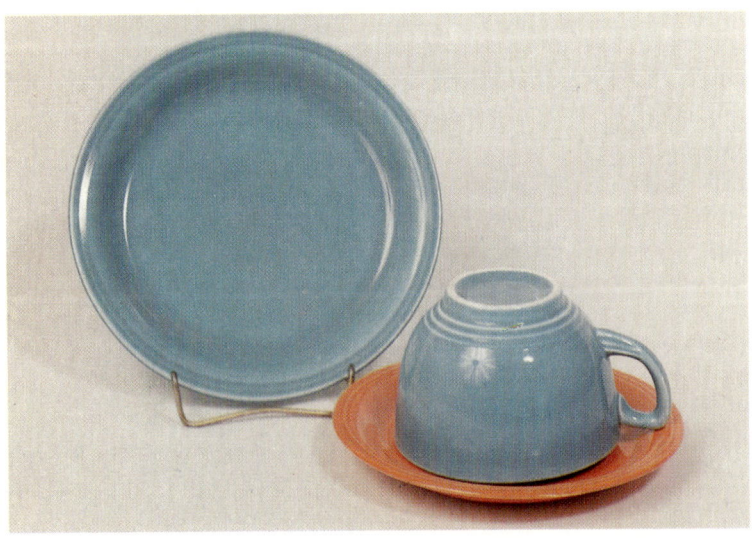

Plate 155

EPICURE

Epicure is a fifties line — with the fifties steamline styling and pastel colors. Anyone who remembers what a great era that was for growing up can tell you about pink and gray. Argyle socks were pink and gray! If your sweater was pink, your skirt or corduroys were gray. Turquoise was popular in home decorating — even down to appliances. And these were the colors of Epicure: Dawn Pink, Charcoal Gray, Turquoise Blue and Snow White.

The designer was Don Schreckengost, who also designed Rhythm. We can find no information pinpointing production dates, but collectors tell us that virtually *all* of their Epicure is stamped 1955.

Plate 156. Coffee pot, 10″: $20.00–30.00. Plate 10″: $4.00–6.00. Nappy, 8¾″ x 3″: $5.00–7.00. Plate, 6½″: $2.00–3.00. Gravy bowl, 7½″: $8.00–10.00. Ladle, 5½″: $10.00–12.00. Covered vegetable: $18.00–25.00. Listed but not shown: Cup and saucer: $5.00–7.50. Individual casserole with lid: $15.00–18.00. Large platter: $6.00–8.00. Pickle (small oval platter) $4.00–6.00. Creamer: $4.00–6.00. Sugar: $5.00–7.00. Salt and pepper shakers: $5.00–7.50, pr. Nappy, 8″: $4.00–6.00. Cereal/soup: $3.00–4.00.

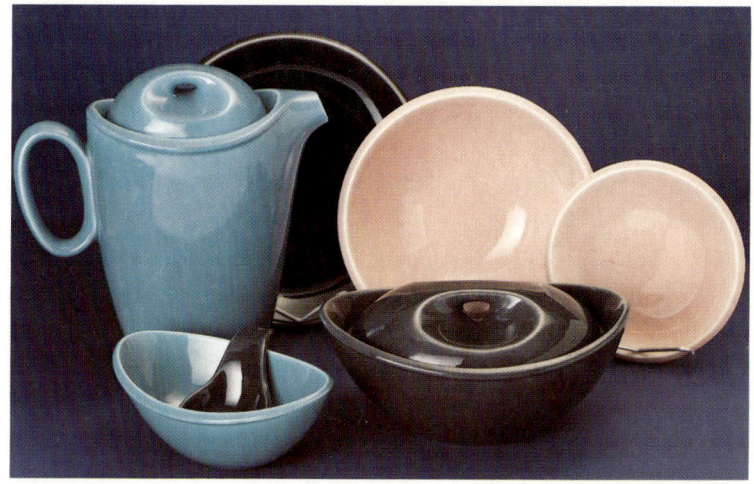

Plate 156

HOMER LAUGHLIN MEXICANA
... the Pattern that Started A Vogue

... so reads a trade paper from May, 1938.

When this Homer Laughlin pattern was first exhibited last July at the House Furnishing Show, it was an immediate smash hit. Its popularity has grown steadily ever since, and retailers have found it a constant and dependable source of profit. It started the vogue for the Mexican motif in crockery decoration which has since swept the country.

And small wonder! For this Mexicana pattern is smart, colorful and attractive. It embodies the old-world atmosphere of Mexico with the modern verve and personality which is so appealing to American Housewives. Applied to the pleasing, beautifully designed Homer Laughlin shapes, it presents a best seller of the first order.

You will often find this line marked 'Mexicana' with a gold backstamp. Although occasionally found with yellow, green and blue bands, red is by far the most plentiful. The Mexican motif tumblers are as compatible with these lines as they are with Fiesta, Harlequin or Riviera.

Plate 157. 36s oatmeal, 6″: $5.00–6.50. Fruit, 5½″: $3.00–5.00. Glass tumbler: $8.00–10.00. Teacup: $5.50–7.00. Saucer: $1.50–2.00. Deep plate: $5.00–6.50. Plate, 9″: $3.00–5.00.

Plate 158. Plate, 10″: $5.00–6.50. Platter, 13″: $8.00–9.00. Plate, 9″: $3.00–5.00. Sauce boat: $6.00–9.00. Oval vegetable, 9″: $6.00–9.00. Cup and saucer: $7.00–9.00. Sauce boat liner: $7.50–10.00. Covered sugar: $5.50–7.50. Creamer: $4.00–5.00.

Mexicana

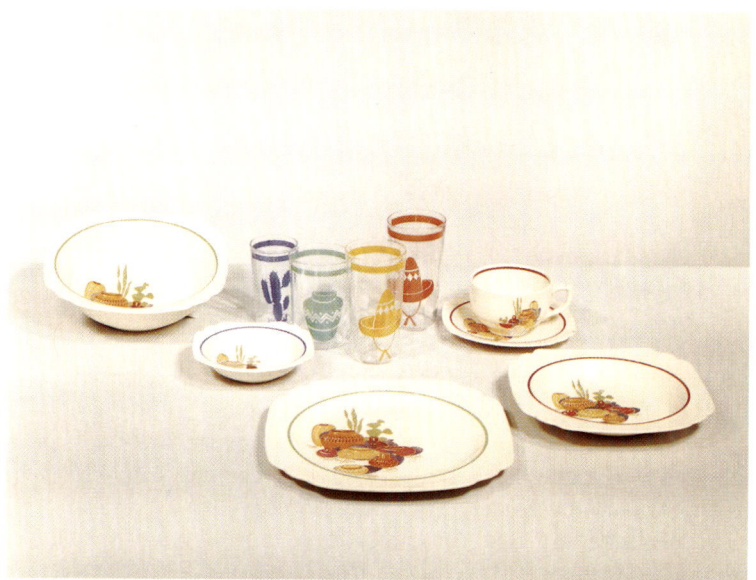

Plate 157

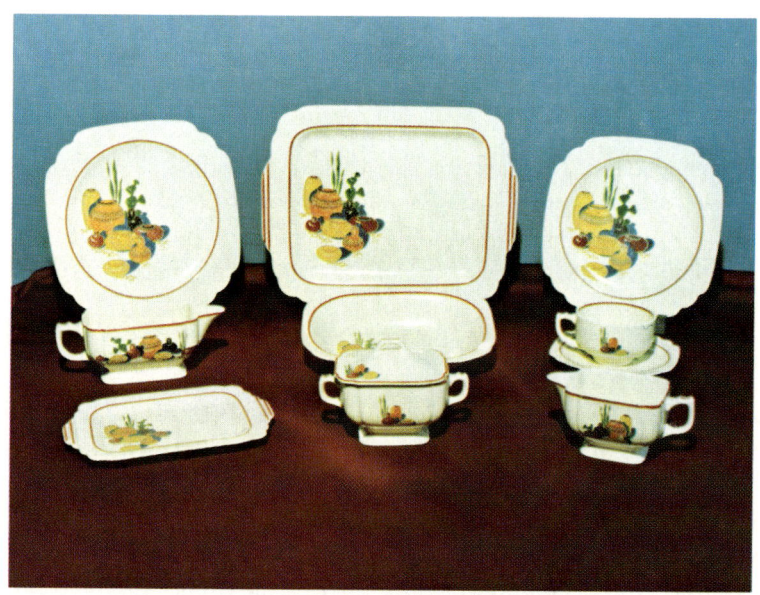

Plate 158

Nor was HLC the only company to 'jump on the bandwagon' — Paden City, Vernon Kiln, Crown, Stetson and many others produced similarly decorated lines with a decided Mexican flavor. Besides Mexicana, Hacienda and Conchita (all decaled Century lines and perhaps their best known), they also made Arizona, decorated with a large green cactus, adobe house, yucca plant and pottery jug . . . and an unidentified ware, shown in Plate 160, that utilized the company's Yellowstone shape and featured pottery jugs and jars, cacti, and a siesta-taking Mexican snoozing under his sombrero. This line has been dubbed Max-i-cana by collectors, and is by no means easy to come by!

Plate 159. Deep plate, 8": $3.00–5.00. Platter, 11": $4.50–7.00. Plate, 7": $2.00–3.00. Oatmeal, 6": $5.00–6.50. Vegetable bowl, 8": $6.00–7.50. Plate, 6": $1.50–2.50. Nappy, 5": $4.00–5.00. Lug soup, 4¾": $6.00–9.00.

Plate 160. Platter, 11½": $4.50–7.50. Platter, 13½": $6.00–9.00. Platter, 10": $4.00–6.50. Creamer: $3.50–4.50. Egg cup: $9.00–12.00. Sugar: $5.50–7.50. Egg cup, rolled edge: $12.00–18.00. Casserole, 8½": $25.00–30.00. Tri-pod candle holders: $60.00–70.00, pr. Sauce boat liner, 8½": $8.00–12.00.

Mexicana

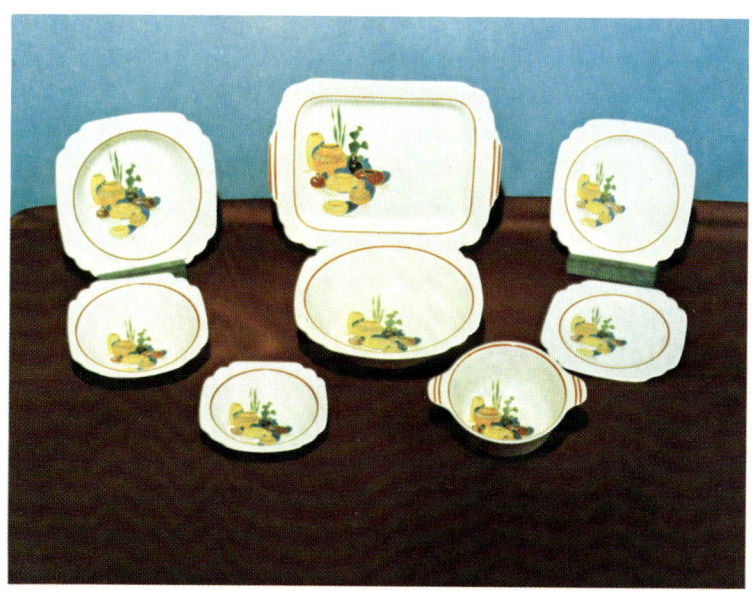

Plate 159

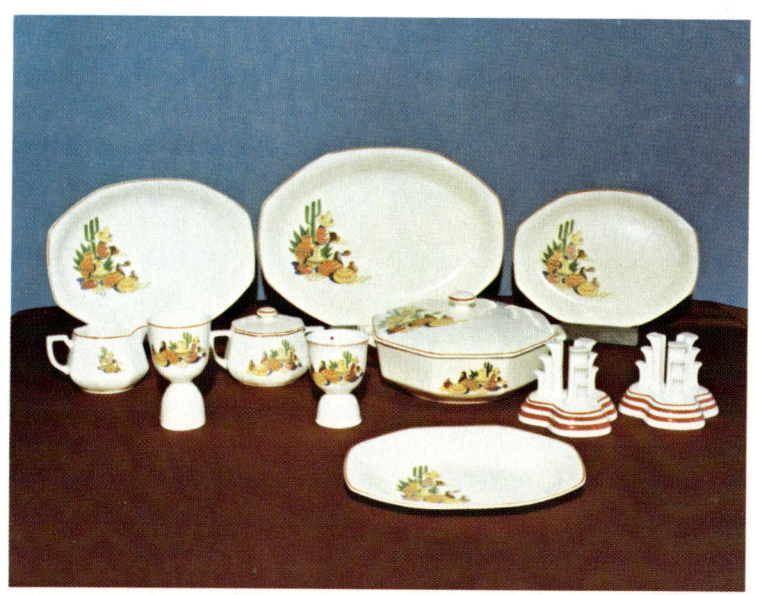

Plate 160

This type of dinnerware became popular during the late thirties; but from the dating codes found on these items, we can conclude that production lasted until near the end of the next decade — quite a long run for so bold a theme!

Plate 161. Plate, 6": $1.50–2.50. Plate, 7": $2.00–3.00. Sauce boat: $6.00–9.00. Lug soup, 4½": $6.00–9.00. Vegetable bowl, 8½": $6.00–7.50. Cup and saucer: $7.00–9.00.

Plate 162. Plate, 9": $3.00–5.00. Plate, 9½": $4.00–5.00. Plate, 6": $1.50–2.50. Vegetable bowl, 9½": $6.00–8.50. Deep plate, 8": $5.00–6.50. Oatmeal, 6": $5.00–6.50. Butter dish, half lb.: $35.00–42.00. Fruit, 5": $3.50–5.00.

Mexicana

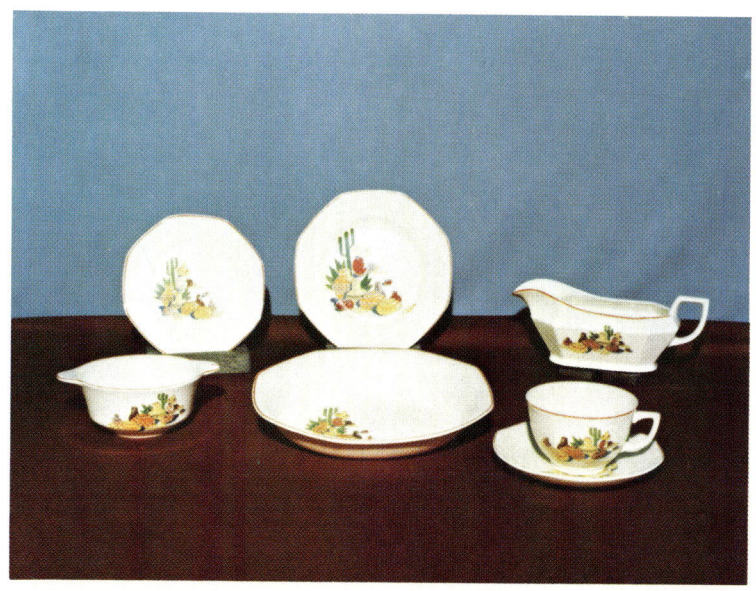

Plate 161

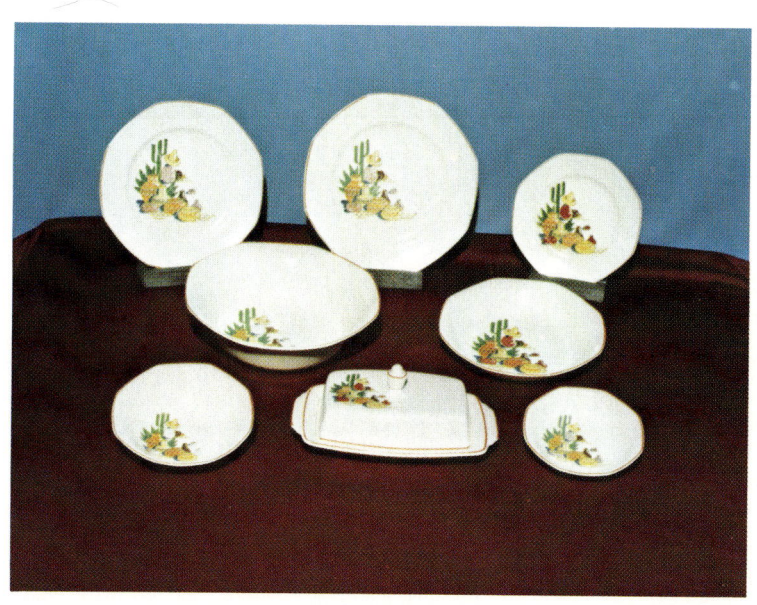

Plate 162

Hacienda

Hacienda! The teapot and butter dish are very hard to find. The bell shown below has the same decal, but it's very doubtful that it was produced at HLC. The white casserole in Plate 165 is on the Nautalis shape — you may find others from this line.

Plate 163. Bell, 5": $20.00–25.00. Butter dish: $90.00–100.00.

Plate 164. Plate, 9": $3.00–5.00. Platter with square well, 11": $7.00–9.00. Plate, 6": $1.50–2.50. Creamer: $3.50–4.50. Sugar with lid: $5.00–6.50. Teapot: $24.00–28.00. Sauce boat: $6.00–9.00. Cup and saucer: $7.00–9.00. Fruit, 5": $3.50–5.00.

Plate 165. Platter with oval well, 11½": $7.00–9.00. Platter with oval well, 13½": $8.00–12.00. Deep plate, 8": $5.00–6.50. Vegetable bowl, 8": $6.00–9.00. Plate, 10": $5.00–6.50. Vegetable bowl, 9": $7.50–8.50. Casserole, Nautalis shape: $35.00–40.00. Oatmeal, 6": $5.00–6.00.

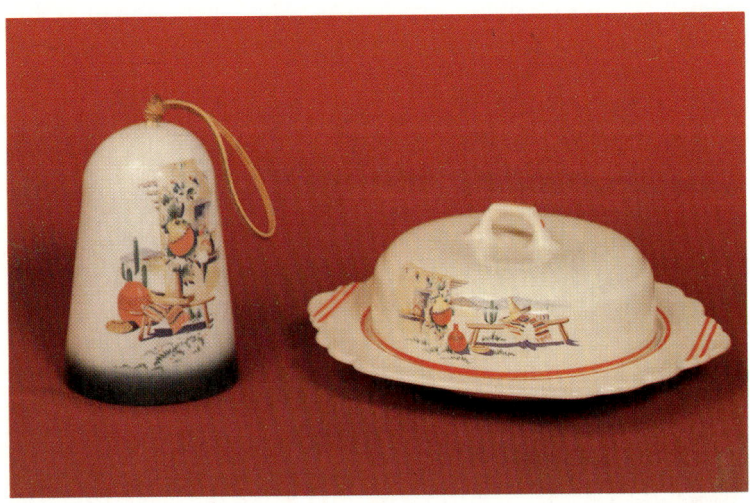

Plate 163

Hacienda

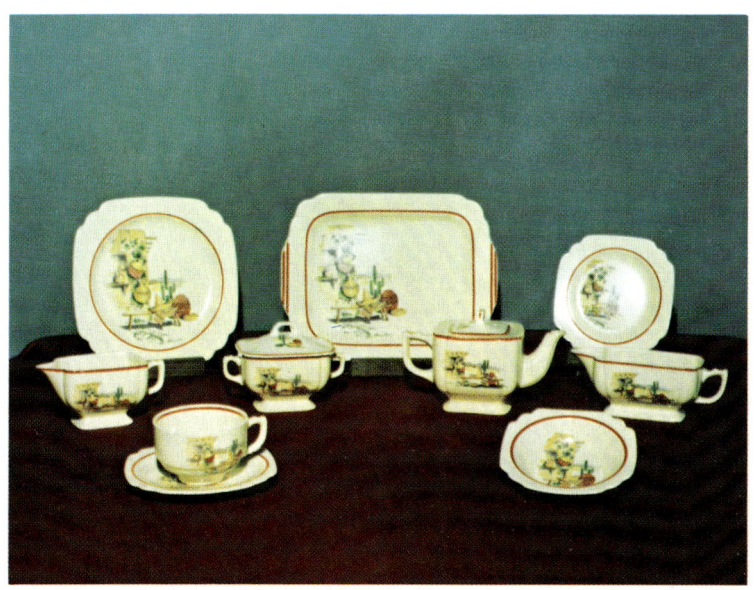

Plate 164

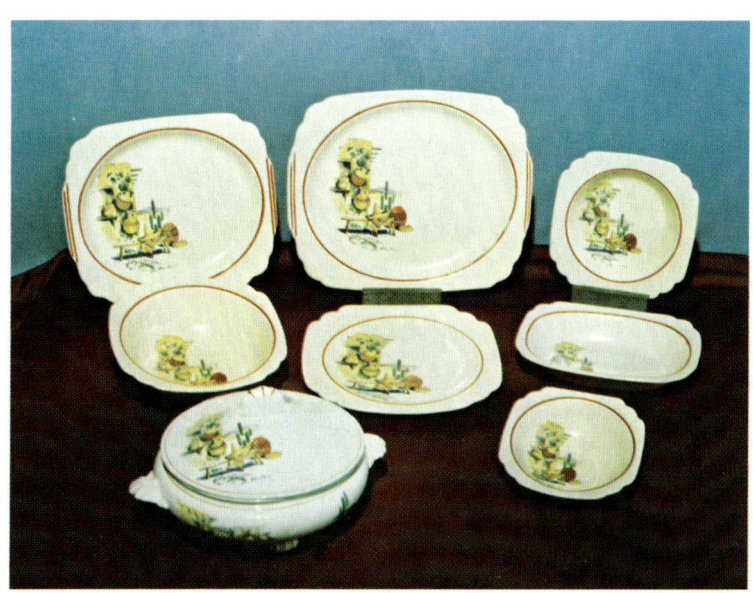

Plate 165

Hacienda

Here are two new 'South of the Border' lines to add — one on Fiesta shapes, the other on Virginia Rose. Max-i-cana's little 'snoozer' looks perfectly content among the pots and cacti, and quite at home on those familiar Fiesta pieces. It's amazing that even now such exciting finds continue to surface! These were discovered just in time to be included in this volume.

Plate 166. Fiesta/Max-i-cana, plate, 10″: $15.00–17.50. Plate, 6″: $3.00–4.00. Cup and saucer: $18.00–22.00. Nappy, 8½″: $20.00–22.00. Platter: $20.00–22.00. Fruit, 5½″: $12.00–15.00.

Plate 167. Virginia Rose with Mexican decal, plate 9″: $5.00–6.00. Platter, 11½″: $7.00–9.00. Vegetable bowl, 8½″: $7.00–8.50.

Hacienda

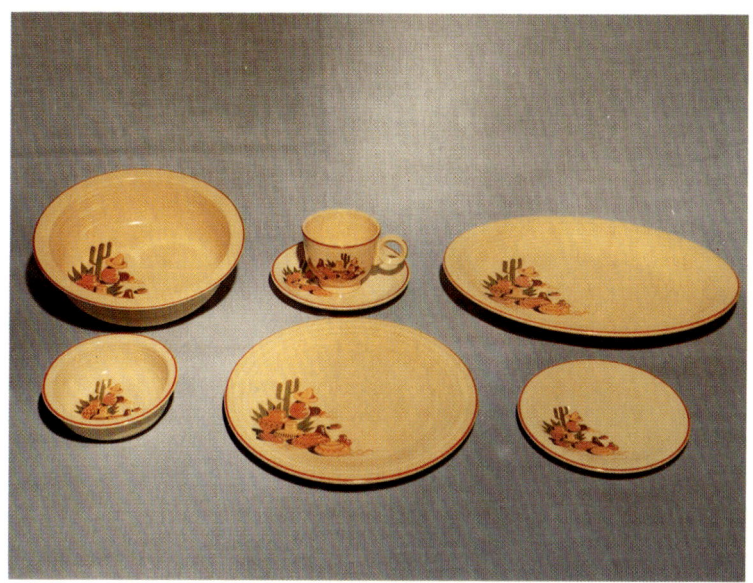

Plate 166

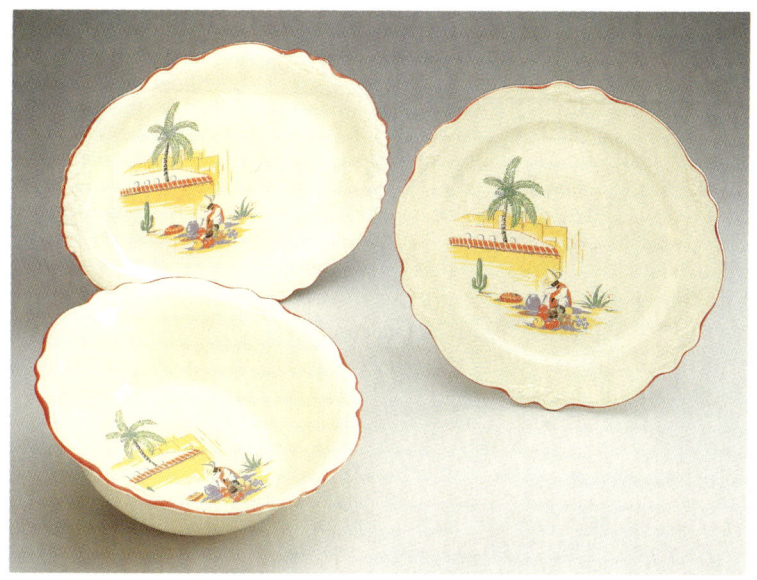

Plate 167

The tablecloth and napkins are of the same vintage . . . the multicolored tumblers are turned to show both sides of one decorated with Spanish dancers, and the one in the center shows the Genuine Fiesta dancing girl! On the right is a cup and saucer in the popular Mexicana pattern on a shape called Swing — one of the most difficult of the Mexican lines to find! Conchita, shown in Plate 169, is occasionally marked with the line name in gold.

Plate 168. Tablecloth and napkins: $30.00–40.00. Tumbler, either style: $5.00–7.50. Cup and saucer: $8.00–12.00.

Plate 169. Platter, 11½": $5.00–7.00. Platter, 13½": $6.00–9.00. Deep plate, 8": $5.00–6.00. Dessert, 5": $3.50–5.00. Plate, 9": $3.00–5.00. Vegetable, 8": $6.00–8.00. Covered sugar: $5.50–7.50. Creamer: $3.50–5.00. Cup and saucer: $8.00–12.00.

KITCHEN KRAFT AND OVEN SERVE

From the very early 1930s Homer Laughlin China was the leading manufacturer of a very successful type of oven-to-table kitchen wares. These lines were called Oven-Serve and Kitchen Kraft. The variety of items offered and the many patterns and decaled lines that were made allow for an endless field of interest for collectors today.

Plate 170. Conchita Kitchen Kraft, large covered jar: $50.00–60.00. Large mixing bowl: $20.00–25.00. Medium covered jar: $50.00–60.00. Covered jug: $75.00–85.00. Cake plate, 10½": $15.00–20.00. Casserole, 8": $30.00–35.00. Under plate, 9": $12.00–18.00.

Kitchen Kraft, Oven Serve

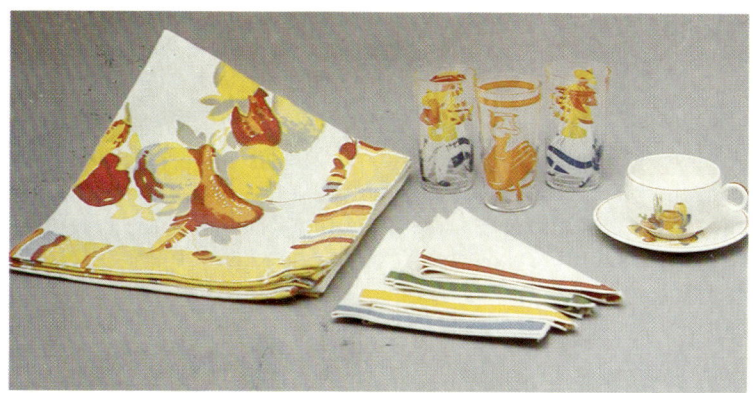

Plate 168

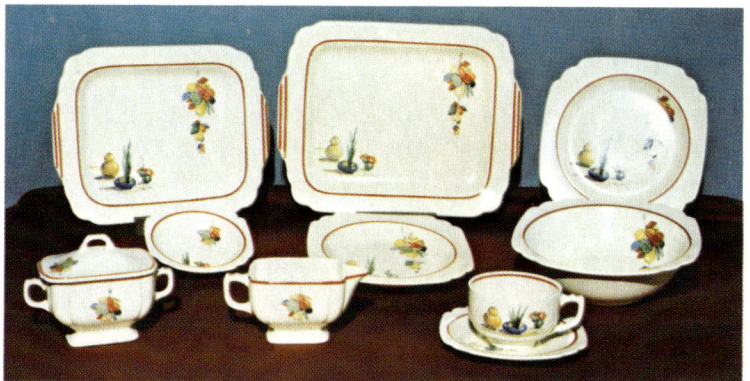

Plate 169

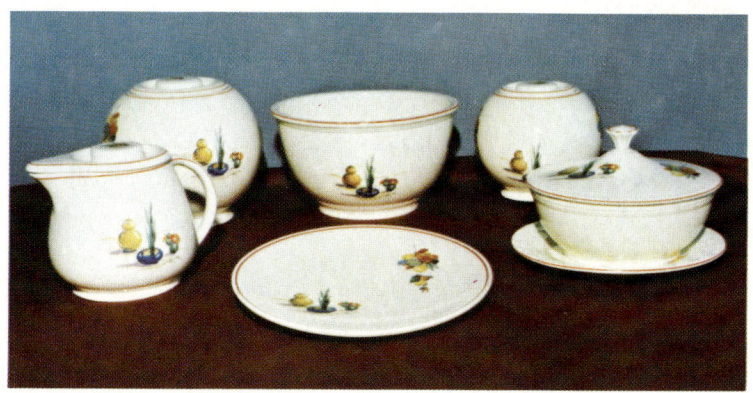

Plate 170

Kitchen Kraft Mexicana (Plates 172-173) is a line very popular with collectors! You may also find in addition to the examples shown here, the small and medium jars, small and medium mixing bowls, and the individual casserole. No Kitchen Kraft Hacienda has ever been reported.

Plate 171. Mexicana casserole (not Kitchen Kraft): $35.00-45.00.

Plate 172. Pie pie plate, 10″: $20.00-25.00. Mixing bowl, 10″: $22.00-28.00. Spoon: $22.00-28.00. Pie server: $22.00-28.00. Fork: $22.00-28.00. Casserole, 8½″: $30.00-35.00. Salt and pepper shakers: $25.00-28.00, pr.

Plate 173. Large covered jar: $50.00-60.00. Cake plate, 10½″: $15.00-20.00. Covered jug: $75.00-85.00. Salt and pepper shakers: $22.00-28.00, pr. Refrigerator jar, unit: $10.00-15.00. Lid: $25.00-30.00.

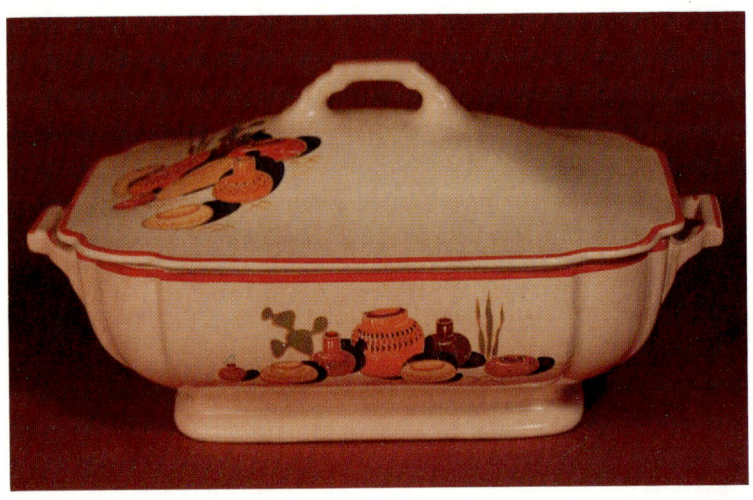

Plate 171

Kitchen Kraft, Oven Serve

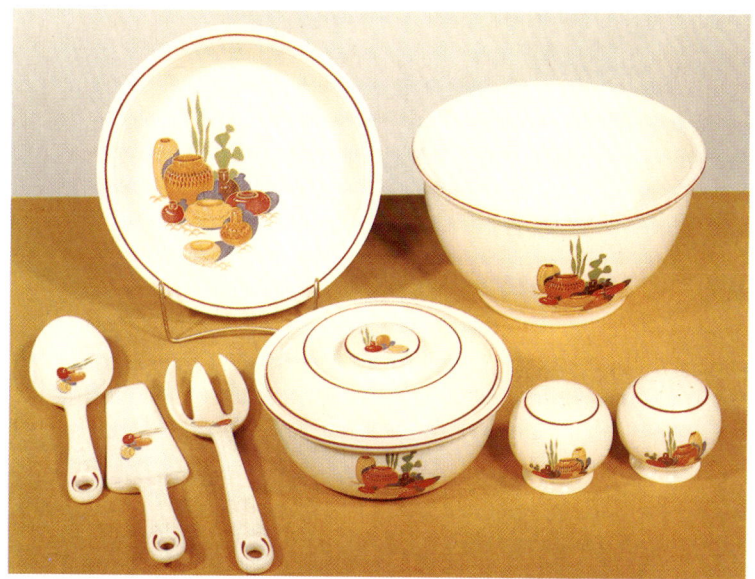

Plate 172

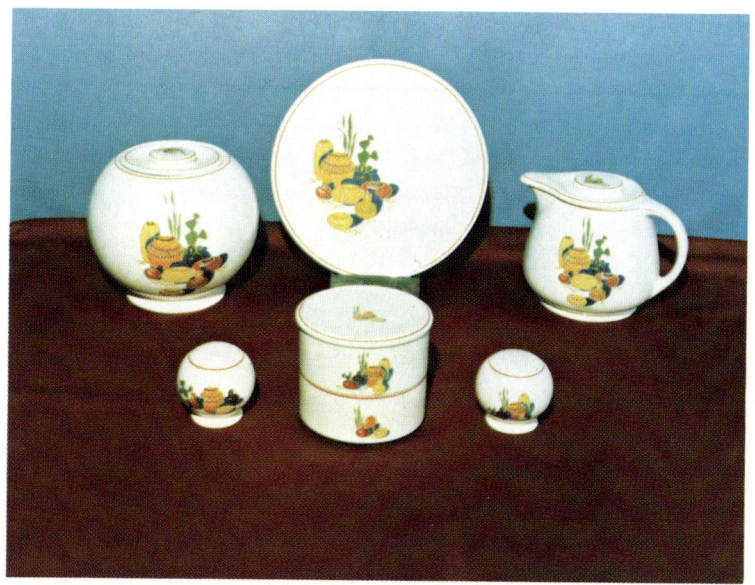

Plate 173

Shown below, the Kitchen Kraft under plate with an unusual decal design. To the right, the ivory Kitchen Kraft with floral decals is very lovely. The jug is rarely found with a cover in these decaled lines. Below is Kitchen Kraft with tulips, marked 'Kitchen Kraft, Oven Serve'.

Plate 174. Kitchen Kraft under plate, 7¼" : $8.00–12.00.

Plate 175. Large, medium or small covered jar: $30.00–35.00. Refrigerator unit: $8.00–10.00, each. Lid: $10.00–15.00. Covered jug: $25.00–30.00. Individual casserole with lid: $22.00–28.00.

Plate 176. Large, medium or small covered jar: $30.00–35.00. Cake plate, 10½": $15.00–20.00. Nested bowls, large: $12.00–18.00; medium: $10.00–15.00; small: $8.00–12.00. Fruit bowl, 14½": $40.00–55.00. Casserole in metal holder, 8½": $15.00–18.00. Cake server: $12.00–15.00. Pie plate, 9½": $10.00–12.00. Salt and pepper shakers: $15.00–18.00, pr.

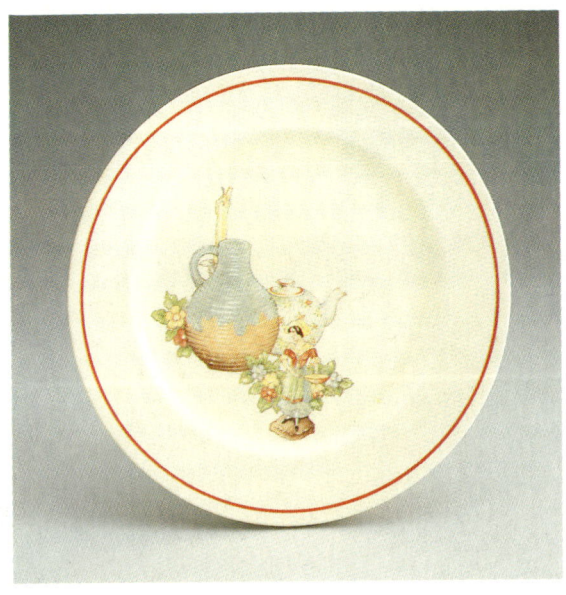

Plate 174

Kitchen Kraft, Oven Serve

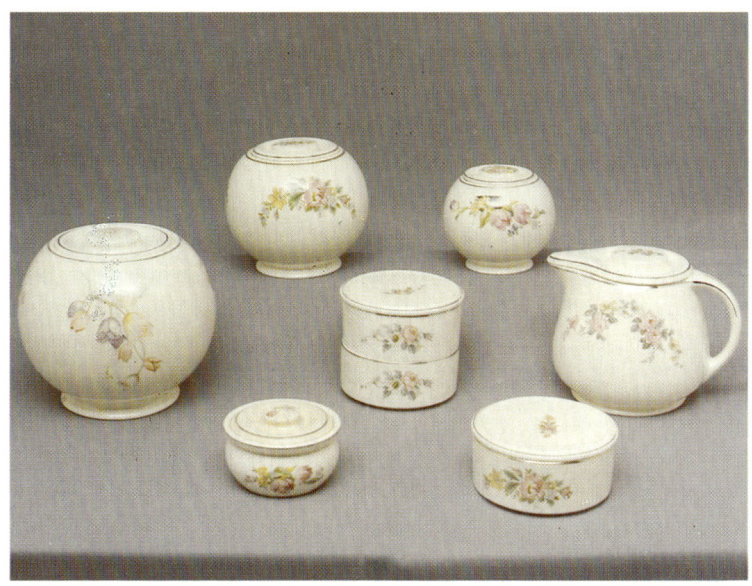

Plate 175

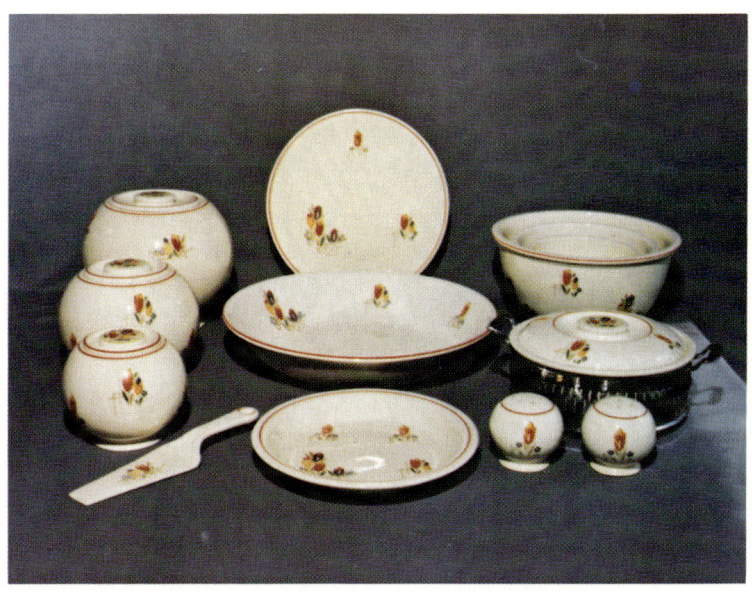

Plate 176

Kitchen Kraft, Oven Serve

These matching pieces must have been a housewife's delight! Here are the 10″ mixing bowl, 10″ pie plate and server... they're all marked 'Kitchen Kraft, Oven Serve'.

Below, Embossed line, Oven Serve. This is the line with the embossed floral pattern that decorates the handles of the Fiesta Kitchen Kraft spoon, fork and server. You will occasionally find other colored glazes and various decal treatments on these shapes. This was quite an extensive line, and many unique pieces were produced. Watch for an almost identical line by T.S.&T.

This label was found on a spoon and fork in a tan-gold glaze.

Guaranteed
To Withstand Changes of
Oven-Dinner Ware
"THE OVEN WARE FOR TABLE SERVICE"
The Homer Laughlin China Co.
Newell, W. Va.

Plate 177. Mixing bowl, 10″: $8.00–10.00. Server: $8.00–10.00. Pie plate, 10″: $10.00–12.00.

Plate 178. Nappy, 10″: $2.00–3.50. Casserole, 8½″: $5.50–7.50. Mixing bowl, 6″: $2.50–3.50. Oval baker, 8″: $2.50–3.50. Plate, 9″: $2.00–3.50. Custard cup: $1.50–2.50. Fruit, 5¾″: $1.50–2.50.

Kitchen Kraft, Oven Serve

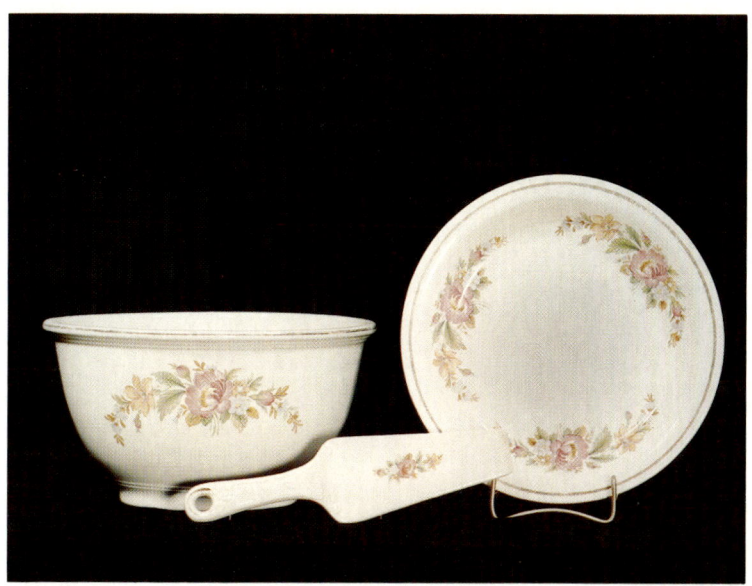

Plate 177

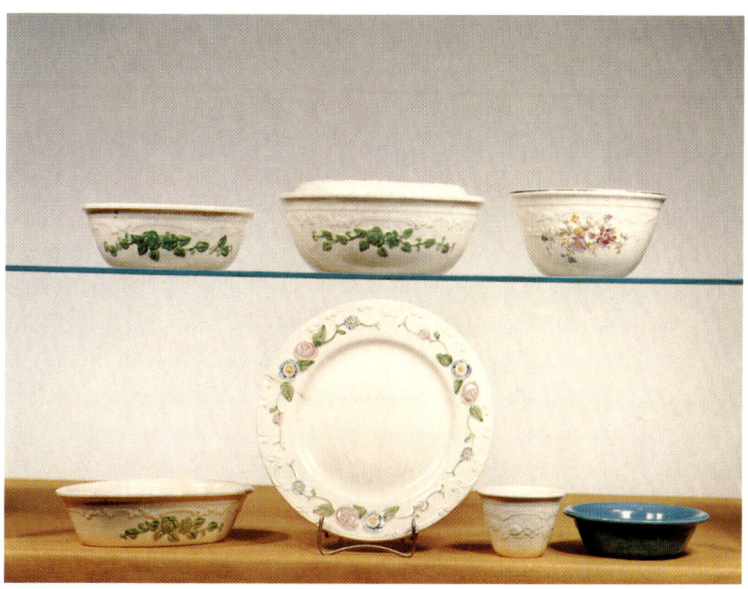

Plate 178

Kitchen Kraft, Oven Serve

Plate 179. Pie plate, 10″, with tulips: $10.00-13.50; with Wild Rose: $10.00-13.50; with floral decal: $10.00-13.50.

Plate 180. Kitchen Bouquet, pie plate, 10″: $10.00-13.50; Platter, 13″: $10.00-13.50.

Plate 181. Cake plate with floral decal: $10.00-13.50; pie plate, 11″: $10.00-13.50; server: $8.00-10.00.

Kitchen Kraft, Oven Serve

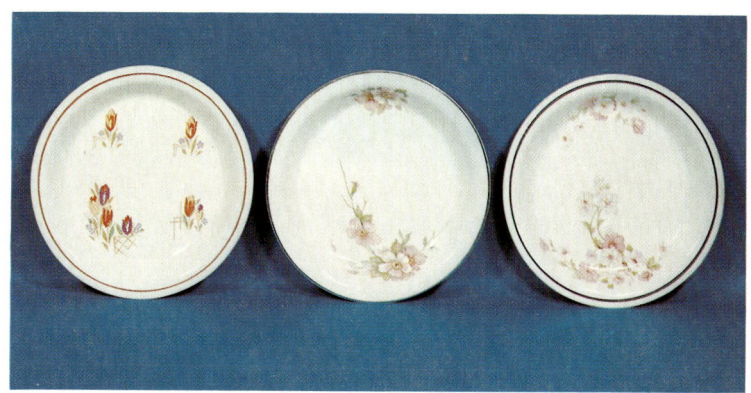

Plate 179

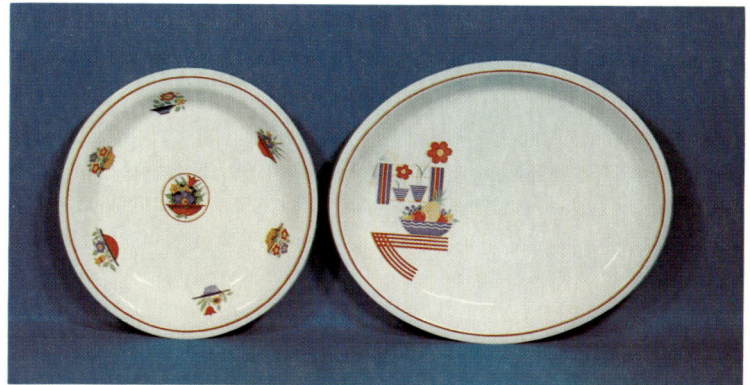

Plate 180

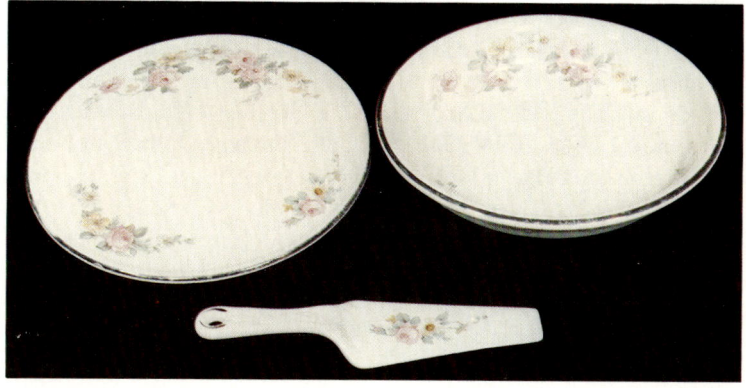

Plate 181

THE AMERICAN POTTER

As a tribute to the American Potter, six pottery companies united their efforts and jointly built and operated an actual working kiln at the 1939-40 World's Fair in New York. A variety of plates, vases, figural items and bowls were produced — marked with an ink stamp 'The American Potter, 1939 (or '40), World's Fair Exhibit, Joint Exhibit of Capitol and Labor.' The Homer Laughlin China Company entry, designed by Fredrick Rhead, is shown in Plate 182. In the center of each plate, you can see the Trylon and the Parisphere, adopted symbols of the Fair. One of these plates as been found with this commemorative message stamped in gold on the back: 'Decorated by by Charles Murphy, 150th Anniversary Inauguration of George Washington as First President of the United States, 1789-1939.'

In Plate 183 are the entries from the other five companies. Although not mentioned on the original pamphlet with the other companies, the pitcher is a World's Fair souvenir marked 'Porcelier Trade Mark, Vitreous Hand Decorated China, Made in U.S.A.'

Plate 182. HLC World's Fair plate, '39 or '40: $32.00–40.00.

Plate 183. Cake set, 'Cronin China Co., Minerva O., National Brotherhood of Operative Potters': $22.00–28.00. Bowl, 'Paden City Pottery, Made in USA', 10″: $20.00–25.00. Plate, 'Knowles, Joint Exhibit of Capitol and Labor', 10¾″: $22.00–26.00. Marmalade bottom, embossed with Trylon and Parisphere and 'New York World's Fair', marked 'Edwin M. Knowles China Co., Semi-Vitreous', 3″: $22.00–28.00, with lid. Pitcher, marked 'Porcelier Trade Mark, Vitreous Hand Decorated China, Made in U.S.A.': $25.00–35.00.

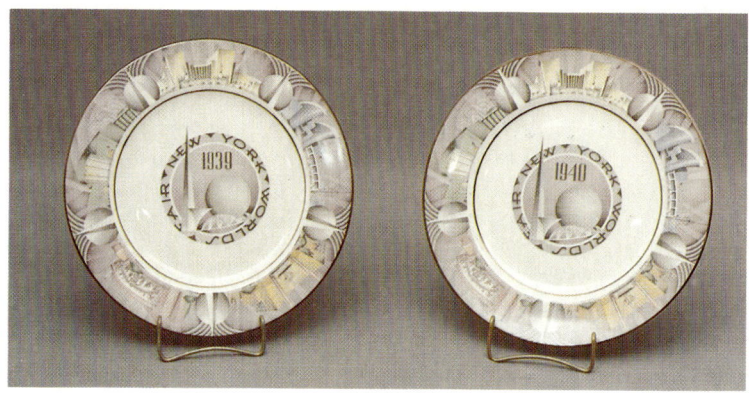

Plate 182

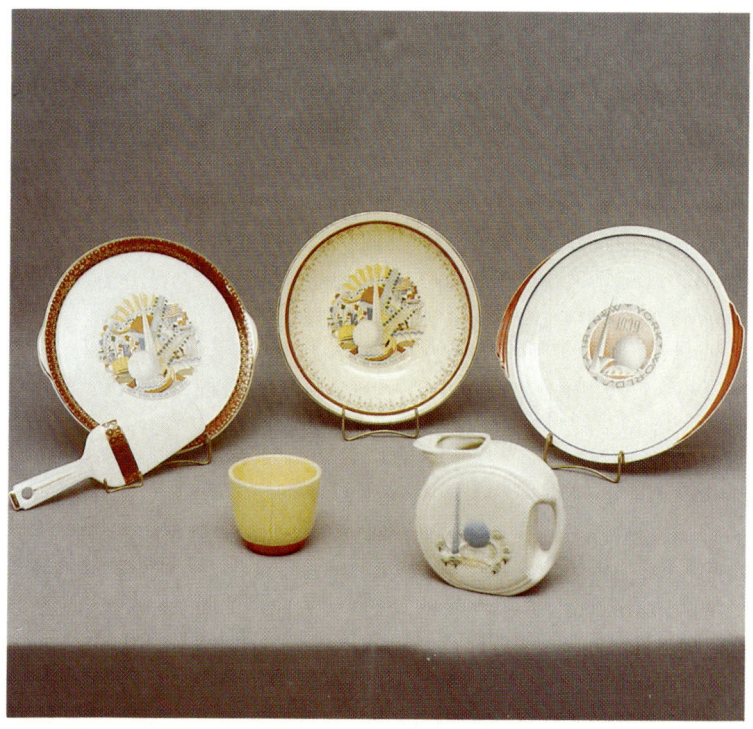

Plate 183

The Potters' Plates are possibly the easiest of the World's Fair items to find. There were two, The Potter at His Wheel, and the Artist Decorating the Vase. They have also been found in turquoise and light green, and are most scarce in light green and ivory. To find one in the original box would be most unusual. Also shown is a cup and saucer embossed with signs of the Zodiac . . . another rarity!

Plate 185 shows an array of the hand turned vases made at the Fair. They are from 1½" to 7" high and all are marked with the 'American Potter' ink stamp. The cobalt blue piece on the far right is a candle holder. Note the individual creamer from the Harlequin line, with 'World's Fair' etched on the side.

Plate 184. Potters' Plate, either view: $18.00–25.00. Original box: $15.00–20.00. Zodiac cup and saucer: $35.00–45.00.

Plate 185. Vases, 5" to 7": $25.00–35.00. Small vases: $20.00–28.00. Candle holder, 2": $22.00–30.00. Individual creamer: $22.00–30.00.

The American Potter

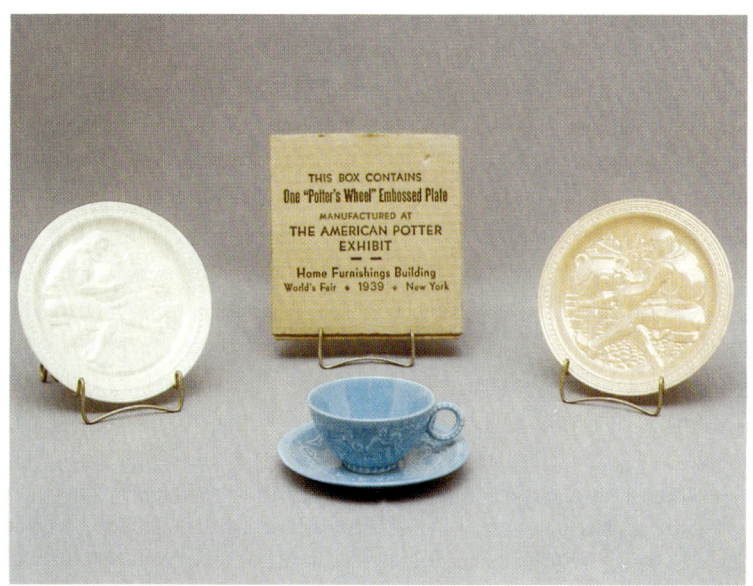

Plate 184

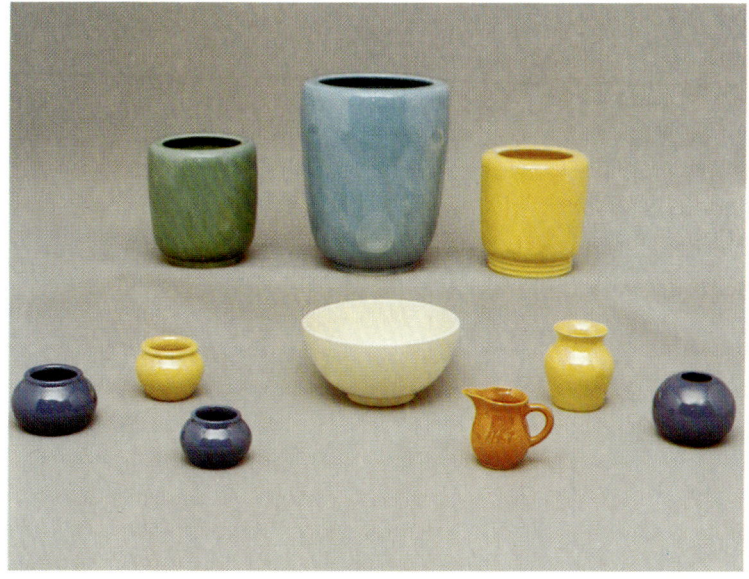

Plate 185

In Plate 186 is experimental ware from the family of Lloyd Dittmer, Ceramic Engineer at HLC during the years of Fiesta's development. The red and cobalt blue Potter's plates were never mass produced.

The plates and ash tray in Plate 187 are souvenirs of the Golden Gate International Exposition of 1939 and 1940. They are marked 'Golden Gate Intern. Expo., Copyright License 63C, Homer Laughlin, Souvenir'.

Plate 187. Golden Gate Expo. Plate, either year: $30.00–35.00. Ash tray: $30.00–35.00.

The American Potter

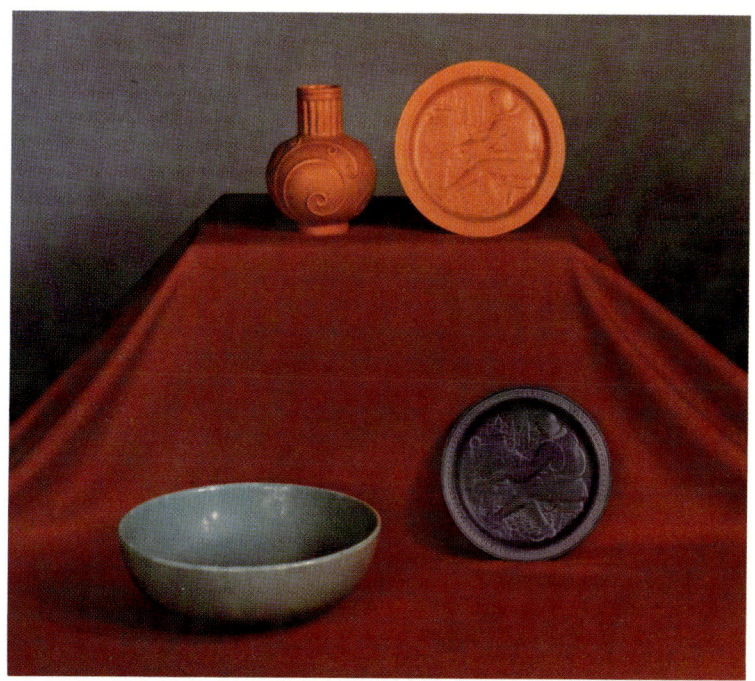

Plate 186

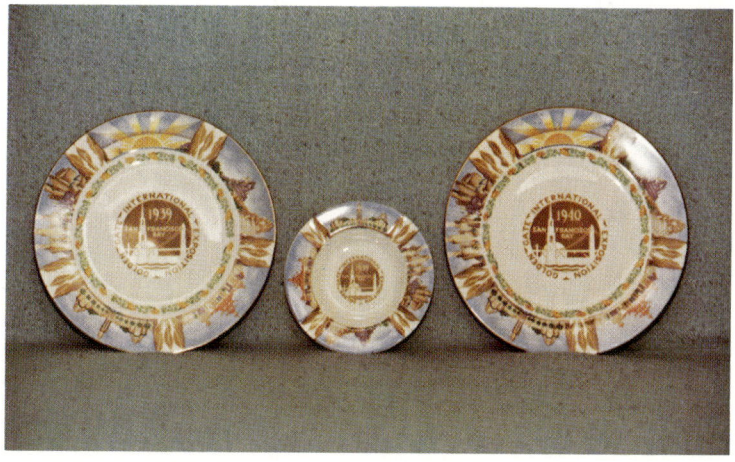

Plate 187

The two figural pitchers shown on the right are each 5″ tall. Martha Washington is marked 'The American Potter, New York World's Fair' with the year 1940 on a raised disk superimposed over a Trylon. George Washington is marked 'First Edition For Collectors, New York's World Fair, 1939'. It is numbered 37. The tall vase measures 7″ and is marked with the ink stamp. On the second row, the figural pitchers are each 2″ tall and are marked. These are sometimes found in bisque, and examples in mauve blue and Harlequin yellow have been reported. The toothpick holder in the center is 2″ high, and the salt and pepper shakers are 2½″. Neither are marked.

In plate 189: the Four Season plates, each measure 4¼″ across. Spring shows a man fishing for trout; Summer depicts a family picnicking; Autumn shows a man hunting with his dog; and Winter, a couple skating.

Plate 188. Martha Washington pitcher, 5″: $26.00–32.00. George Washington pitcher, 5″: $20.00–25.00. Vase, 7″: $25.00–35.00. Either 2″ pitcher: $18.00–22.00; in bisque: $10.00–12.00; in colored glazes: $30.00–40.00. Toothpick holder: $20.00–25.00. Salt and pepper shakers: $20.00–25.00, pr.

Plate 189. Four Seasons bowls: $20.00–25.00, each.

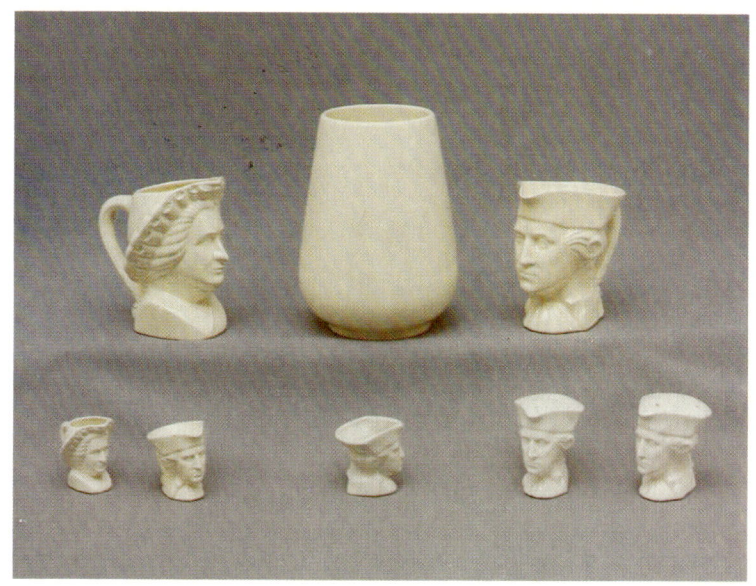

Plate 188

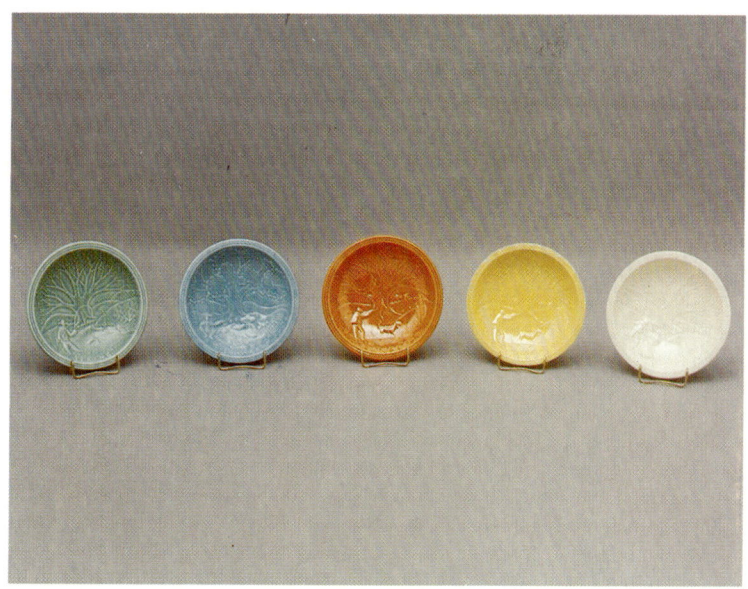

Plate 189

LAUGHLIN ART CHINA

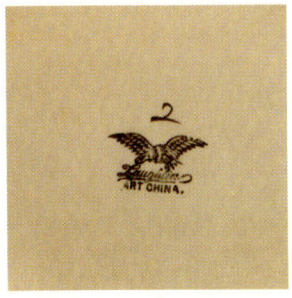

Plate 190

In the early 1900s in an attempt to enter the art pottery field, HLC produced a unique line of art china. It was marked in gold or black with the eagle and the line name, 'Laughlin Art China'. Examples of this ware are very rare. Several decorating techniques were employed; most are decaled wares but occasionally you will find a hand decorated piece that is artist signed, such as the dog vase in Plate 195.

Plate 191. Ruffled bowl, 9¾": $65.00–75.00. Bowl with handles, 4" x 11¾": $80.00–90.00. Vase, 8": $65.00–75.00. Plate, 9½": $20.00–25.00.

Plate 192. Mug, Jacobean design: $20.00–25.00. Tankard with Monk: $70.00–80.00. Mug with Monk: $20.00–25.00.

Plate 193. Jardiniere, flow blue, 10" x 14½": $275.00–300.00.

Plate 194. Vase, artist signed, 8": $100.00–125.00.

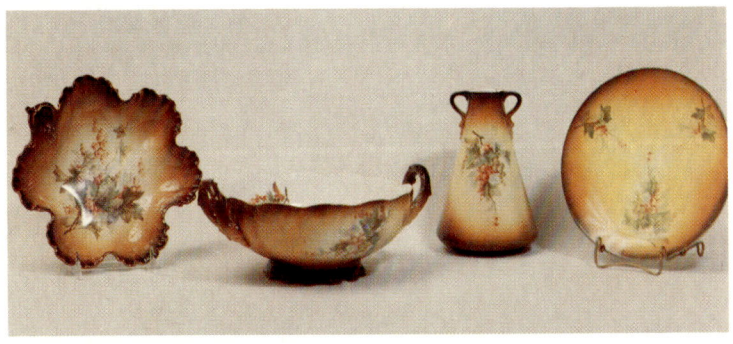

Plate 191

Laughlin Art China

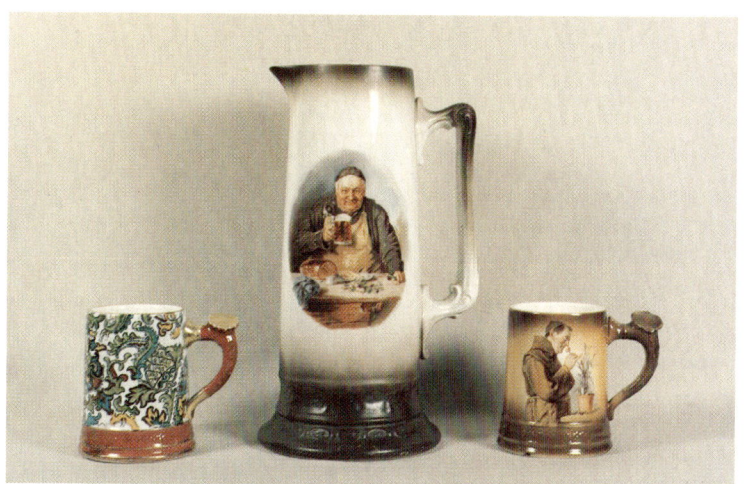

Plate 192

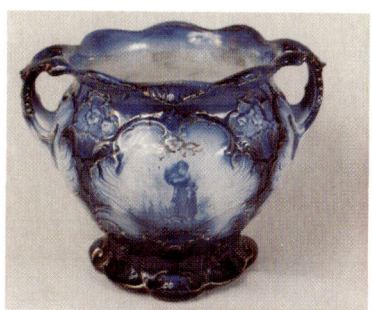

Plate 193

Plate 194

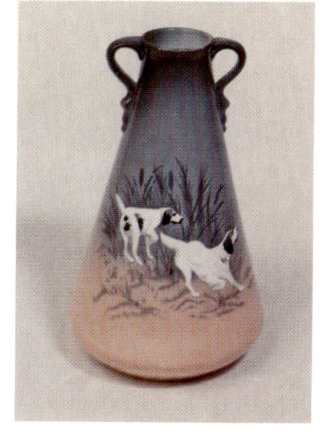

INDEX

Advertising mugs ... 69
A.D. Coffee cups ... 49, 119
A.D. Coffee pot ... 49
Amberstone ... 91
American Potter ... 185
Animals ... 123
Art china ... 192
Ash tray ... 53, 71, 117
Baker ... 111
Batter set ... 135, 137
Box ... 69, 185
Bud vase ... 55
Buick mugs ... 69
Bulb candle holders ... 55
Butter dish ... 117, 132
Cake plate ... 45
Cake plate, KK ... 103
Calendar plate ... 73
Candle holder ... 55, 119
Carafe ... 51
Carnival ... 162
Casserole ... 47, 111, 131, 159
Casserole, KK ... 101
Casuals ... 89
Casualstone ... 92
Century, decals ... 143
Child's sets ... 139-141
Chop plate ... 37, 71
Coffee cups ... 41
Coffee pot ... 41
Conchita ... 175
Compartment plates ... 37
Comport ... 49
Cream soup ... 39, 109, 129
Creamer ... 43, 115, 133
Creamer, stick handle ... 41
Decals ... 82

Deep plate	39, 109, 129
Demitasse cups	49, 119
Demitasse pot	49
Dessert bowl	39
Disk pitcher	43
Dogwood	151
Dripolator	61
Egg cups	41, 113
Embossed line	182
Epicure	163
Experimental ware	31, 33-35, 189
Fiesta pamphlet	83
Fiesta/Mexicana	173
Fiestawood	59, 61, 71
Figure-8 tray	56, 57
Floral Fiesta	75
Four Seasons plates	191
French casserole	55
Fruit bowl	45, 129
Fruits	39, 45, 109
Gravy boat	47, 115, 131
Golden Gate Expo	189
Hacienda	170, 171
Handled chop plate	55
Hankscraft	87
Harlequin brochure	107
Ice pitcher	51
Individual creamer	56, 57, 115, 121
Individual salad	39, 112
Individual sugar & creamer on tray	56
Individual tea pot	31
Ironstone	95
Jam dish	61
Jar, covered	101
Jubilee	59, 157
Jug, covered	99, 133
Jug, 2 pt.	51
Jug, 22 oz.	115
Jug, water	113
Juice pitcher	57, 59, 131, 136
Juice tumblers	57, 58, 131
Kitchen Kraft	98, 175, 182

Lamps	65, 121
Lazarus	41
Lids	47, 98
Marmalade	53, 115
Max-i-cana Yellowstone	167
Metal holders	59, 61, 63, 103
Mexicana	165, 176, 177
Mixing bowls	47, 101, 120
Mixing bowls, KK	101
Monterey Modern	87
Mugs	67, 69
Mustard	53
Napkin holder	79
Nappy	45, 112, 129
Newspaper ad	83
Novelty creamer	115
Nut dishes	117
Oatmeal	109, 129
Onion soup	51
Orange Tree bowls	147
Paper items	82
Perfume bottle	117
Pie plate	103, 177, 179, 182, 183
Pitcher	43, 113
Plate	37, 109, 127
Platter	45, 102, 109, 127
Popcorn set	80
Potters plate	187
Priscilla	151
Quickut flatware	80
Refrigerator jar	98, 99
Relish tray	49, 63, 117
Rhythm	159
Rhythm Rose	149
Salad bowl	45, 47
Salt and peppers	43, 103, 115, 159
Salt and peppers, KK	103
Saturday Eve. Post	83
Sauceboat	47, 115, 131
Serenade	153
Sit 'n Sip	69
Spoon, Fork, Server, KK	103

Spoon rest	119, 158
Sta-brite	61
Stack set	98
Store display	85
Sugar	43, 115, 133
Sweets comport	53
Syrup	53, 117, 133
Tablecloth	63, 175
Tango	155
Tankard	117, 121
Teacups	41, 113, 129
Teapot	53, 113, 129
Tid-bit	59
Tin Ware	79
Tom & Jerry	41, 67, 71
Tripod candle holder	55
Tulip	179
Turkey platter	73
Tumbler	47, 113, 115, 135, 175
Tumbler, handled	133
Two pt. jug	51
Under plate	178
Utility tray	43
Vases	55, 187
Virginia Rose	145, 146, 173
Washington, George, pitcher	191
Washington, Martha, pitcher	191
Wells Art Glaze	161
Wooden handle	71
World's Fair plate	185
Zodiac cup	187